# NEW YORK

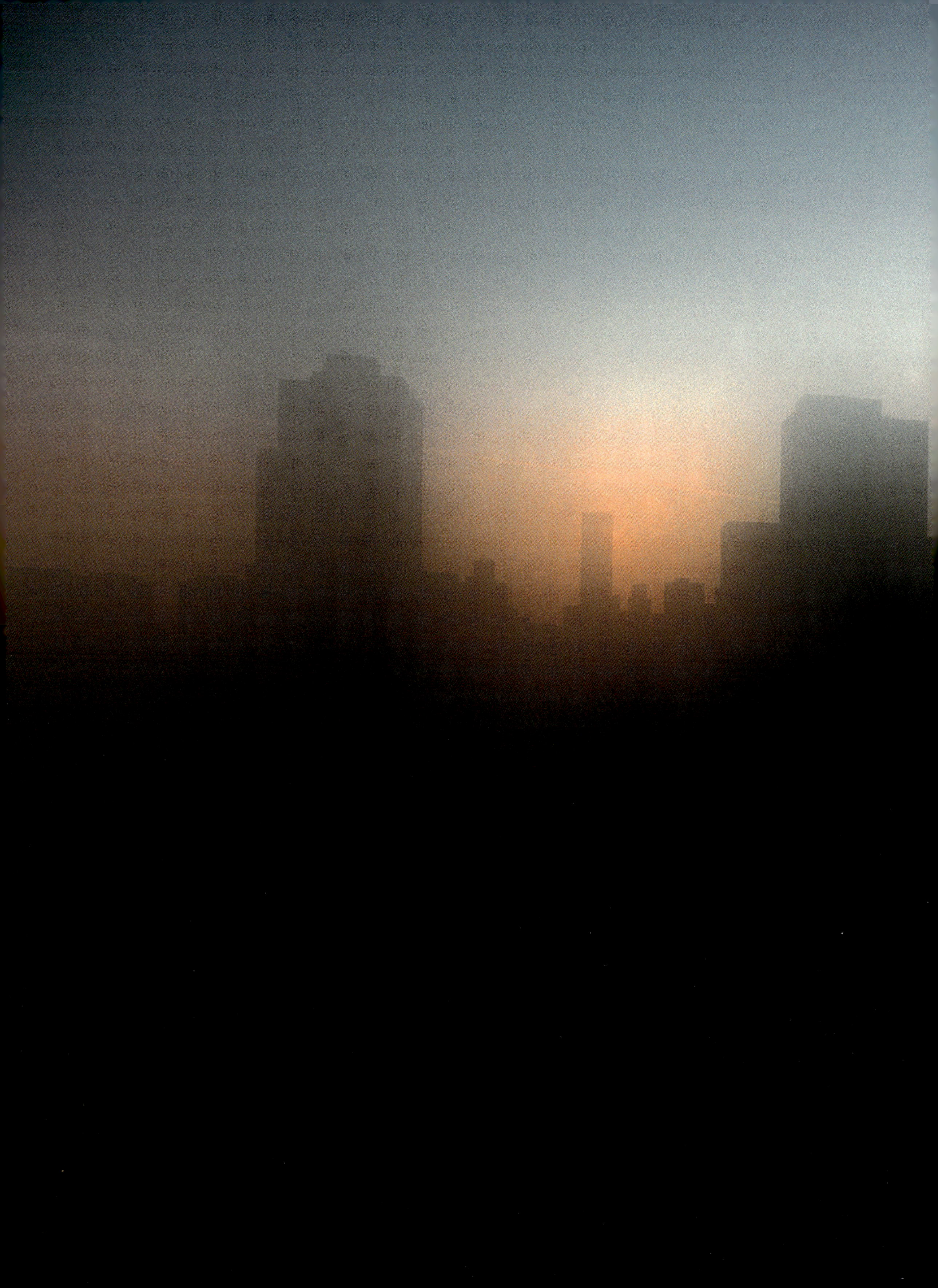

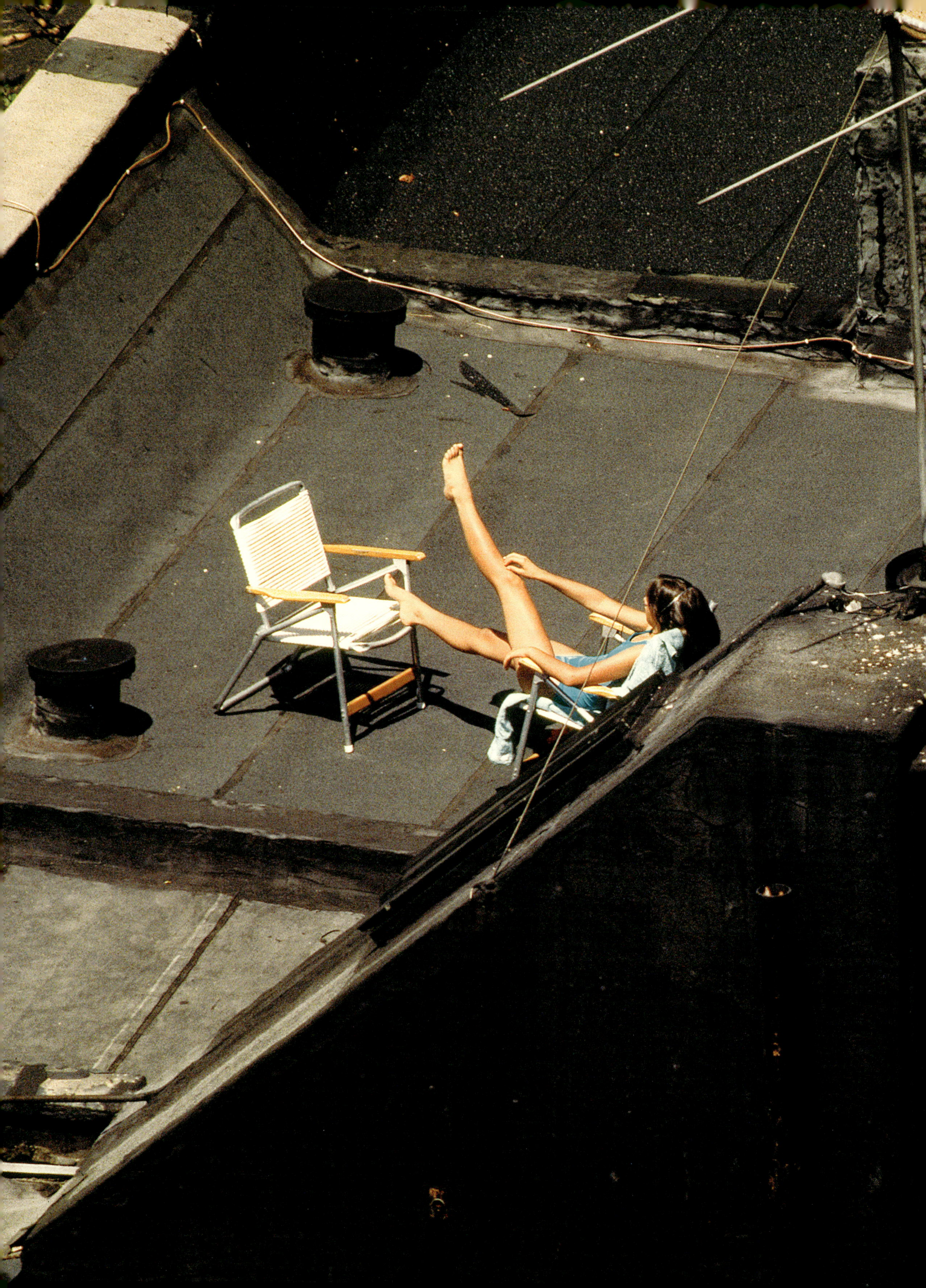

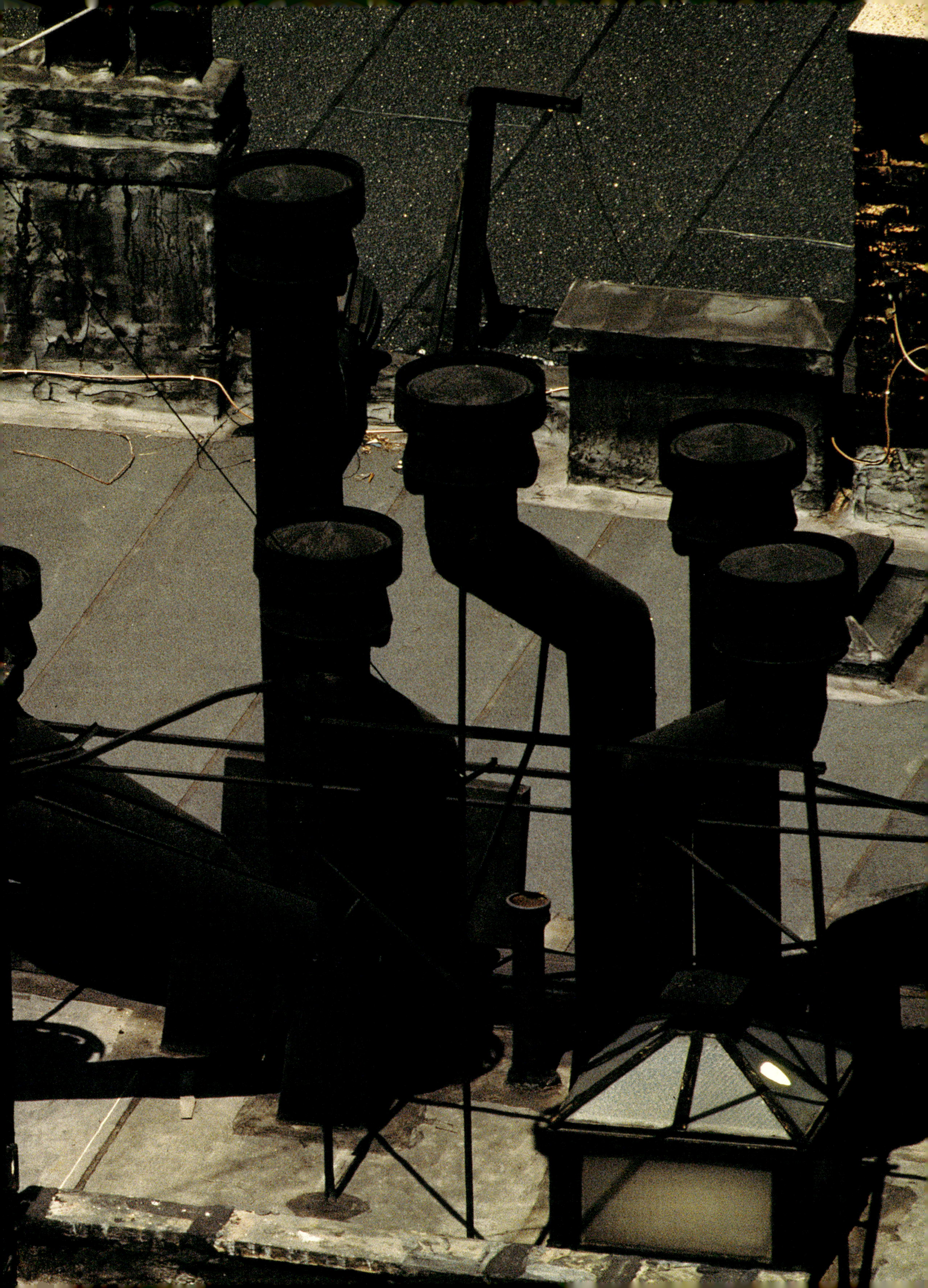

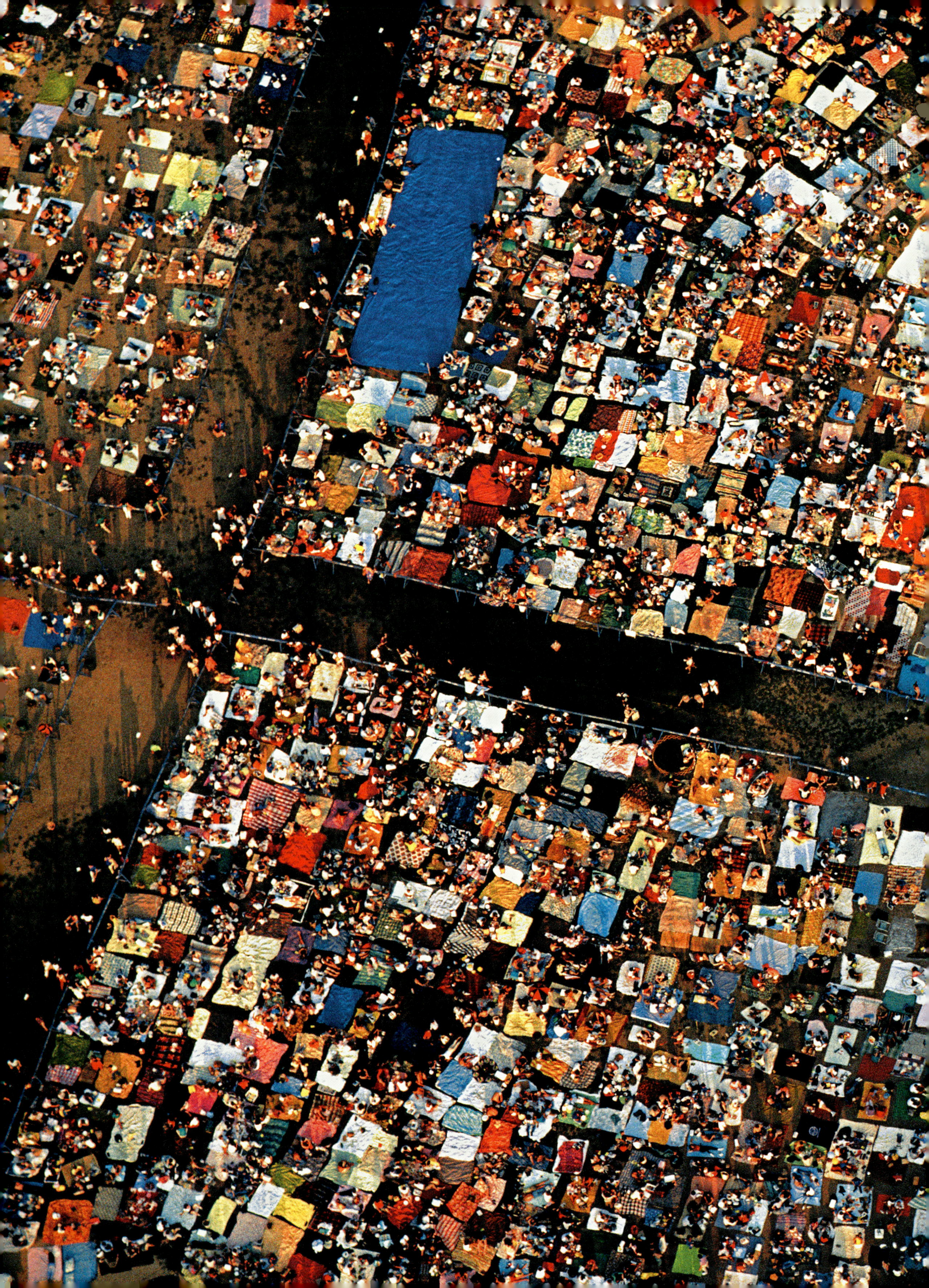

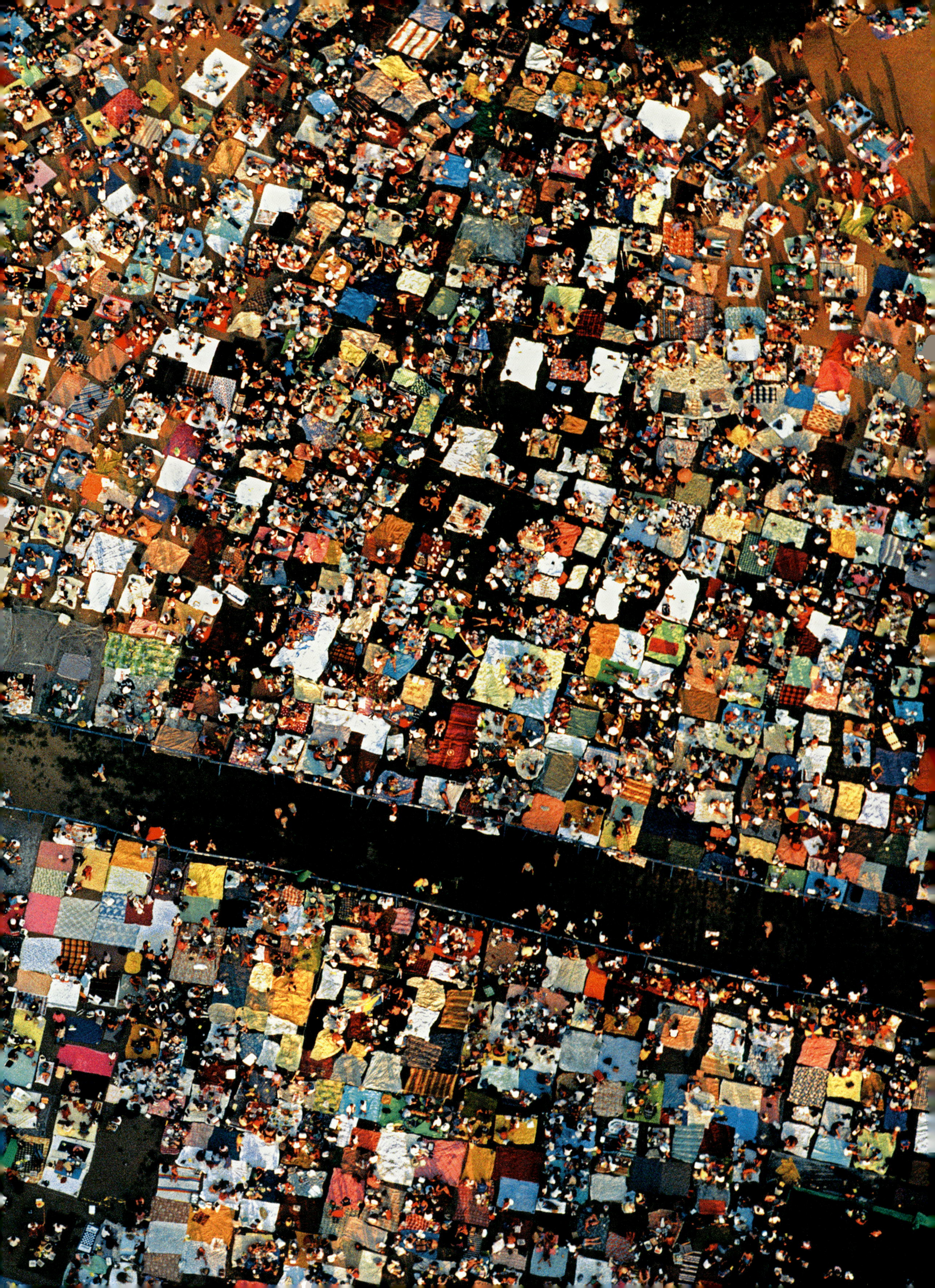

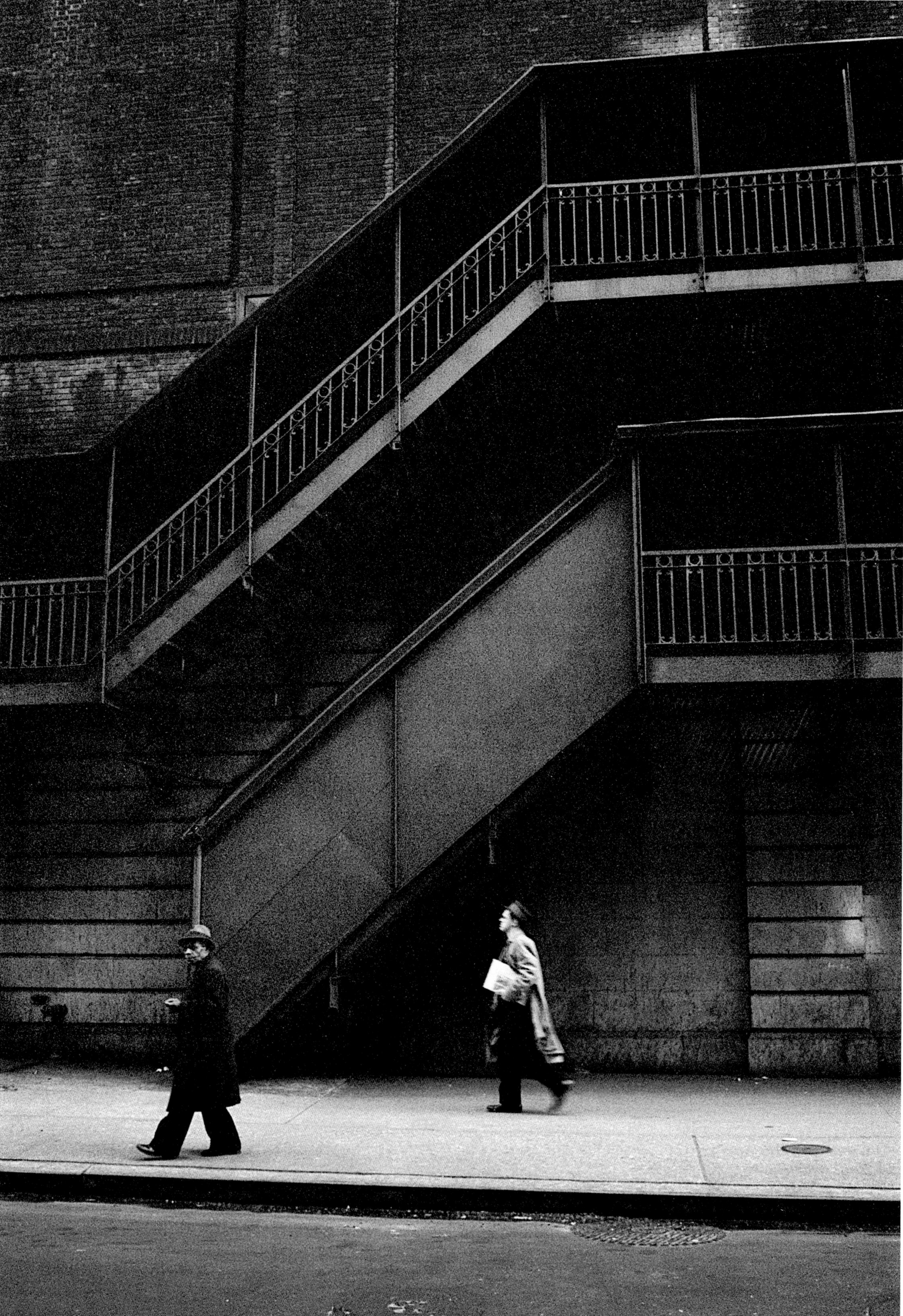

# NEW YORK
# THOMAS HOEPKER

teNeues

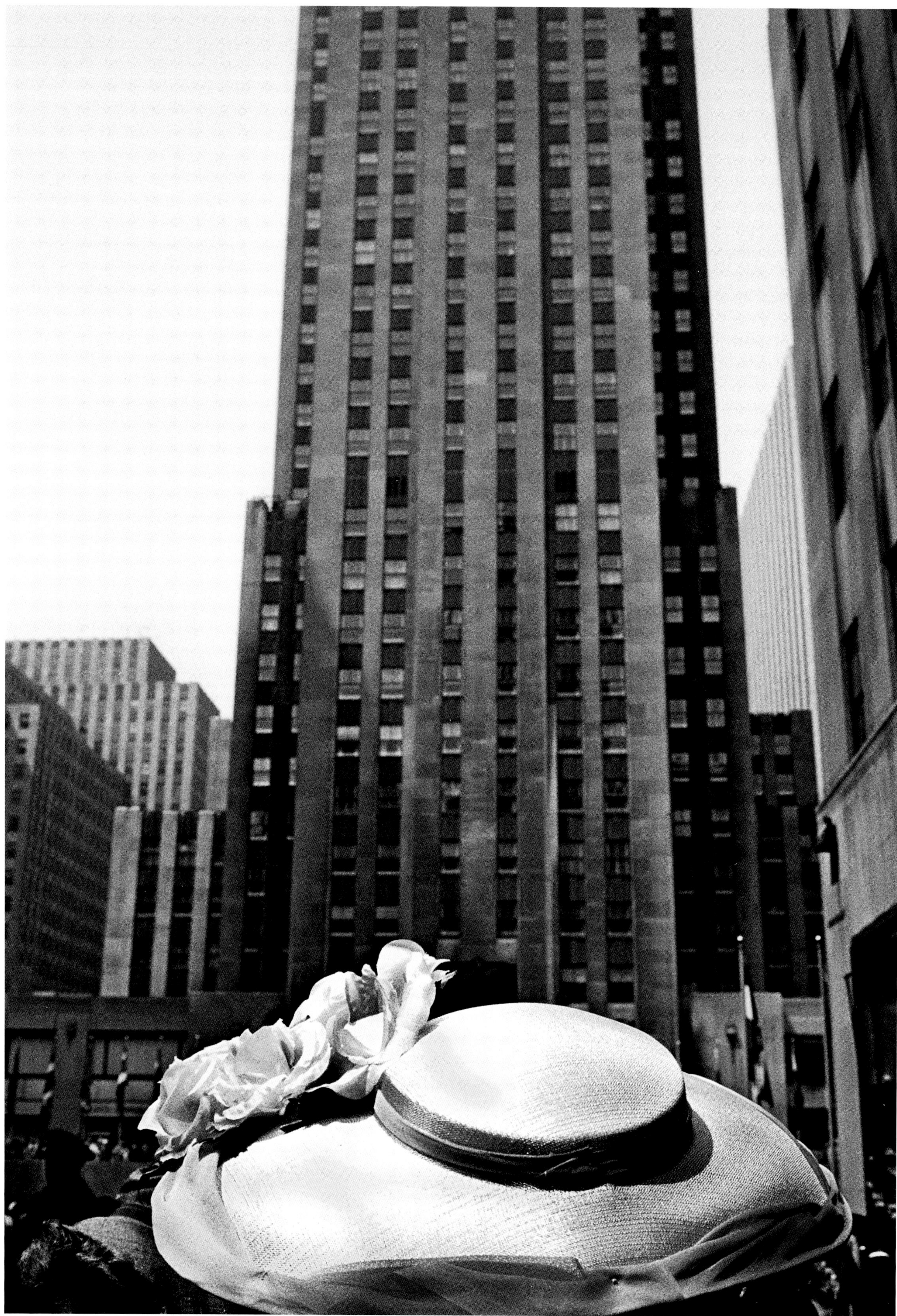

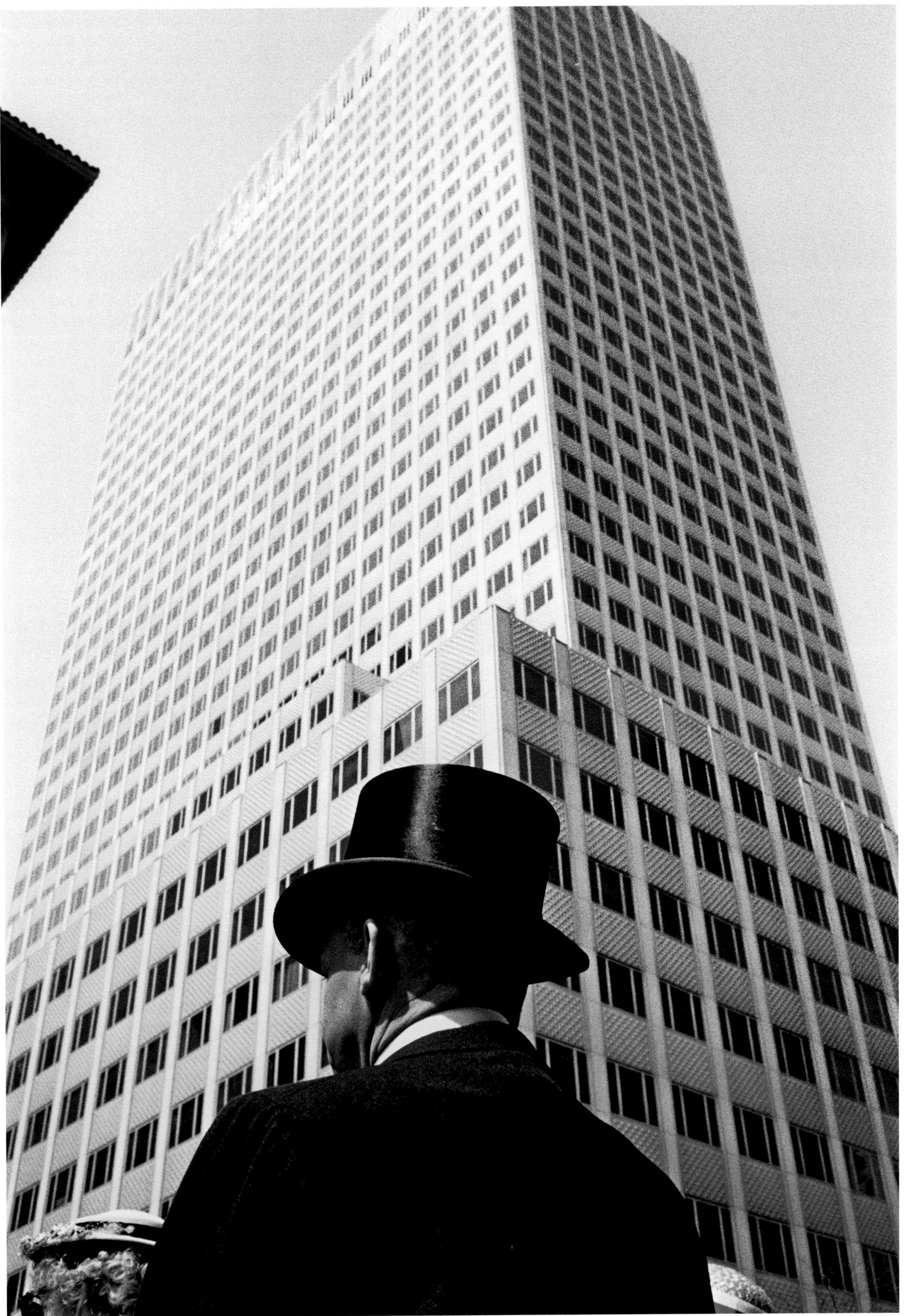

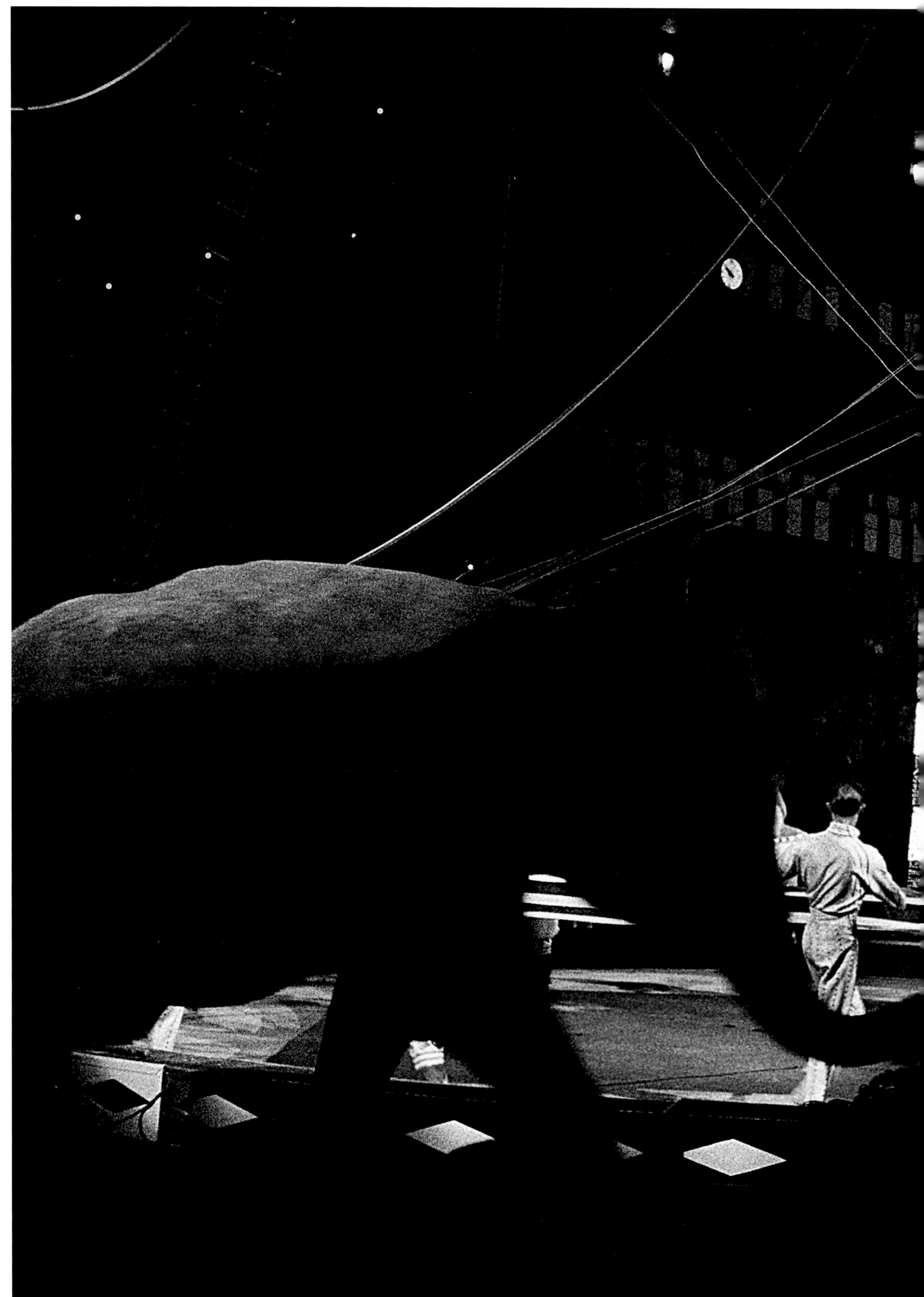

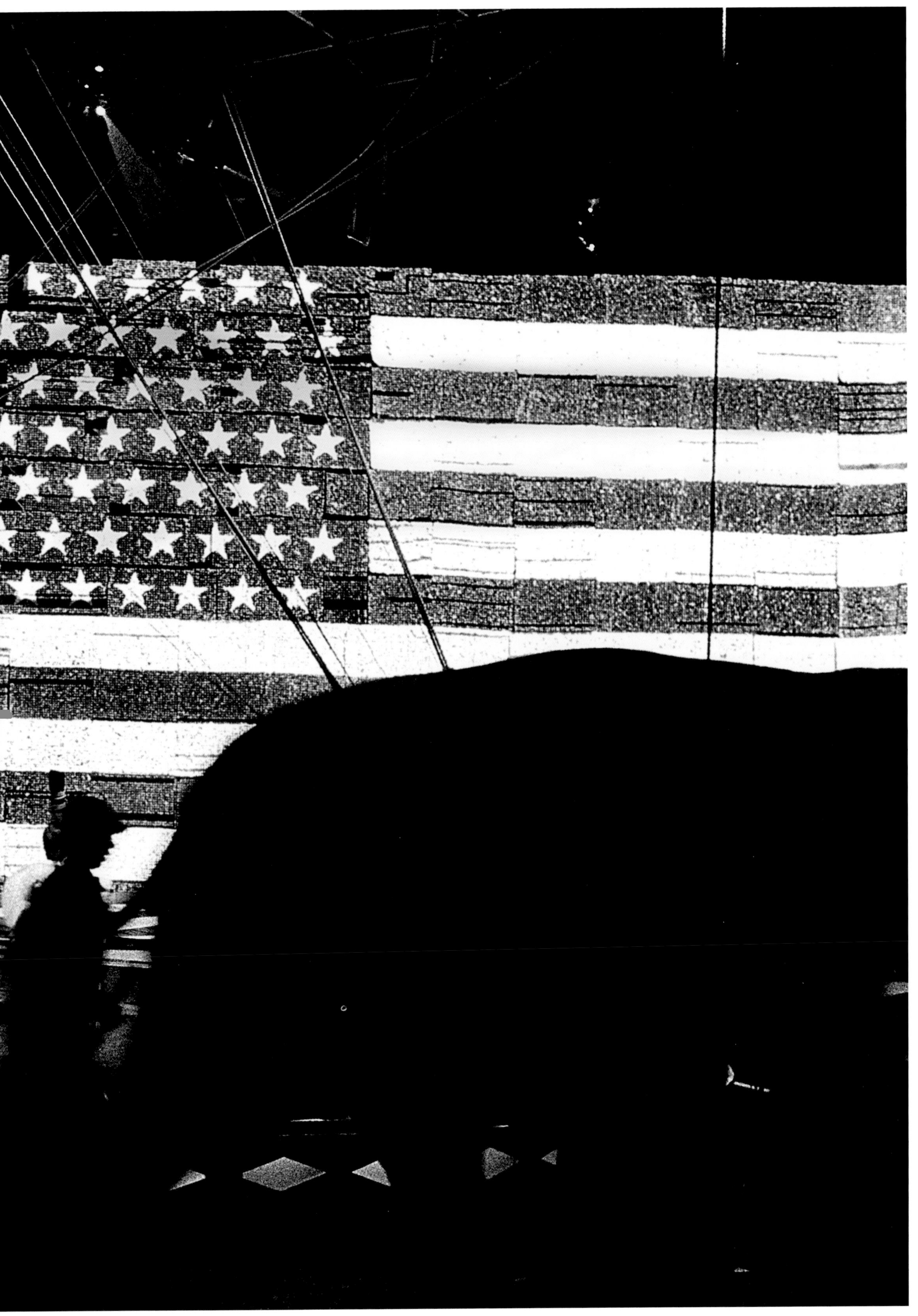

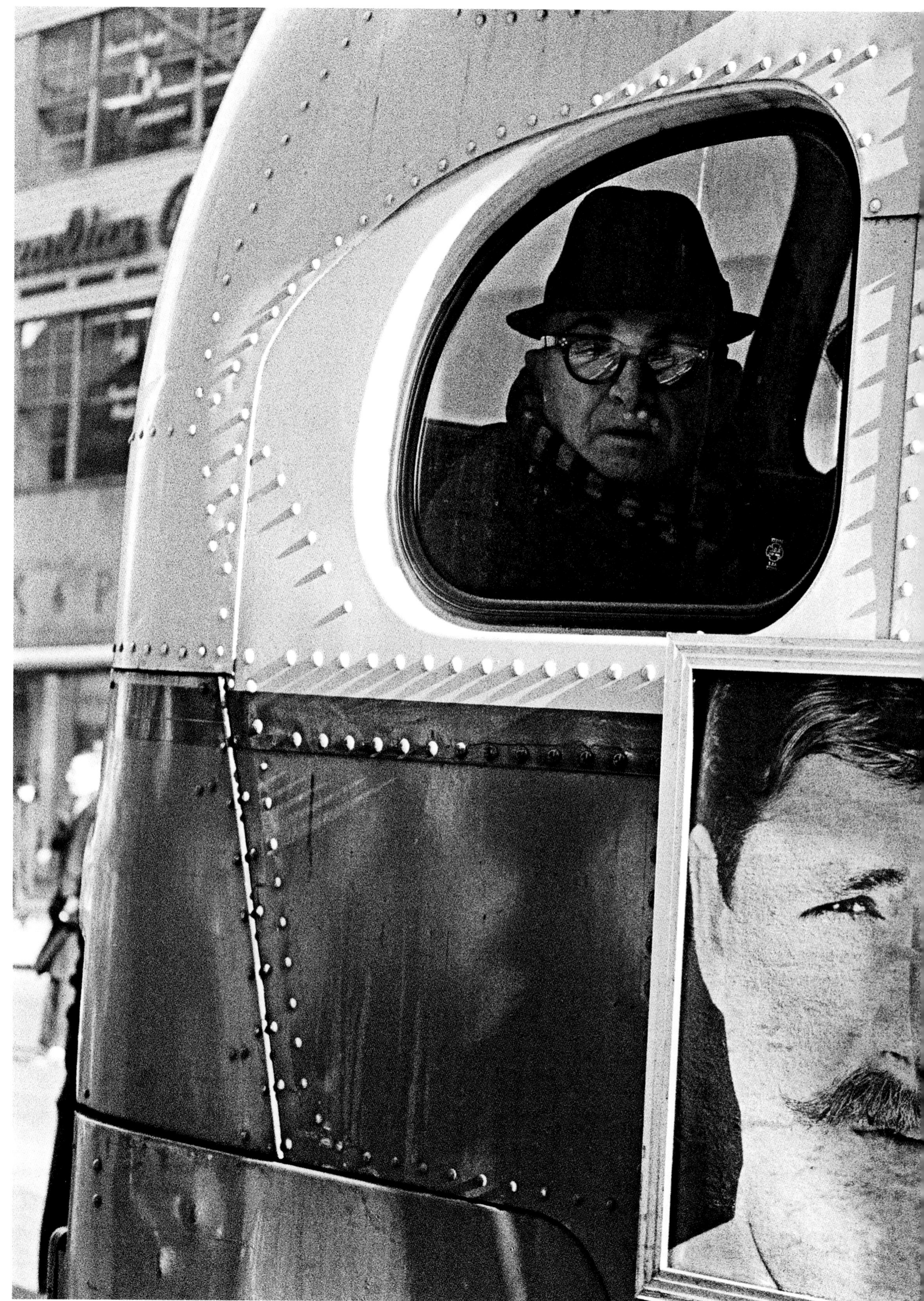

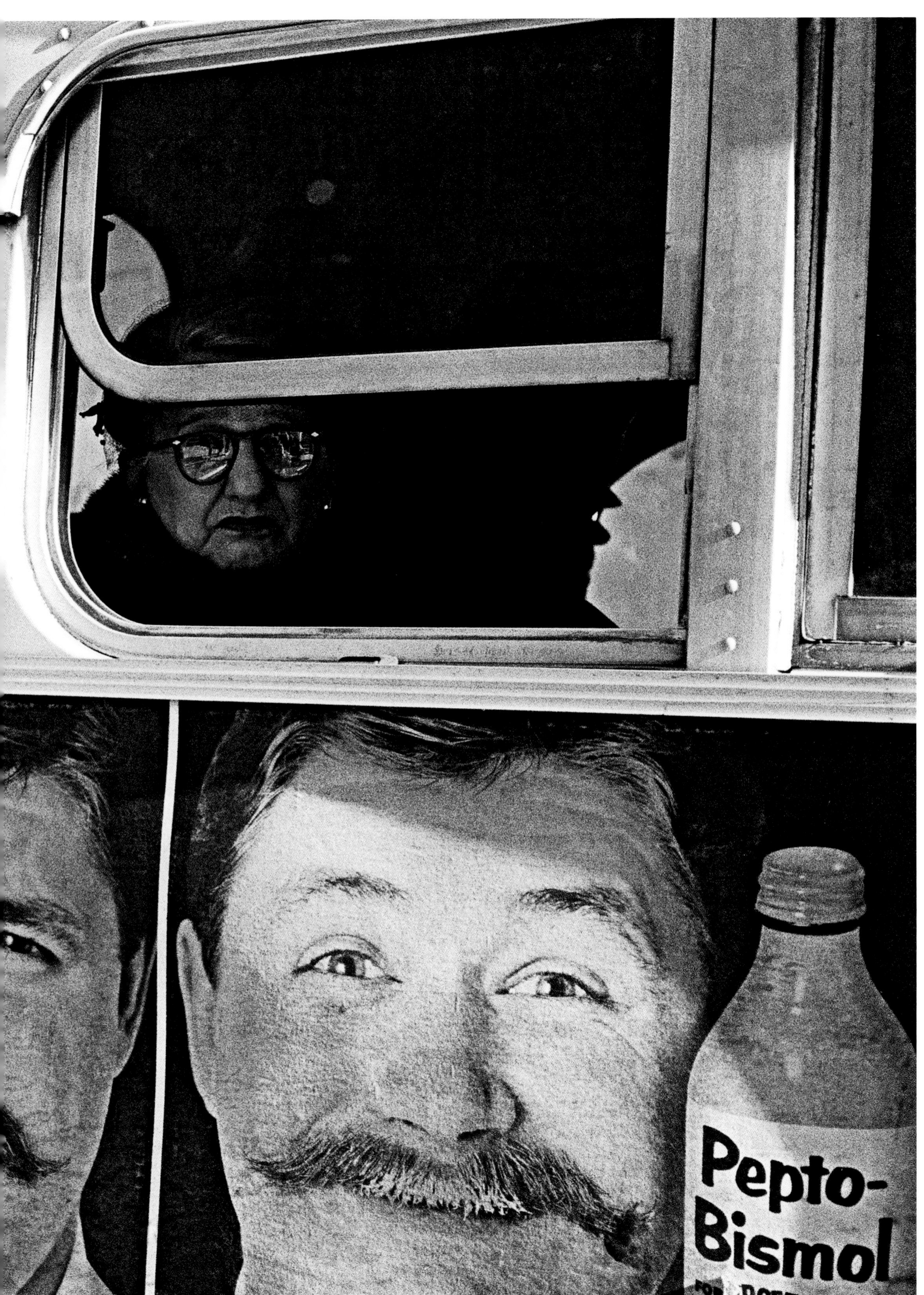
Pepto-
Bismol
FOR UPSET STOMACH

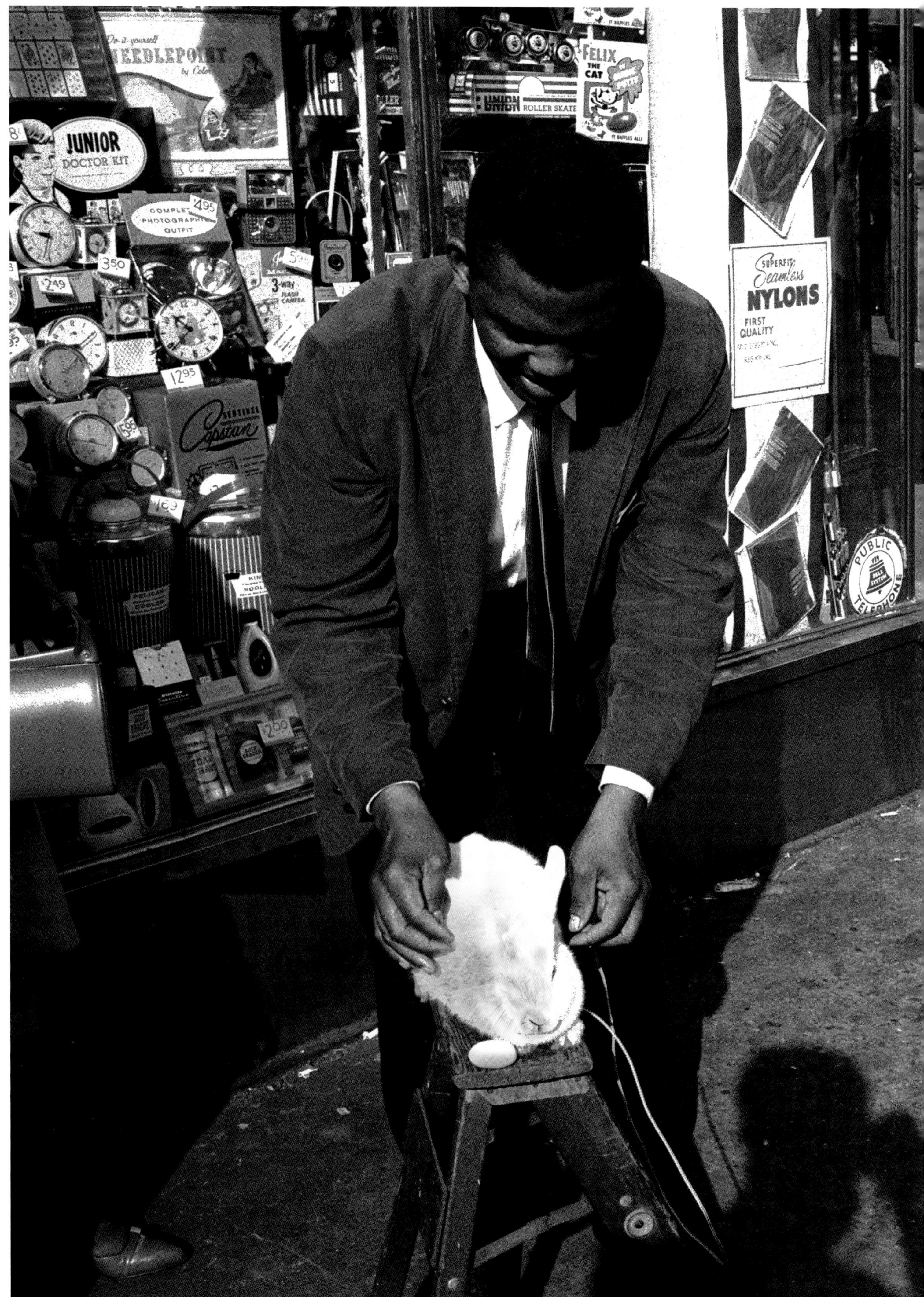
Do-it-yourself
NEEDLEPOINT
by Color
JUNIOR
DOCTOR KIT
COMPLETE
PHOTOGRAPHIC
OUTFIT
3-way
FLASH CAMERA
SENTINEL
Capstan
FELIX
THE
CAT
IT BAFFLES ALL!
UNION
ROLLER SKATE
Superfit
Seamless
NYLONS
FIRST
QUALITY
PUBLIC
TELEPHONE

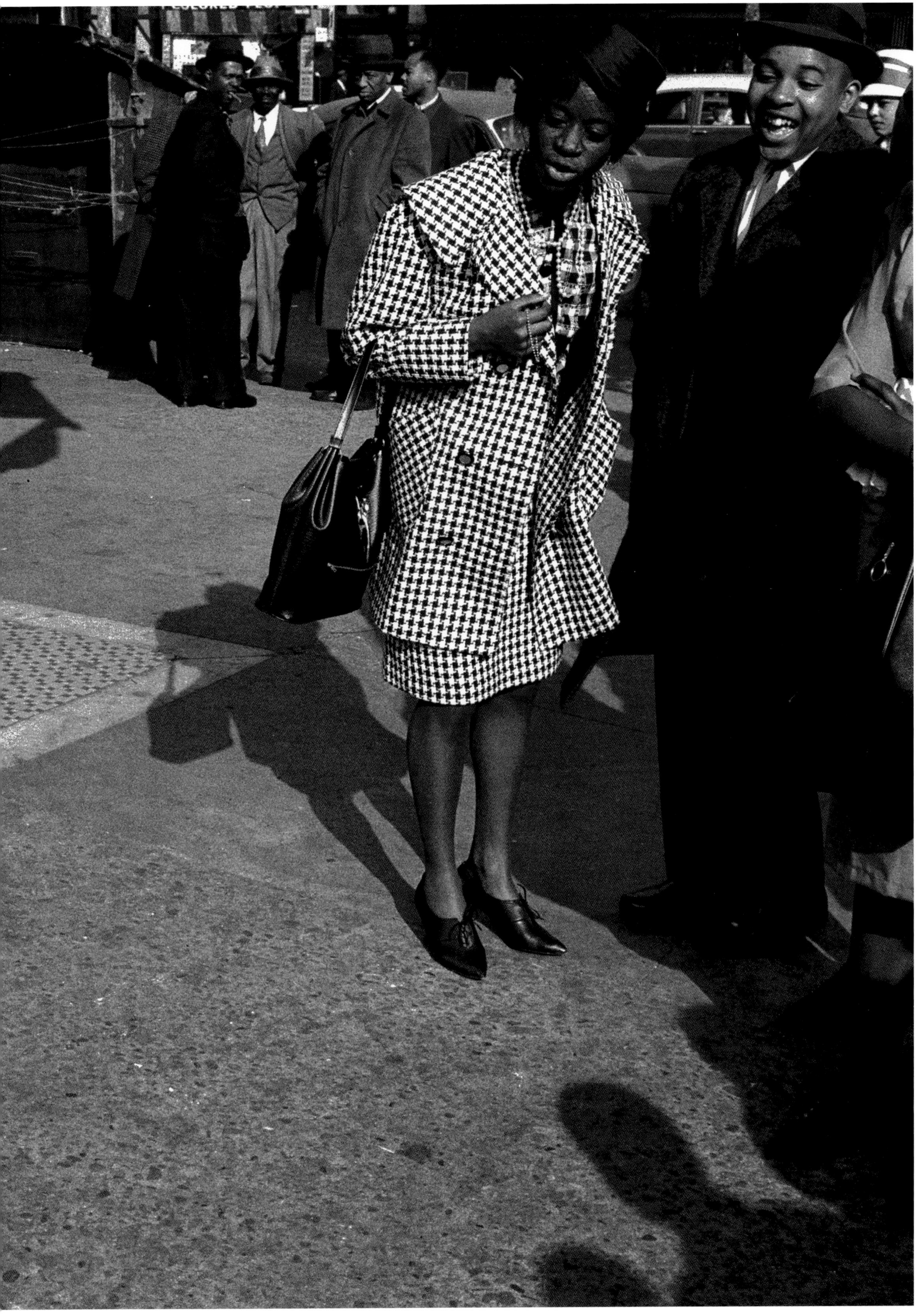

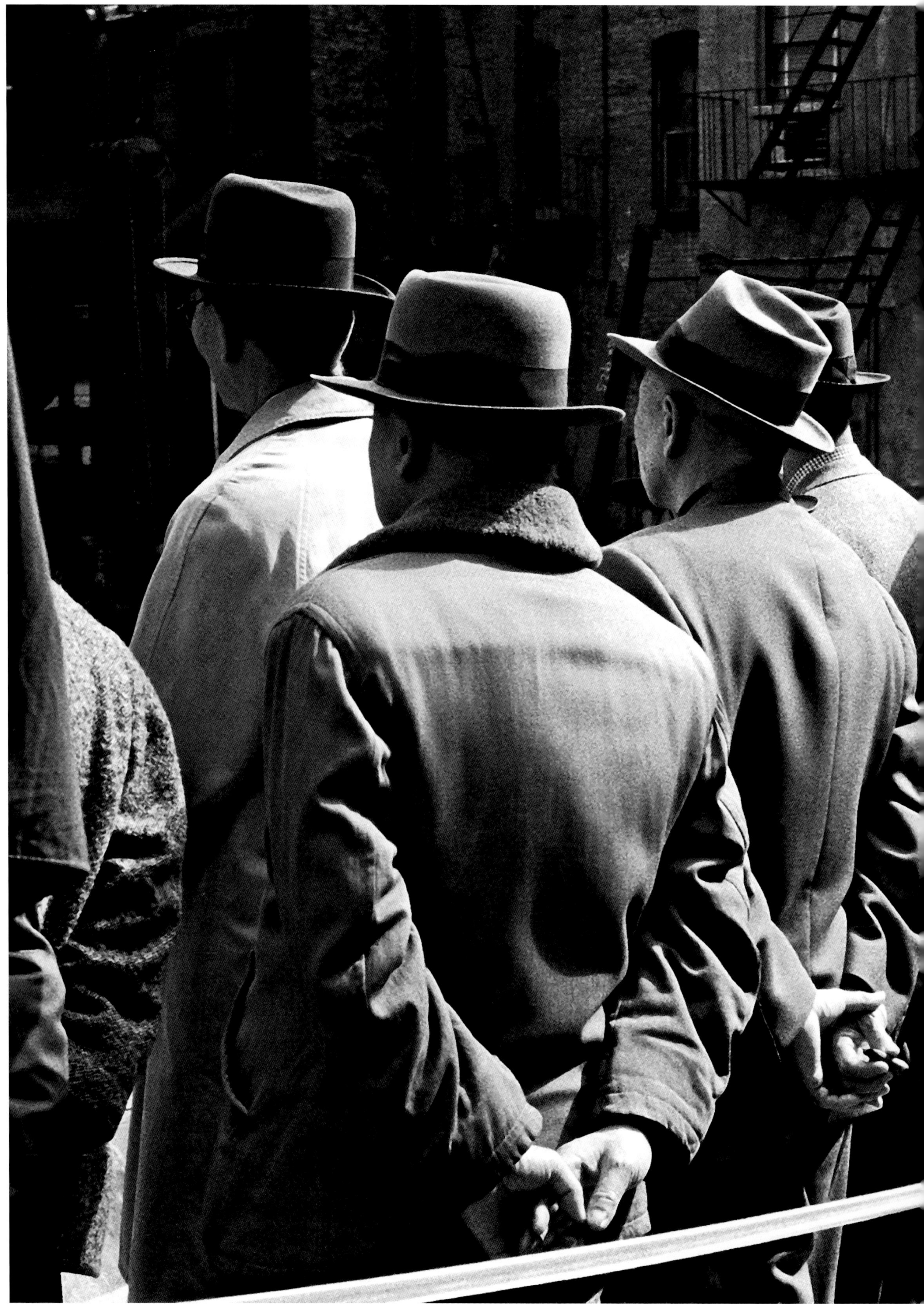

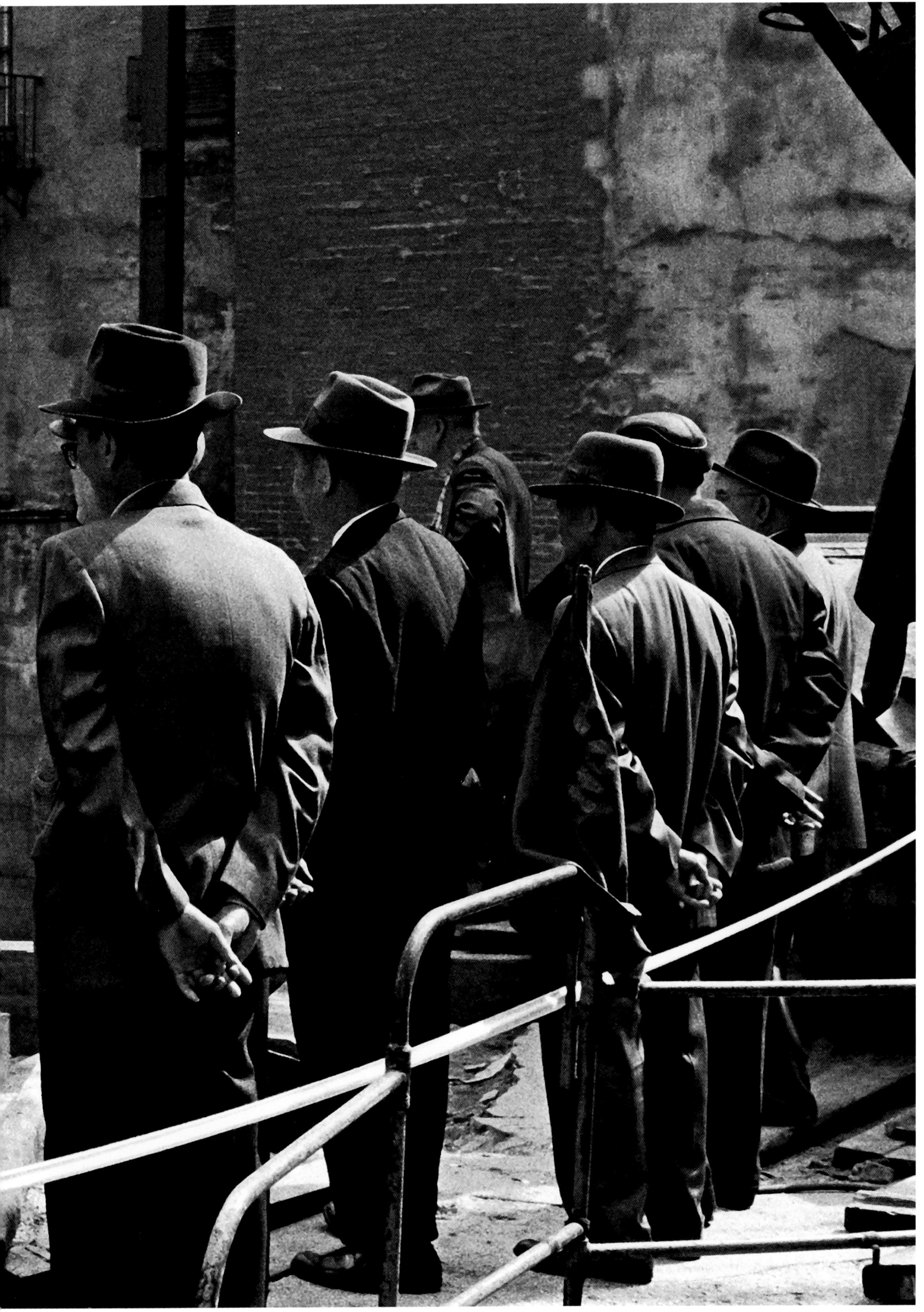

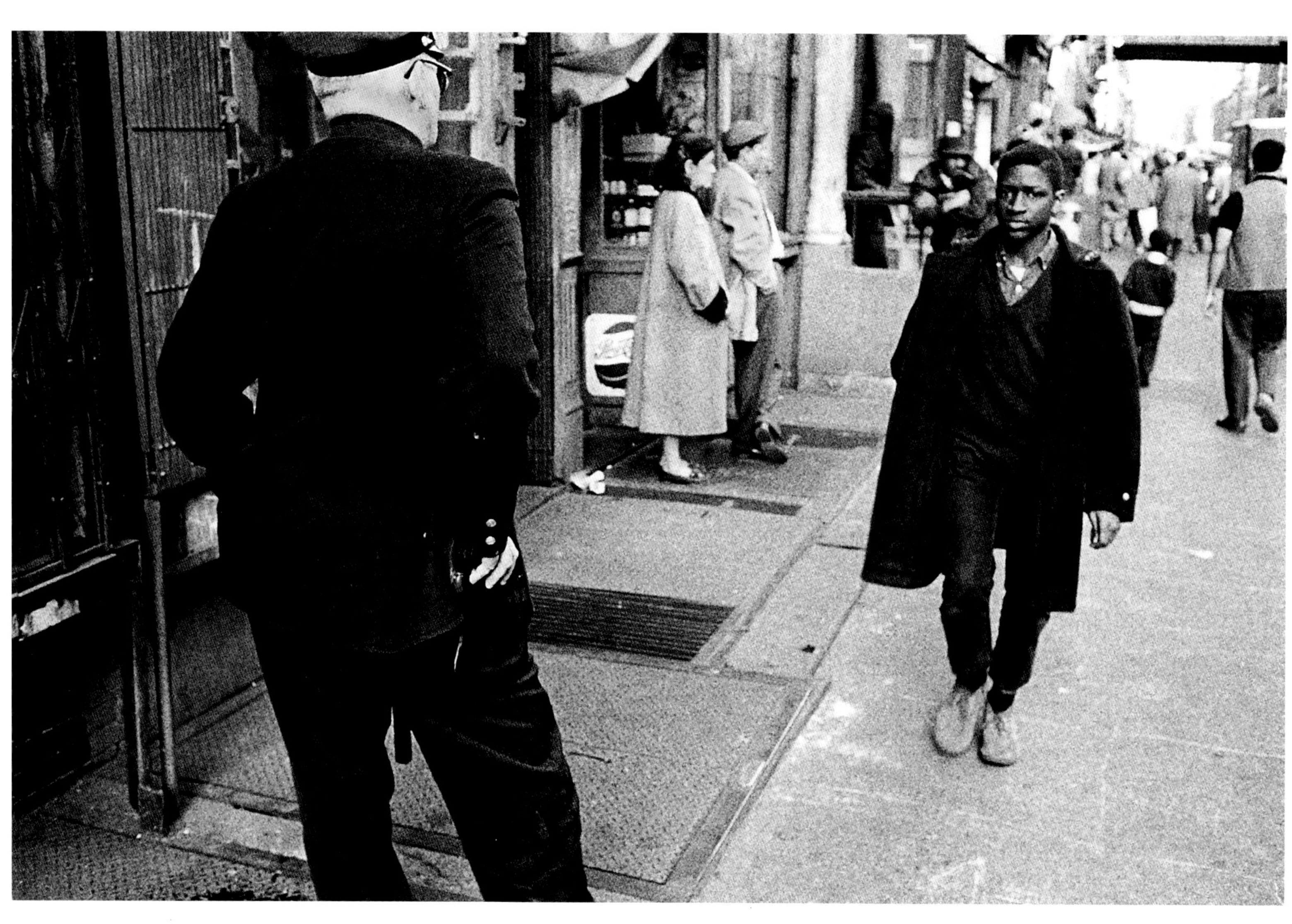

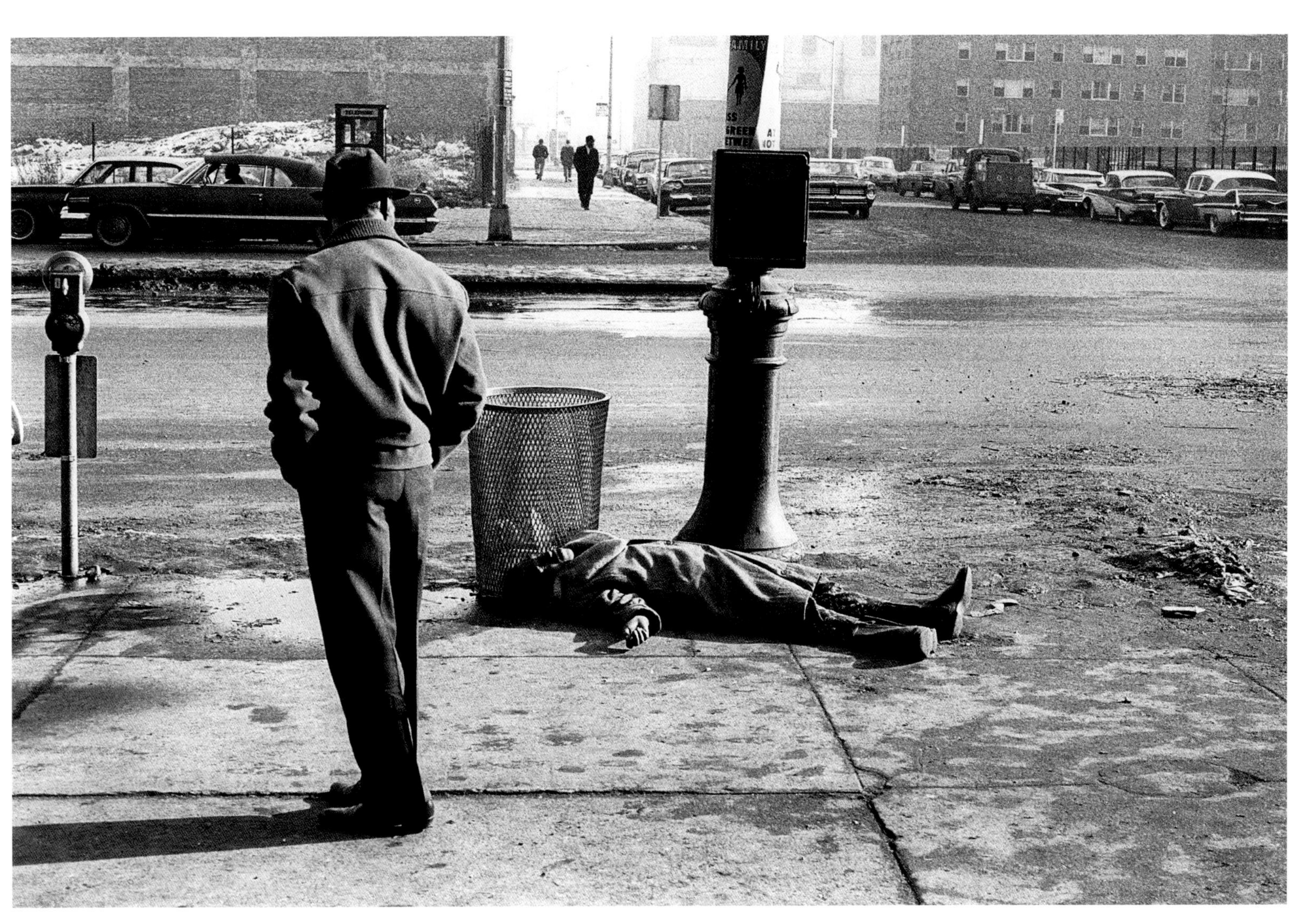

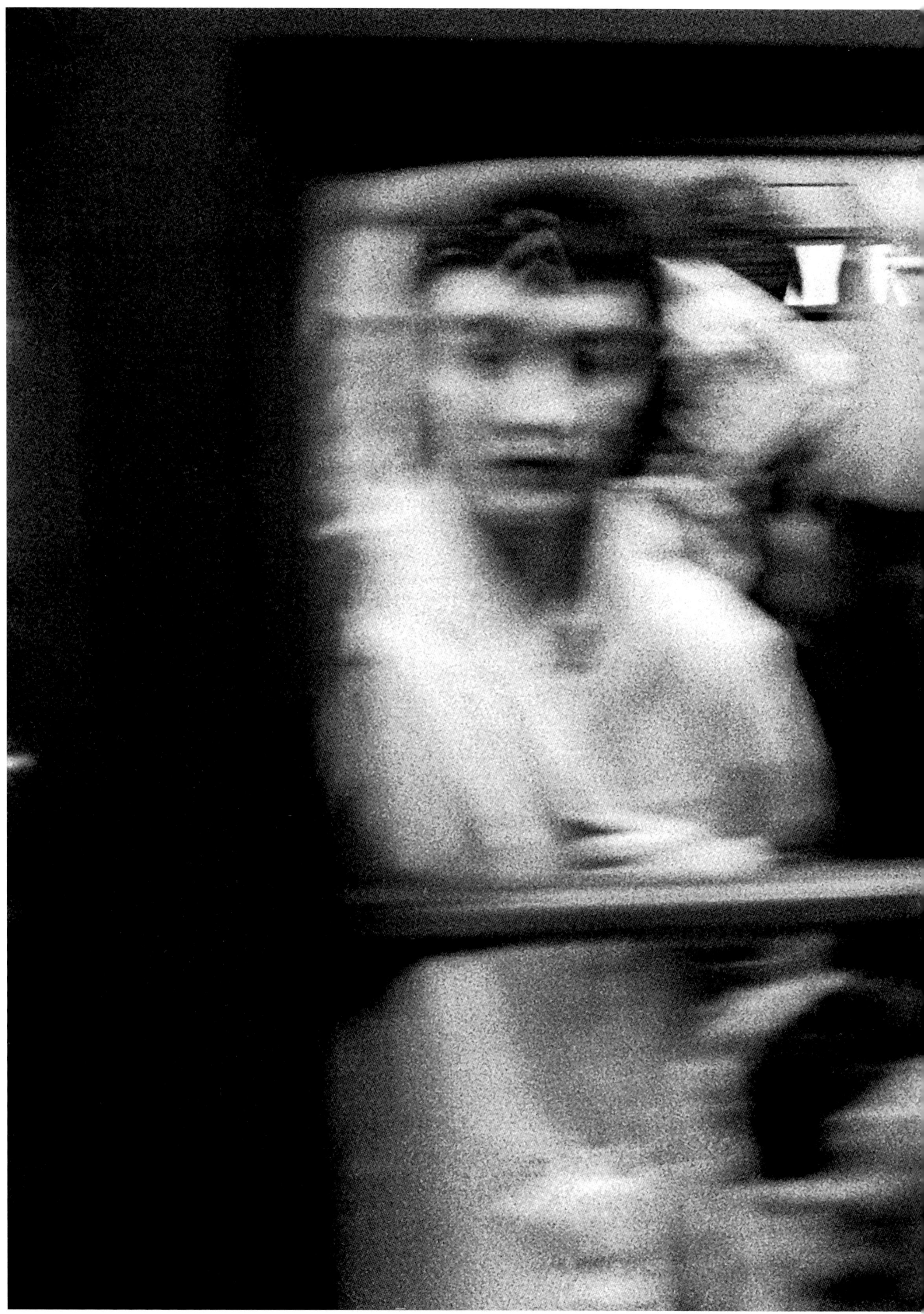

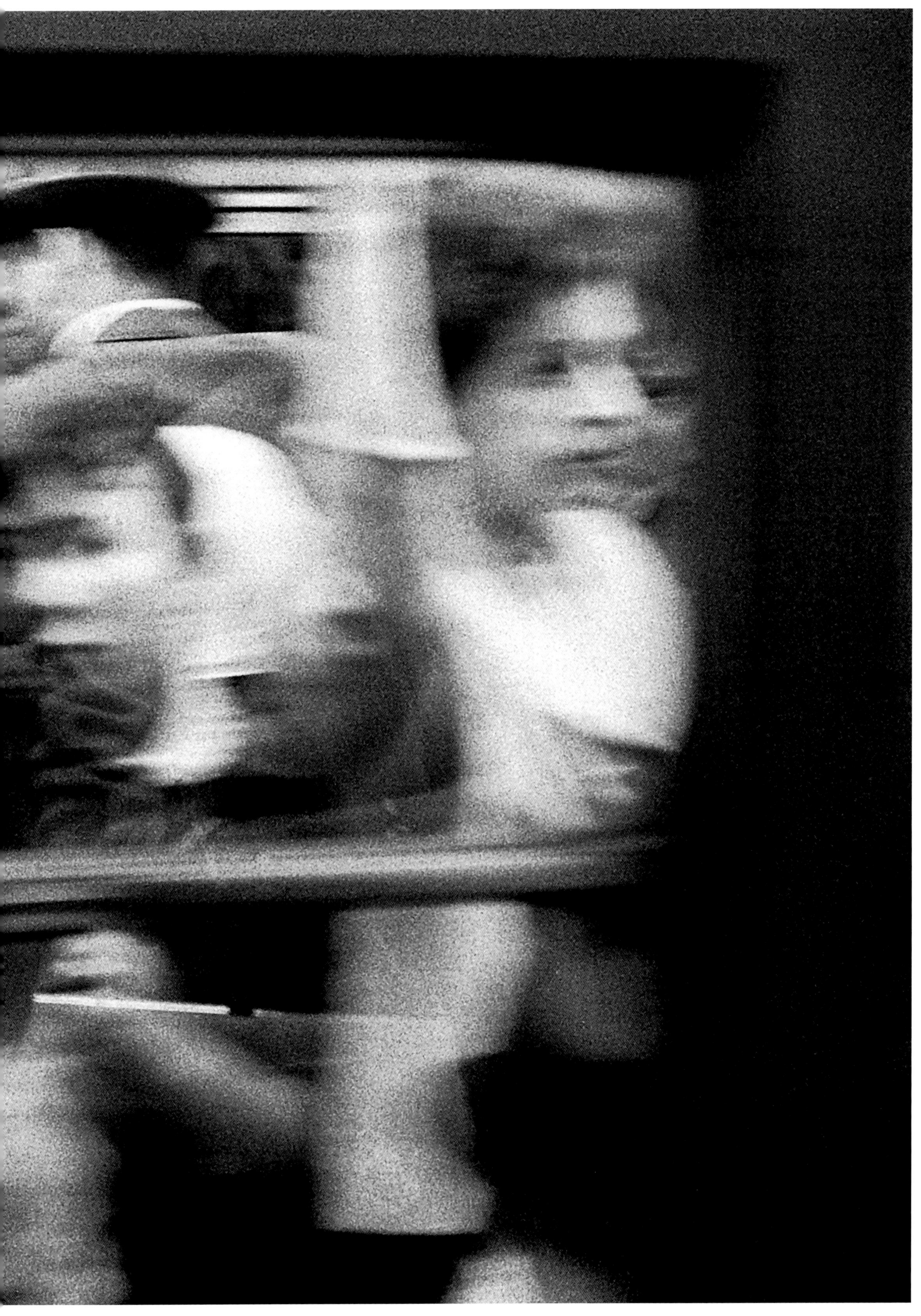

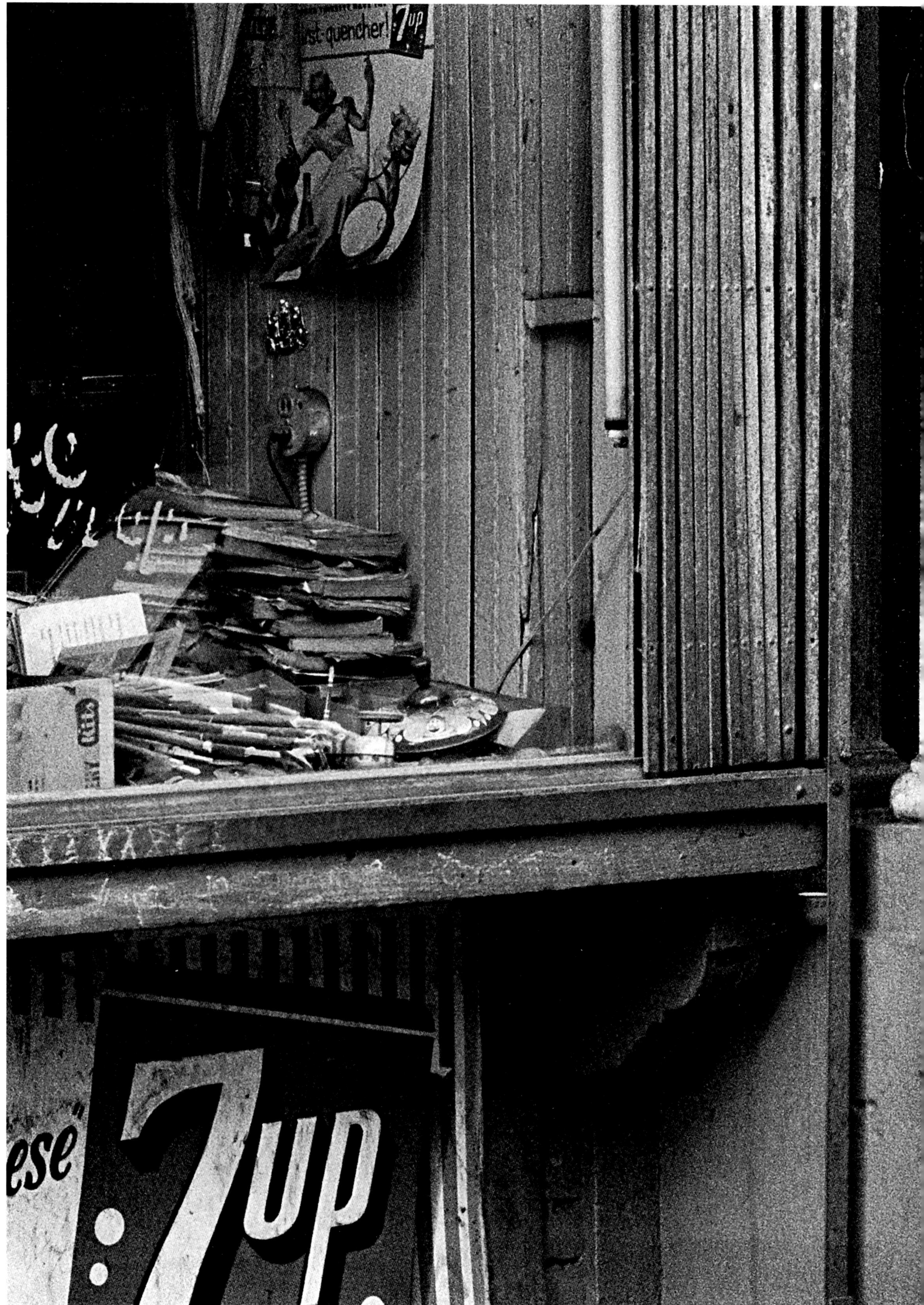
st-quencher! 7up
ese 7up

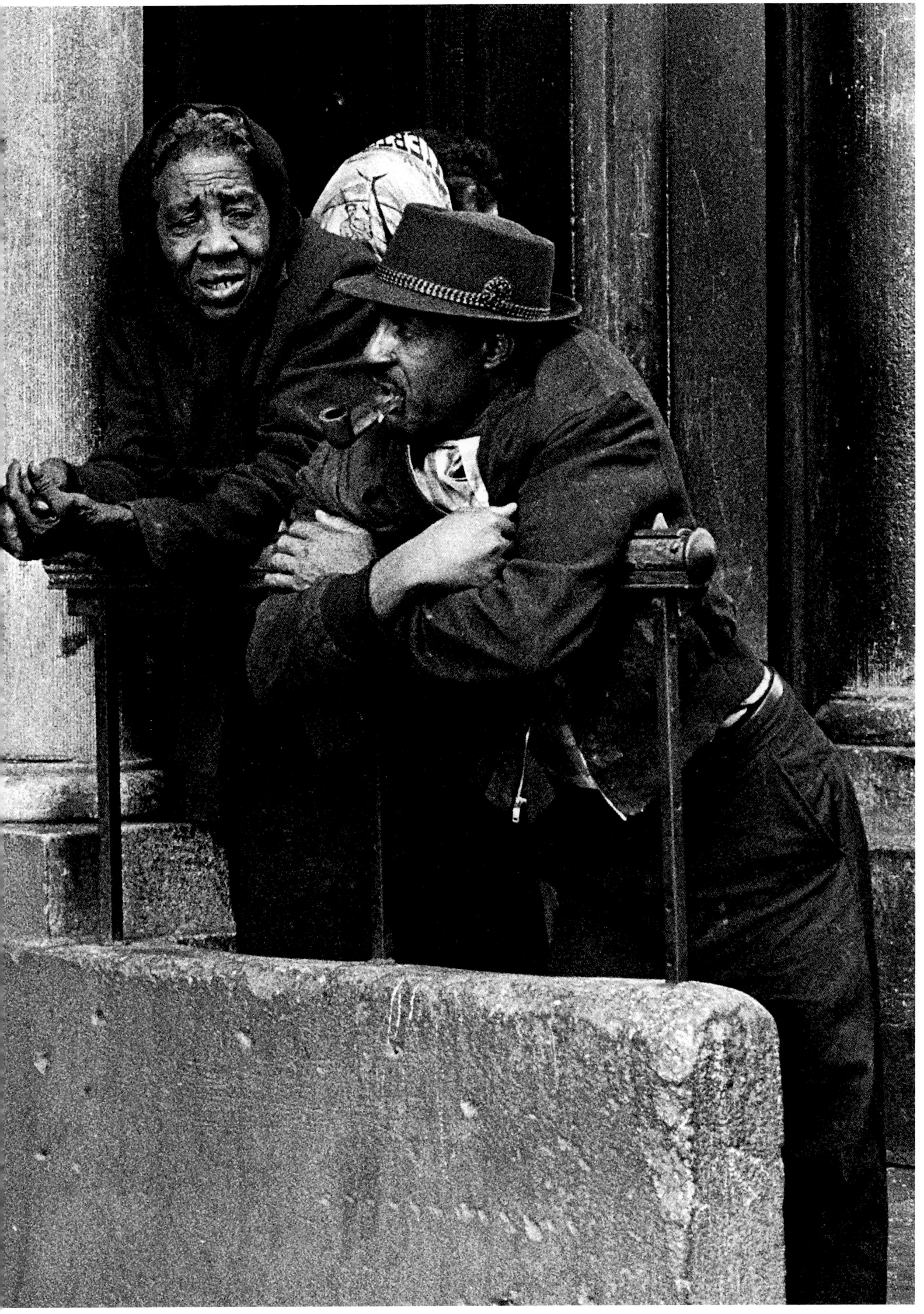

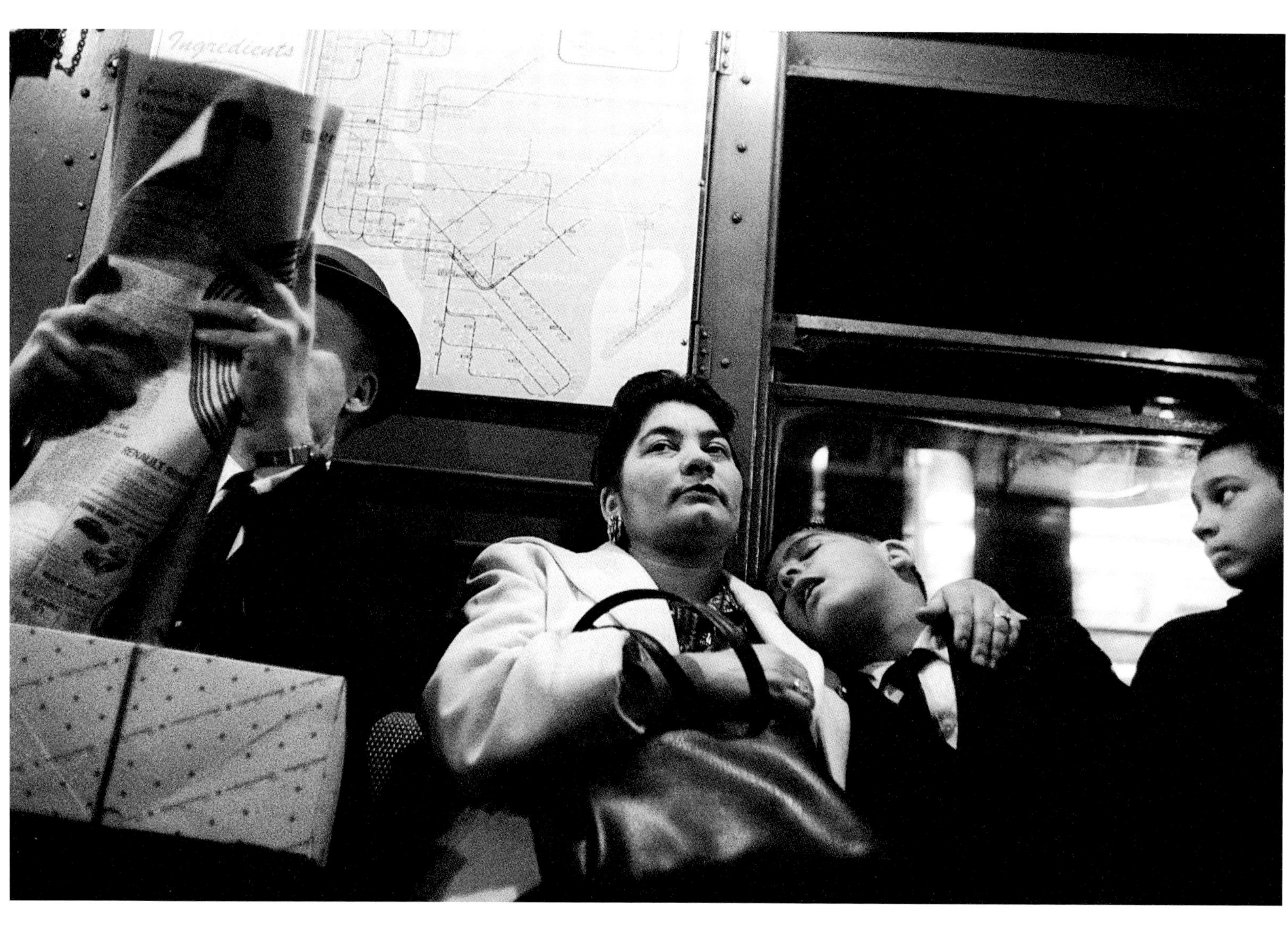
Ingredients

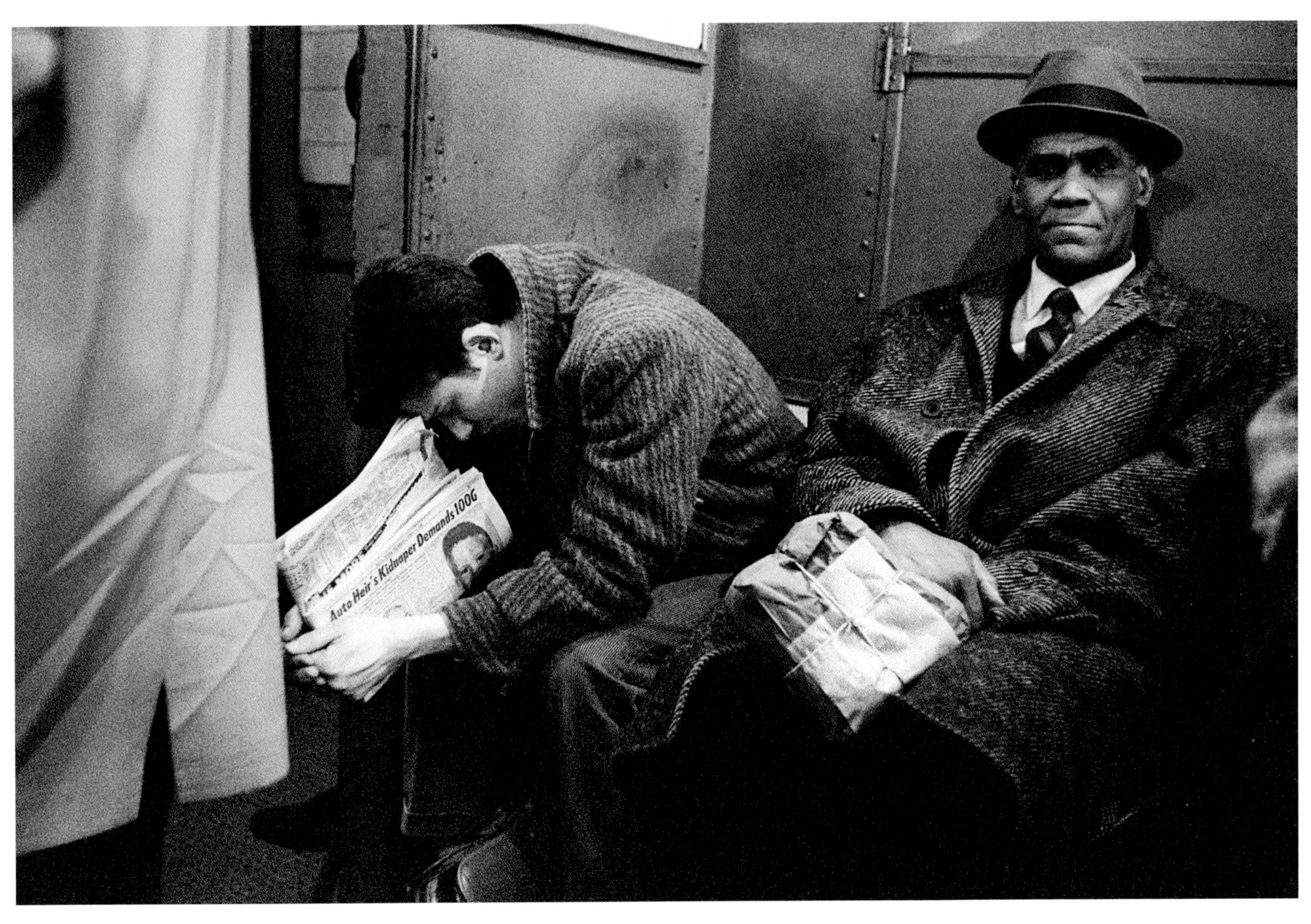
Auto Heir's Kidnaper Demands 100G

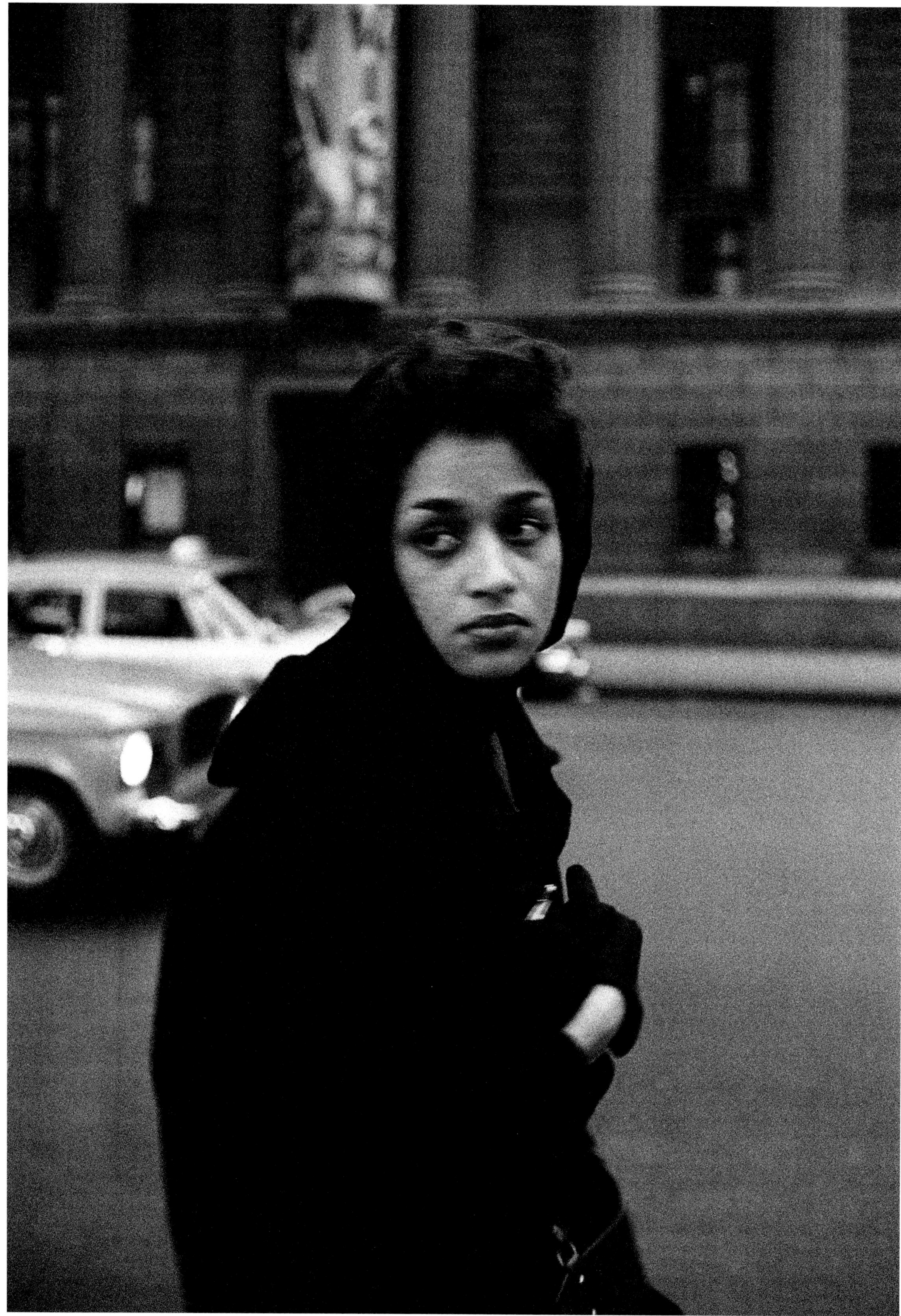

Everyone who walks the streets of New York with their eyes wide open takes imaginary snapshots and carries albums full of them in their heads. They mostly collect faces and when pressed will recall them in astonishing detail. My father, for example, knew a barber who said that he was just sixteen when he saw the most beautiful woman he ever saw in his life. She was disembarking from the Staten Island Ferry as he was boarding, their eyes met for a moment and he never forgot her. Walt Whitman has a poem called "A Broadway Pageant," written more than hundred and fifty years ago, in which he describes the people milling on its sidewalks: farmer, merchant, fisherman, mechanic, and along with them, the singing girl, the dancing girl, the unknown emperor, the great poet, and unacknowledged hero, crowding into the city from all directions, from Altay Mountains and far-flowing rivers of China, from Tibet, Assyria, Malaysia, and from hundreds of other places. It is no wonder Thomas Hoepker has felt at home in New York for more than fifty years, since faces in the crowd and the secrets they may be hiding are his obsession too.

Unlike Paris, Rome, and many other great cities, New York is not conventionally beautiful. There is order to the Old World. What is architecturally ugly and what is beautiful are carefully segregated. Not so in New York, where buildings tend to be thrown together more or less haphazardly. One can take a walk in London in complete confidence that one's aesthetic ideas are not going to be upset. In Manhattan, on the other hand, one may turn a corner to find a skyscraper made of glass next to a dilapidated shack fronting a small parking lot with cars stacked up on top of one another by some clever mechanical contrivance, or glimpse a spire of a cathedral reflected in a store window full of manicurists at work on a block of several boarded-up stores and buildings. If Aristotle was right that "the mark of a poet is to see a connection between seemingly incongruous things," New York makes poets of us all.

Not just poets, of course. Sights, like the ones that I'm describing, in which reality and illusion is not easily differentiated, make one think of photomontage, the art of combining several photographs into a single picture. They give New York a fantastic quality even in broad daylight.

In his fascination with the city, Hoepker encounters beauty where no one expects to find it. Like his photograph of a bright red armchair facing three abandoned and gutted brick buildings where someone once sat, or that terrifying and very famous one in which five people are seen sunning themselves and chatting quietly on the bank of East River while behind them on the spot where the twin towers collapsed in Manhattan earlier that day, black smoke and dust rise into the clear September sky. This is what Paul Rosenfeld, writing about Alfred Stieglitz called "the full majesty of the moment," which the mind is not able to retain in its fullness and the camera can. Again and again Hoepker captures in his photographs what even the most sensitive and alert observer has overlooked. That is where the delight and the shock of looking at the images in this book comes from, the recognition that while every living eye has stories to tell, the eye of a great photographer not only tells them better, but tells them so they may last.

— Charles Simic

Jeder, der mit weit geöffneten Augen durch New York geht, macht im Geiste Schnappschüsse und hat ganze Alben dieser imaginären Bilder im Kopf. Er sammelt Eindrücke von Gesichtern und kann sich, wenn nötig, erstaunlich detailliert an sie erinnern. Mein Vater zum Beispiel kannte einen Herrenfriseur, der ihm erzählte, er habe mit nur sechzehn Jahren die schönste Frau seines Lebens gesehen. Sie kam von der Staten Island Fähre, als er gerade einstieg, und ihre Blicke begegneten sich für einen kurzen Moment. Er hat sie nie vergessen. Vor mehr als einhundertfünfzig Jahren verfasste Walt Whitman ein Gedicht mit dem Titel „Festzug auf dem Broadway", in dem er die Menschen auf den belebten Gehsteigen beschrieb: den Bauern, den Kaufmann, den Fischer, den Mechaniker, und daneben das singende Mädchen, das tanzende Mädchen, den unbekannten Kaiser, den großen Dichter, den verkannten Helden – Menschen, die aus allen Himmelsrichtungen in die Stadt strömten: aus dem Altaigebirge und von den Ufern der endlosen Flüsse in China, aus Tibet, Assyrien, Malaysia und aus Hunderten von anderen Orten. Es ist also kein Wunder, wenn Thomas Hoepker sich seit mehr als fünfzig Jahren in New York zu Hause fühlt, denn auch er ist besessen von den Gesichtern in der Menge und den Geheimnissen, die sie vielleicht verbergen.

Anders als Paris, Rom und viele andere großartige Metropolen ist New York nicht im herkömmlichen Sinne schön. In der Alten Welt herrscht eine gewisse Ordnung. Schöne und hässliche Architekturen sind sorgfältig voneinander getrennt. Nicht so in New York, wo sich die Gebäude tendenziell mehr oder weniger planlos aneinanderreihen. Man kann in dem vollen Vertrauen durch London spazieren, dass die eigenen ästhetischen Vorstellungen nicht erschüttert werden. In Manhattan dagegen kann hinter der nächsten Ecke ein gläserner Wolkenkratzer neben einer verfallenen Bretterbude und einem kleinen Parkplatz auftauchen, auf dem sich dank einer cleveren mechanischen Konstruktion die Autos stapeln. Oder man erblickt mitten in einem Straßenblock mit hier und da vernagelten Geschäften und Gebäuden den Turm einer Kathedrale, der sich in einem Schaufenster voller Nagelpflegerinnen bei der Arbeit spiegelt. Wenn Aristoteles recht hatte, dass es „das Merkmal eines Dichters ist, einen Zusammenhang zwischen scheinbar unvereinbaren Dingen zu sehen", dann macht New York uns alle zu Dichtern.

Aber natürlich nicht nur zu Dichtern. Anblicke wie die gerade beschriebenen, in denen Illusion und Wirklichkeit kaum voneinander zu unterscheiden sind, lassen uns an Fotomontagen denken, an die Kunst, mehrere Fotografien zu einem Bild zusammenzufügen. Selbst am helllichten Tag verleihen sie New York etwas Fantastisches. In seiner Faszination für die Stadt begegnet Hoepker der Schönheit, wo sie niemand vermutet. Etwa in der Aufnahme eines knallroten, auf drei verlassene und ausgeschlachtete Klinkerbauten blickenden Sessels, in dem einmal jemand saß; oder in der erschreckenden, weltberühmt gewordenen Fotografie von fünf jungen Leuten, die am East River in der Sonne sitzen und entspannt plaudern, während im Hintergrund, dort, wo Stunden zuvor die Zwillingstürme eingestürzt sind, dunkler Rauch und Staub in den klaren Septemberhimmel über Manhattan aufsteigt. Das ist es, was Paul Rosenfeld in einem Essay über Alfred Stieglitz mit „der ganzen Herrlichkeit des Augenblicks" meinte, deren Fülle sich nicht mit dem Verstand, wohl aber mit der Kamera bewahren lässt. Wieder und wieder fängt Hoepker in seinen Fotografien ein, was selbst dem sensibelsten und aufmerksamsten Beobachter entgeht. Hier liegt der Grund, warum uns das Betrachten der Bilder in diesem Buch begeistert und schockiert: in der Erkenntnis, dass zwar jedes offene Auge Geschichten zu erzählen hat, das Auge des Fotografen sie aber nicht nur besser erzählt, sondern auch so, dass sie die Zeit überdauern.

— Charles Simic

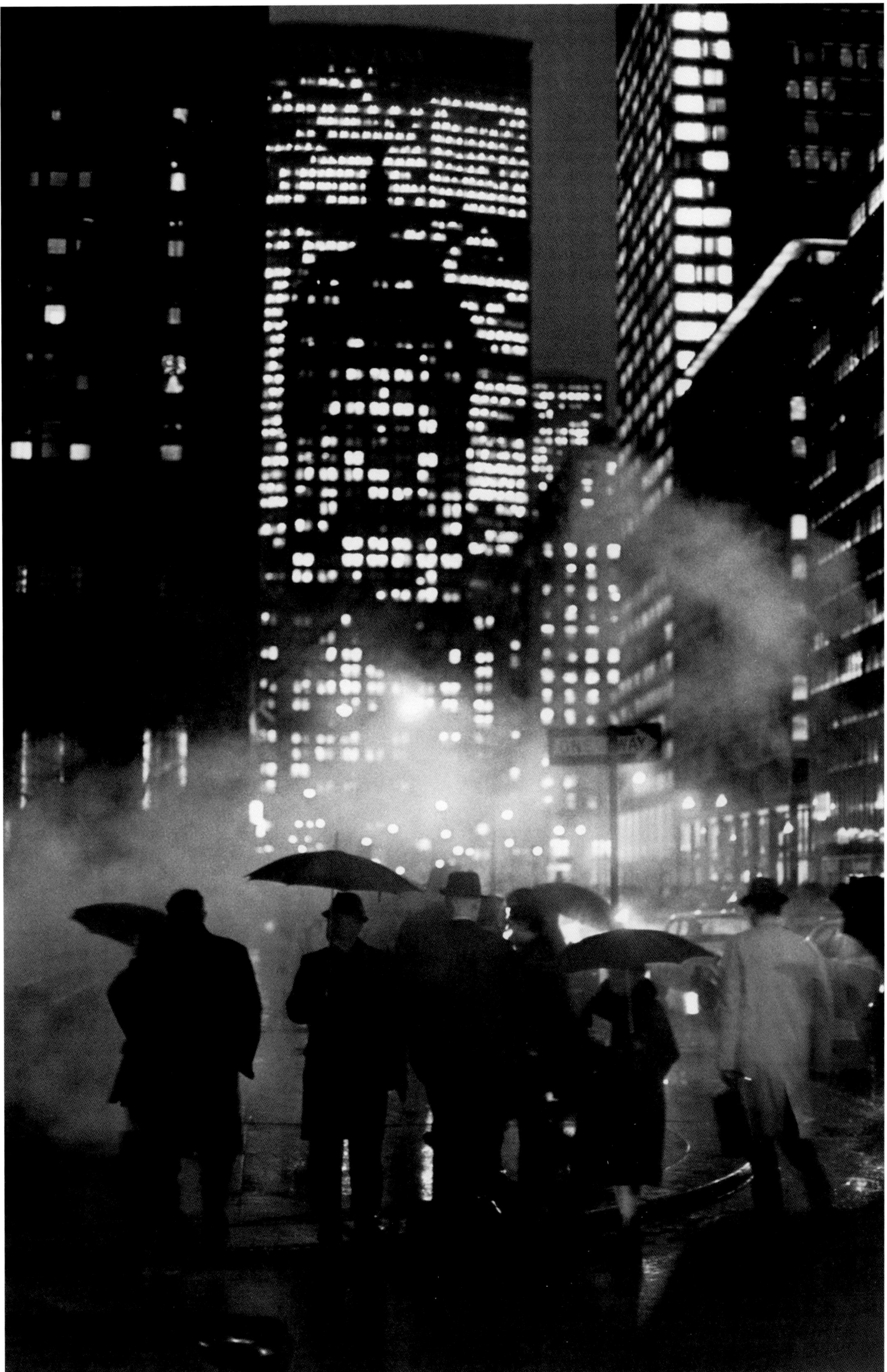

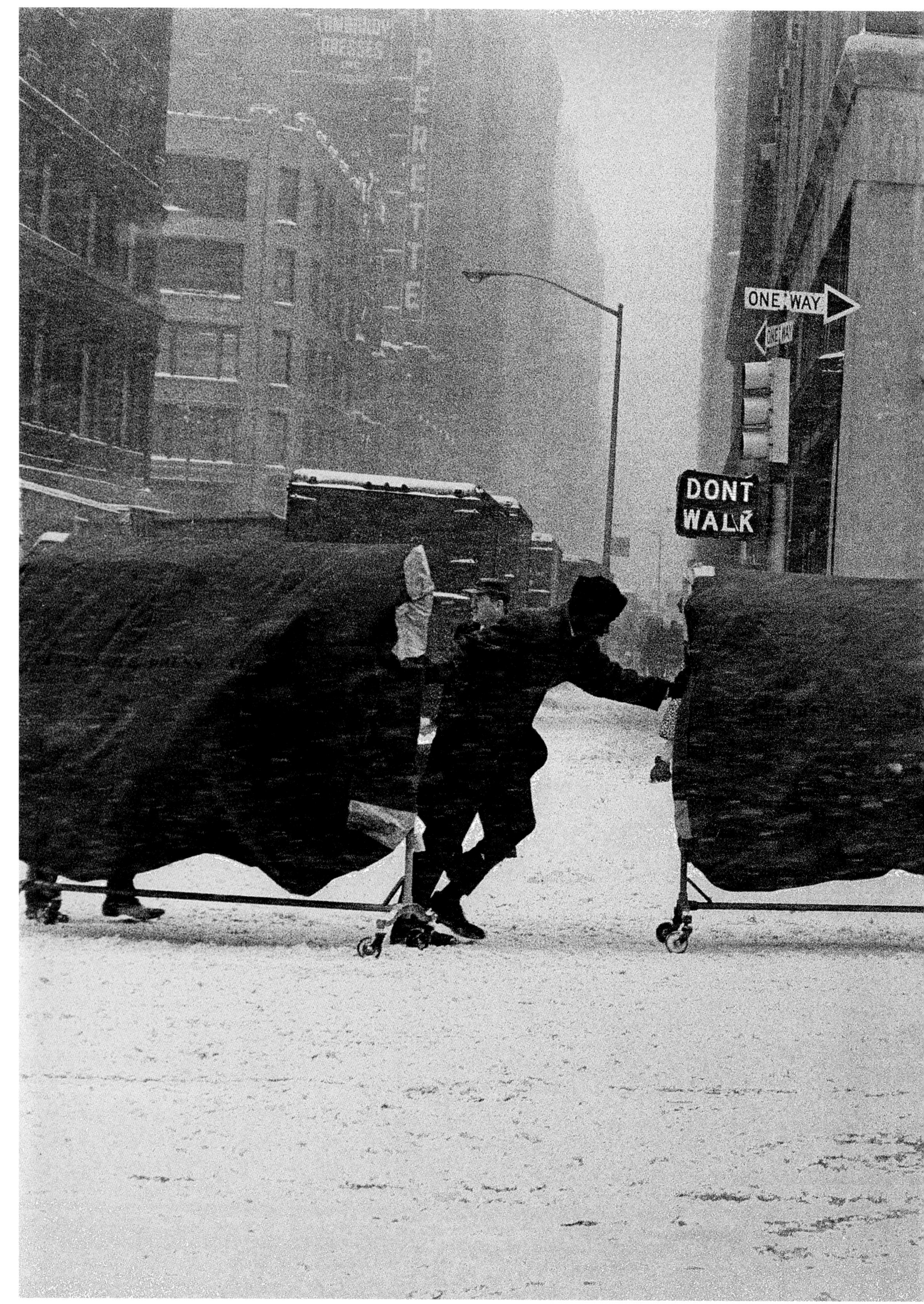
ONE WAY
ONE WAY
DONT
WALK

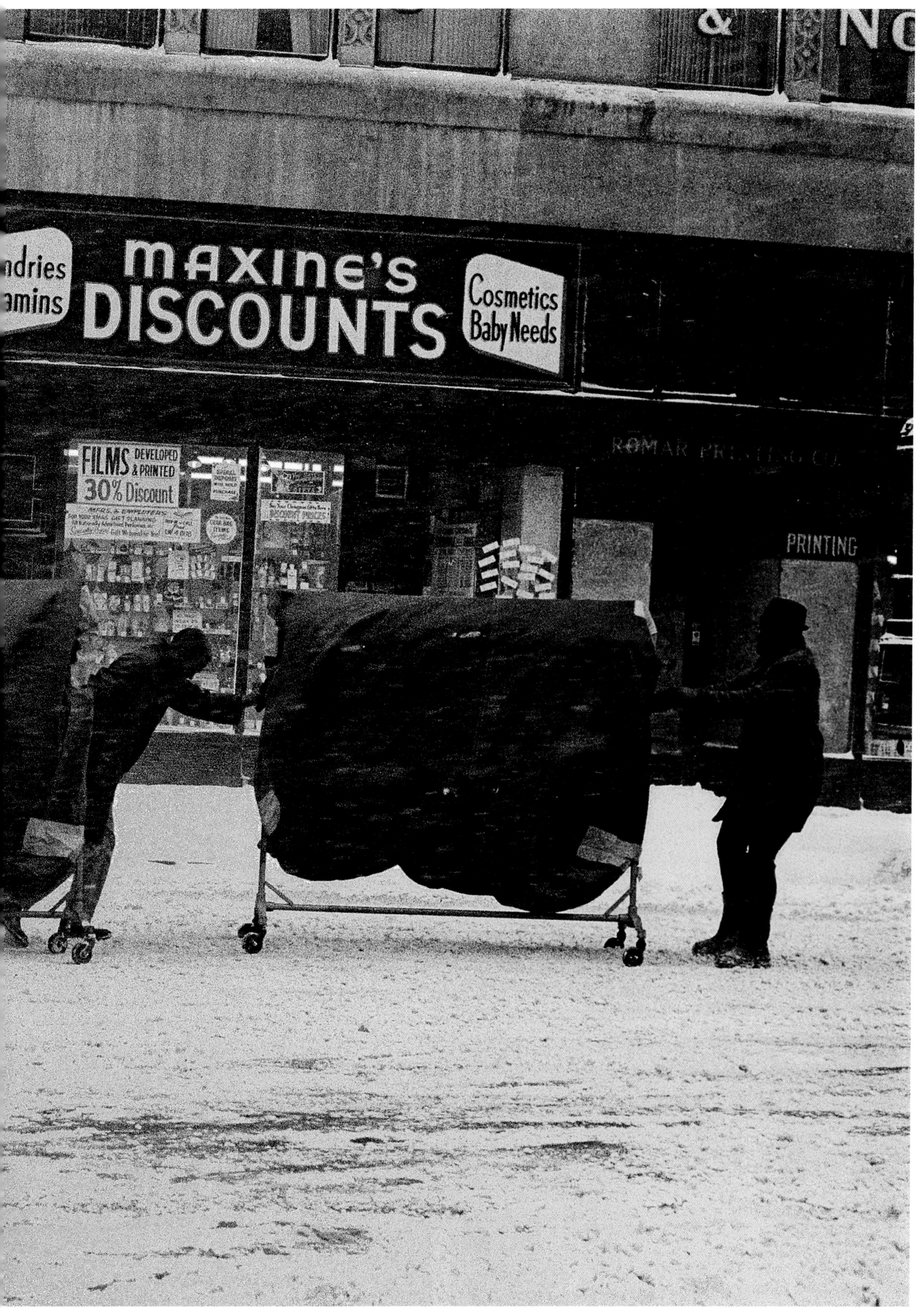

ndries
amins
maxine's
DISCOUNTS
Cosmetics
Baby Needs
FILMS DEVELOPED & PRINTED
30% Discount
PRINTING

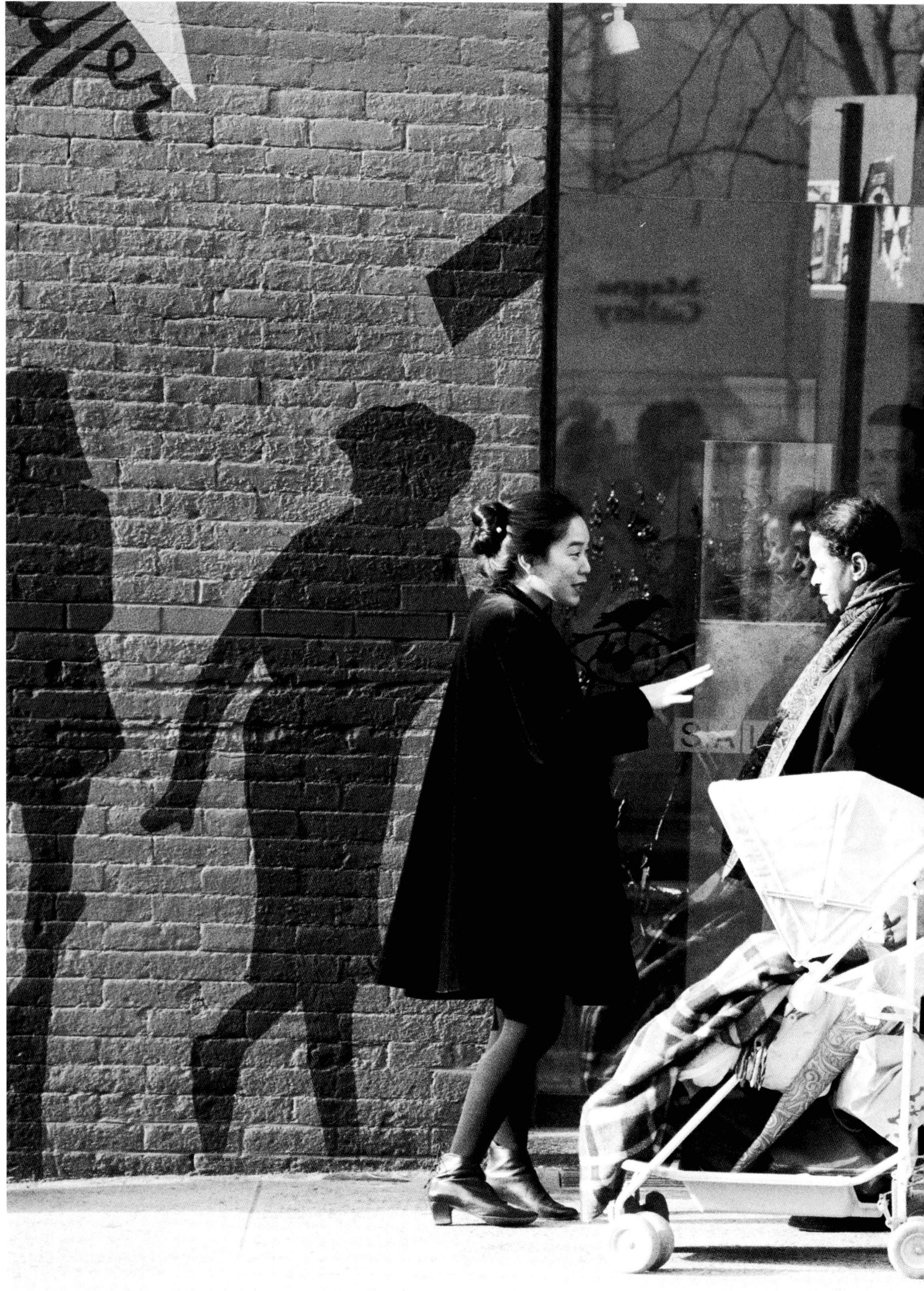

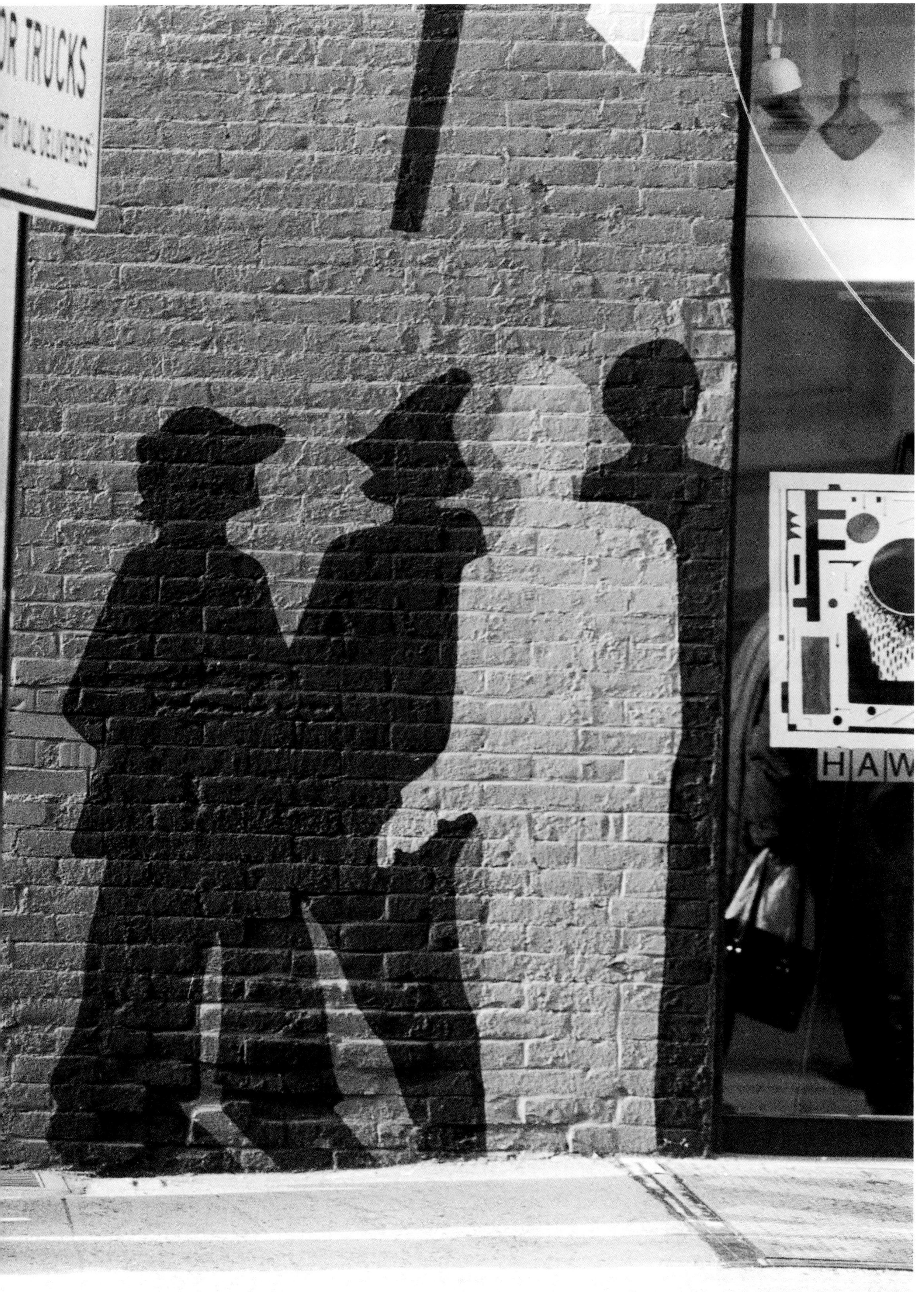
OR TRUCKS
FT LOCAL DELIVERIES
HAW

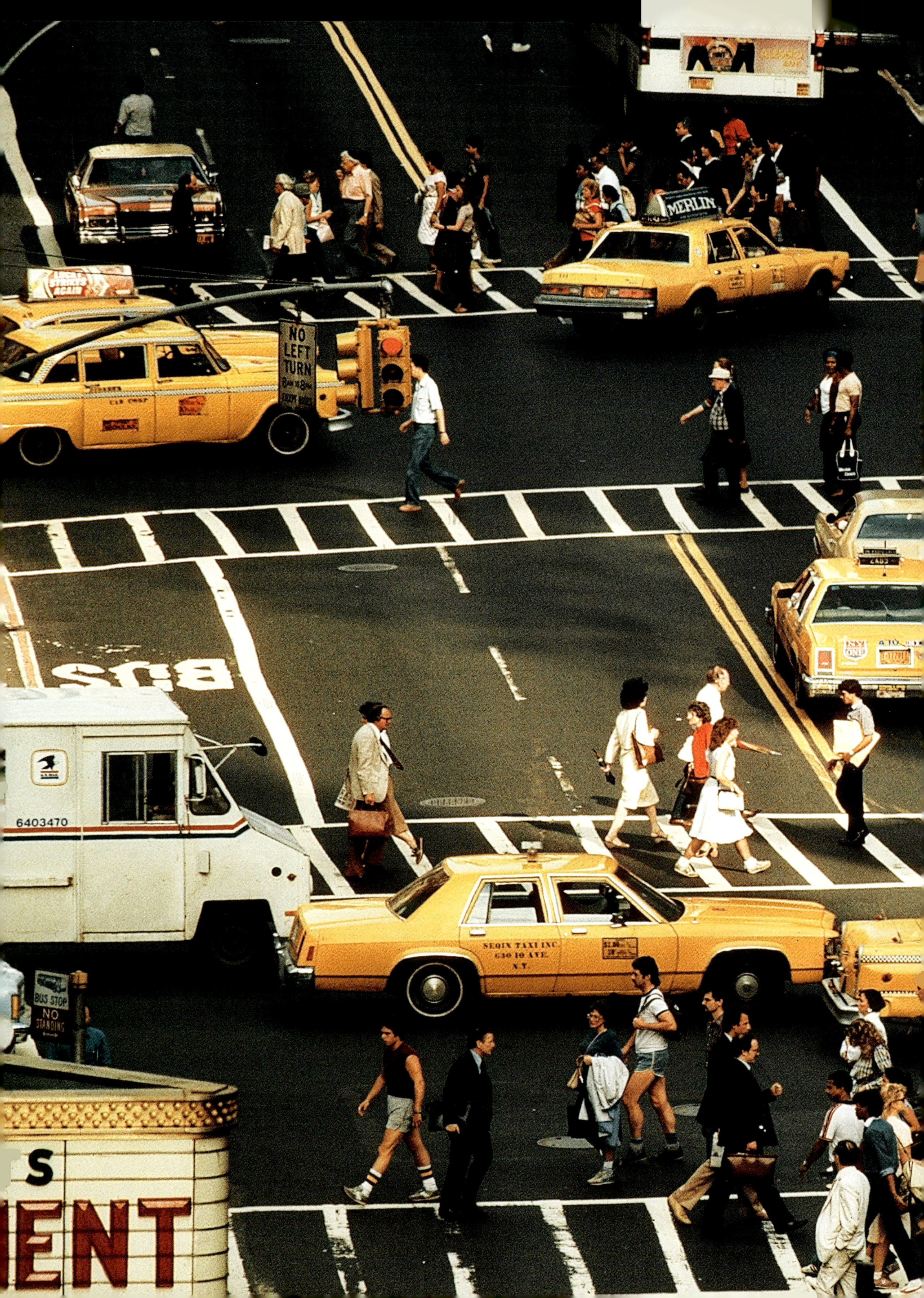
LOCAL
STRIKES
AGAIN
NO
LEFT
TURN
8AM TO 8AM
EXCEPT BUSES
MERLIN
BUS STOP
NO
STANDING
U.S. MAIL
6403470
SEQIN TAXI INC
636 10 AVE
N.Y.
BUS
ENT
S
ALESSIO

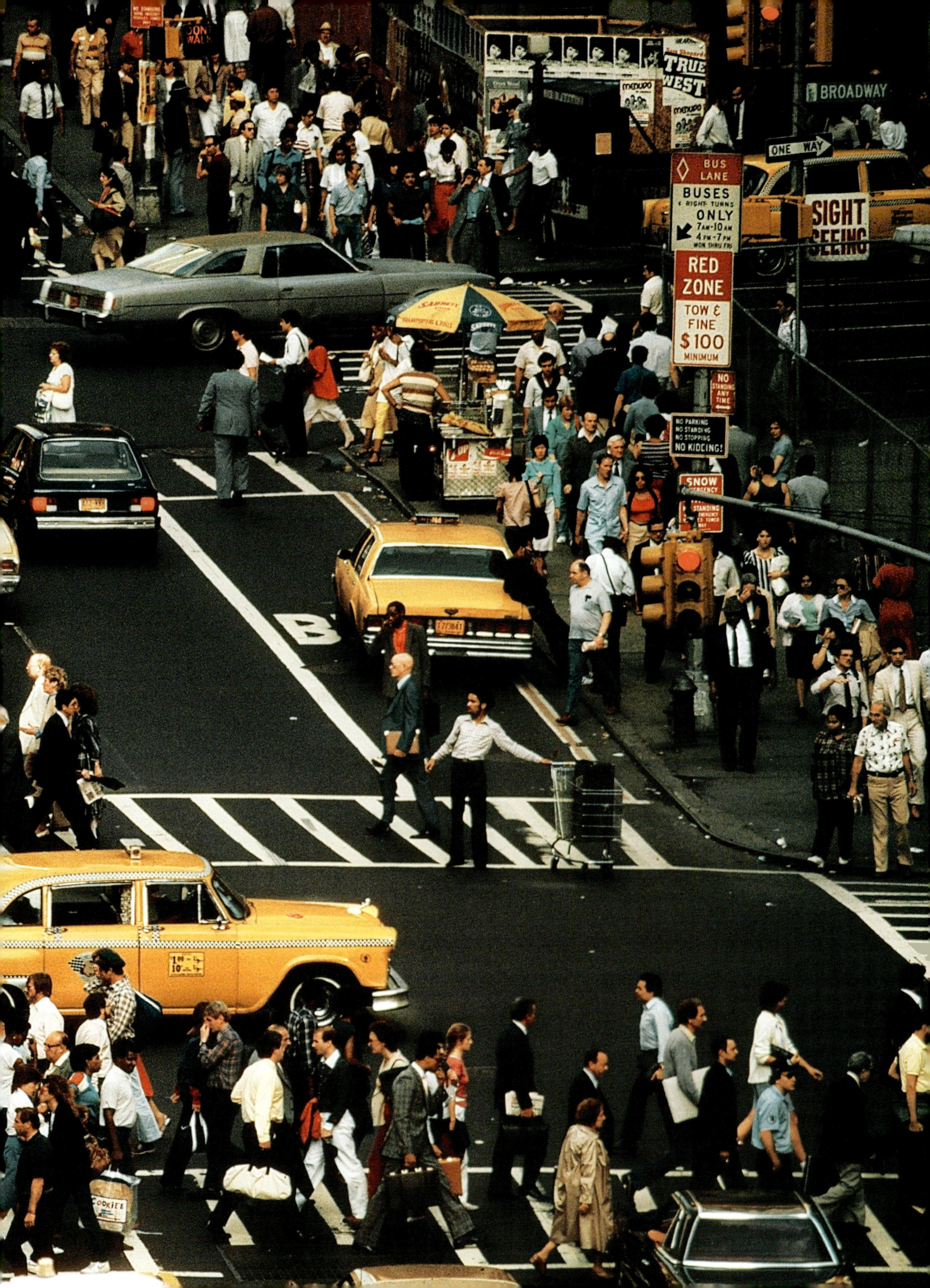

TRUE
WEST
BROADWAY
ONE WAY
SIGHT
SEEING
BUS
LANE
BUSES
& RIGHT TURNS
ONLY
7AM-10AM
4PM-7PM
MON THRU FRI
RED
ZONE
TOW &
FINE
$100
MINIMUM
NO STANDING
ANY TIME
NO PARKING
NO STANDING
NO KIDDING!
SNOW
EMERGENCY
COOKIES

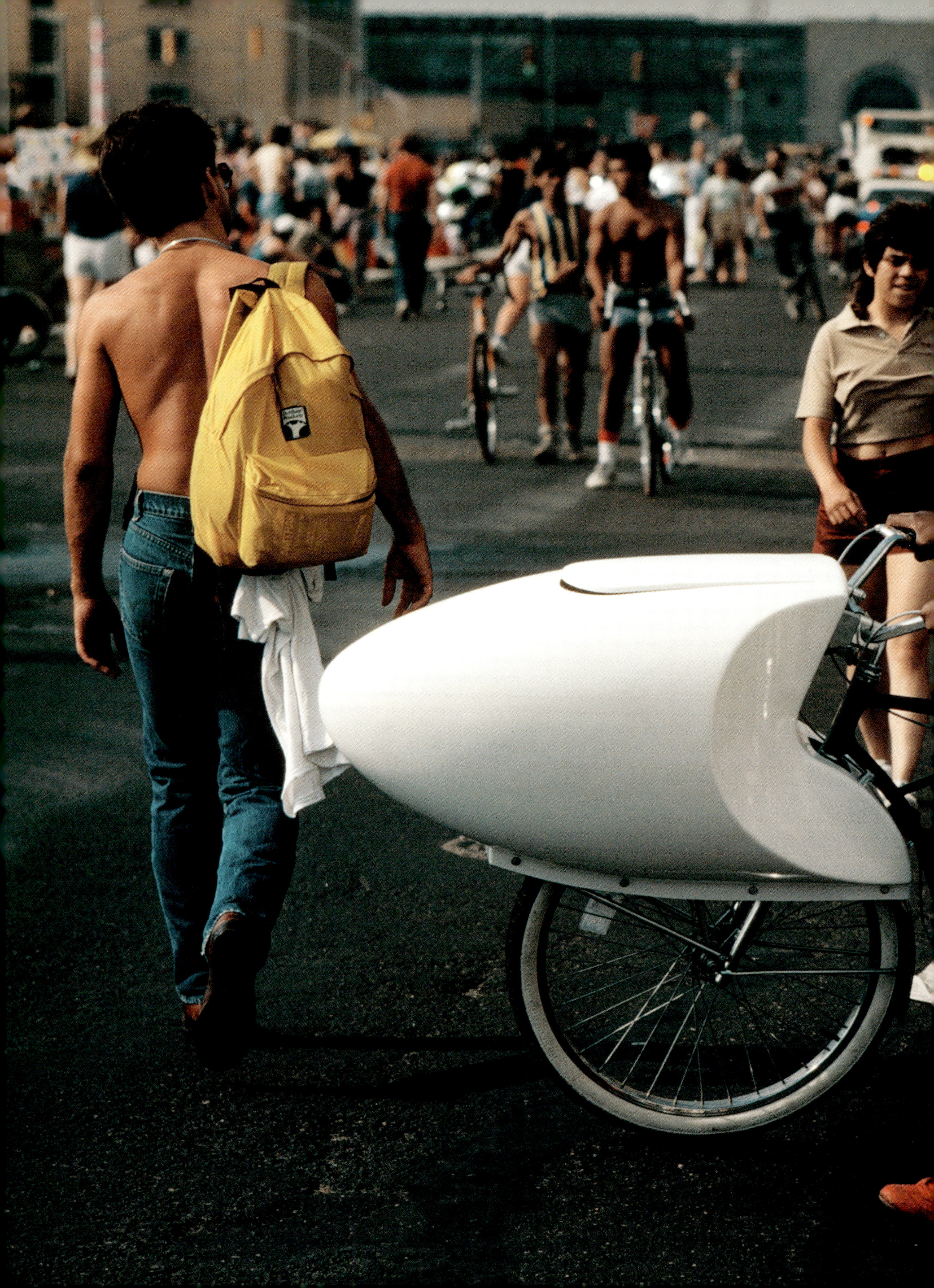

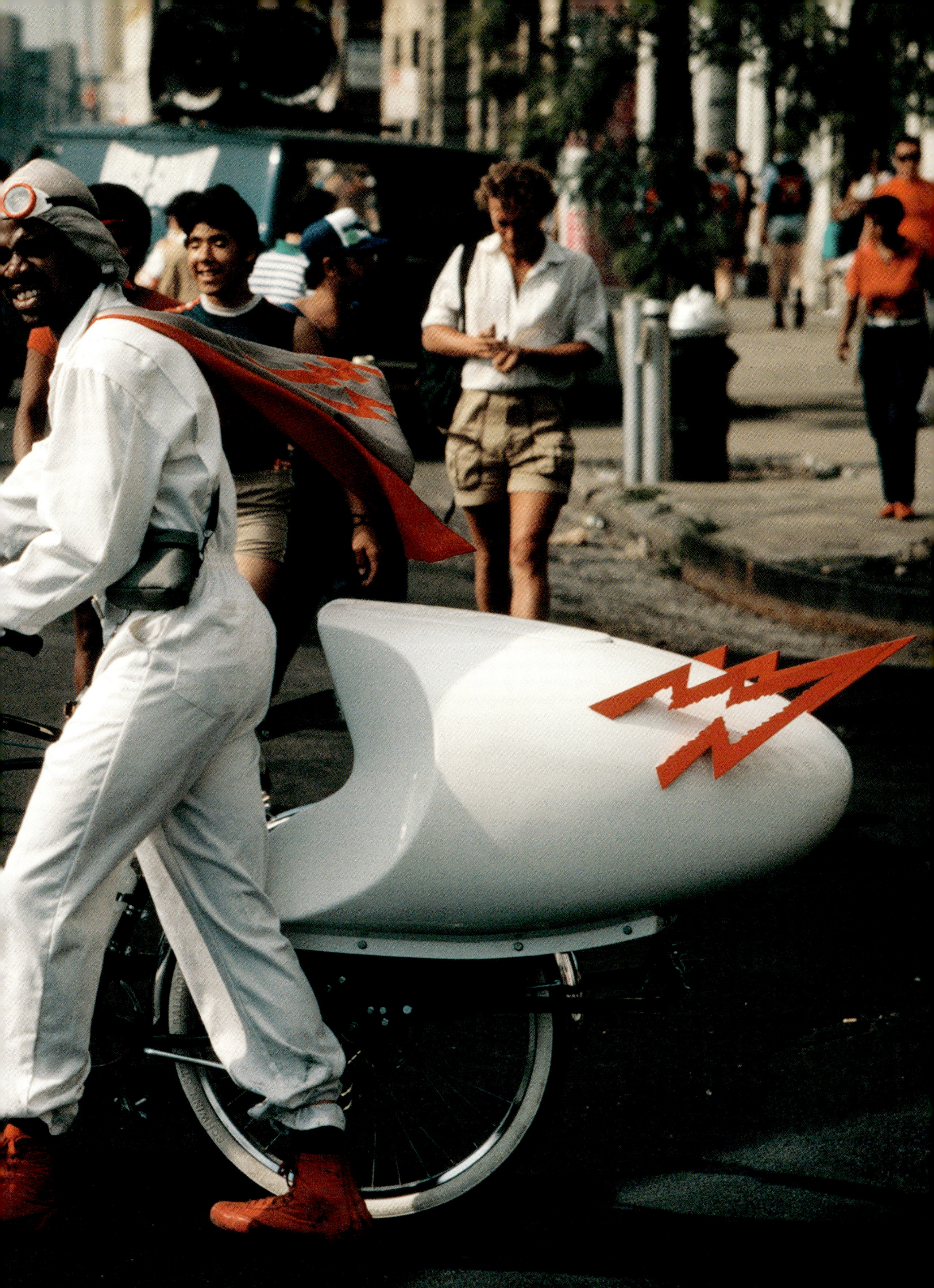

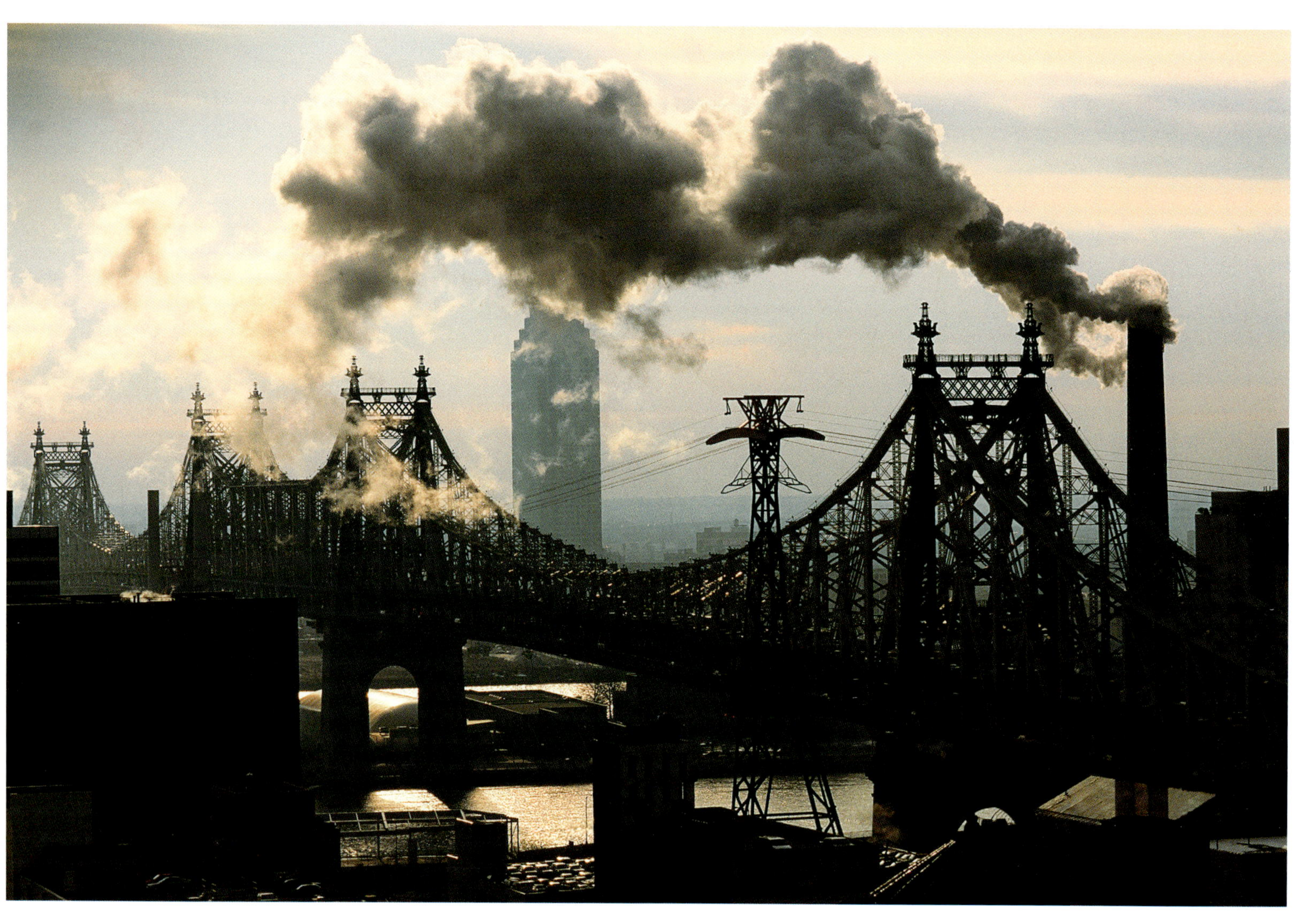

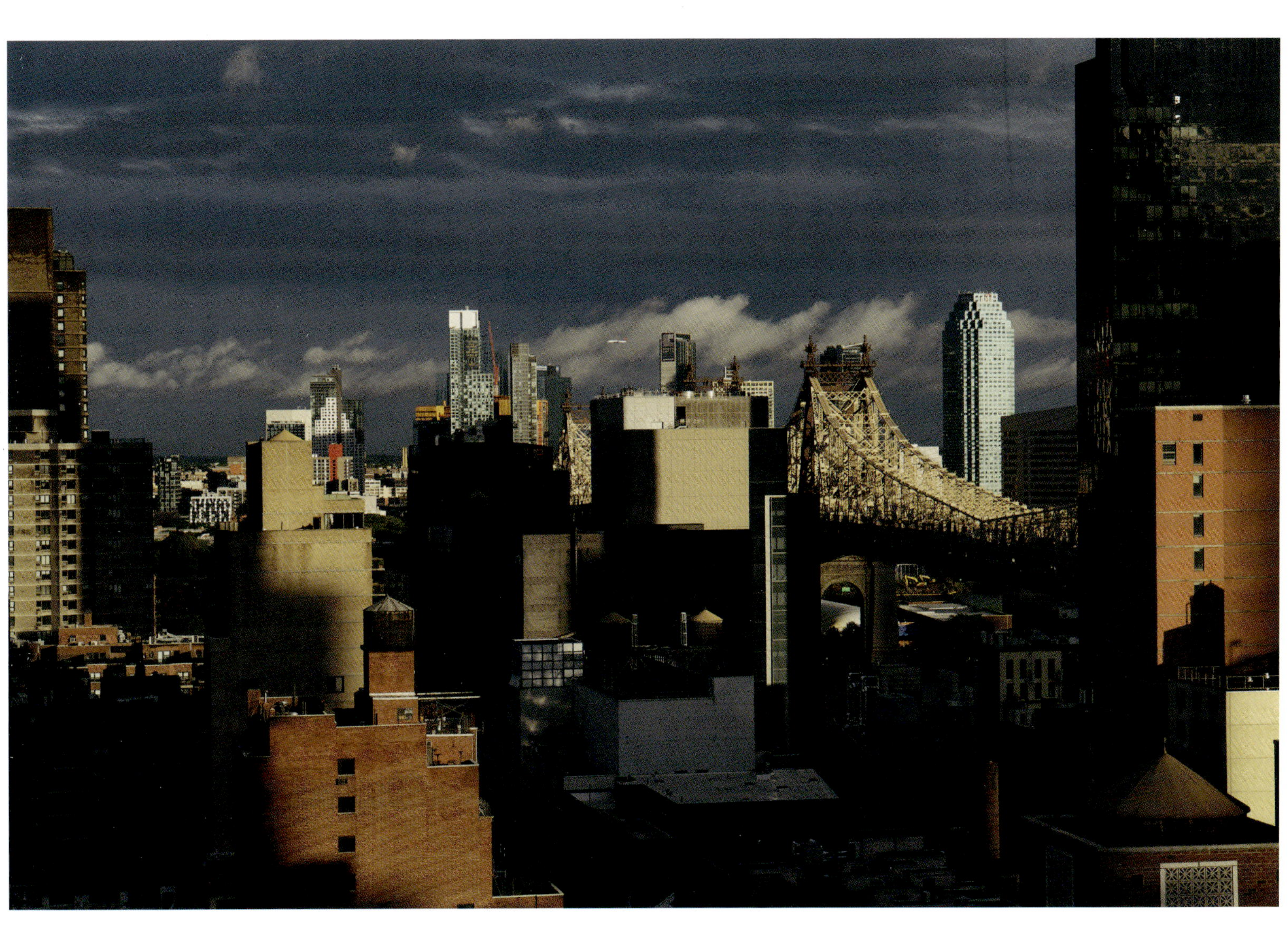

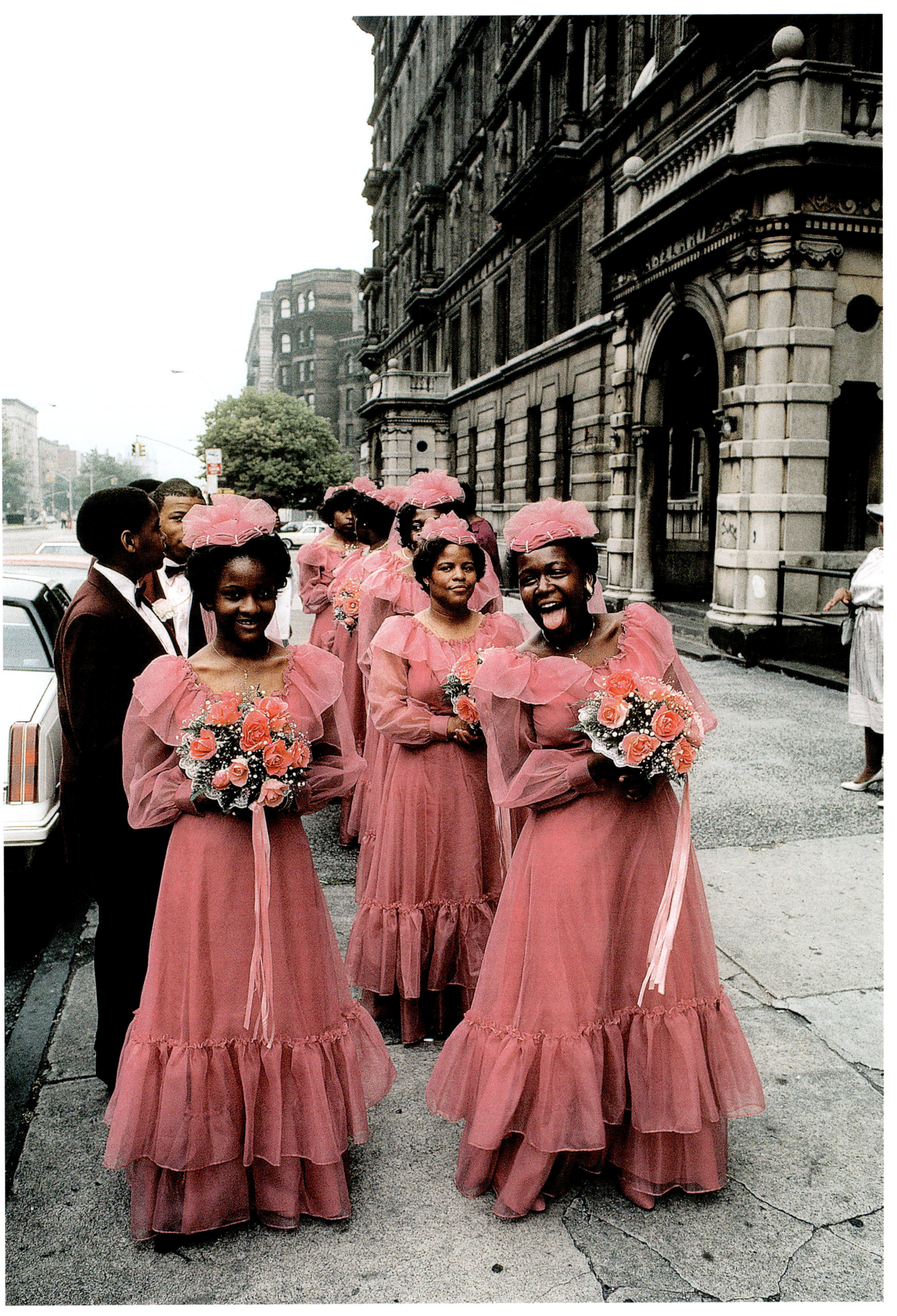

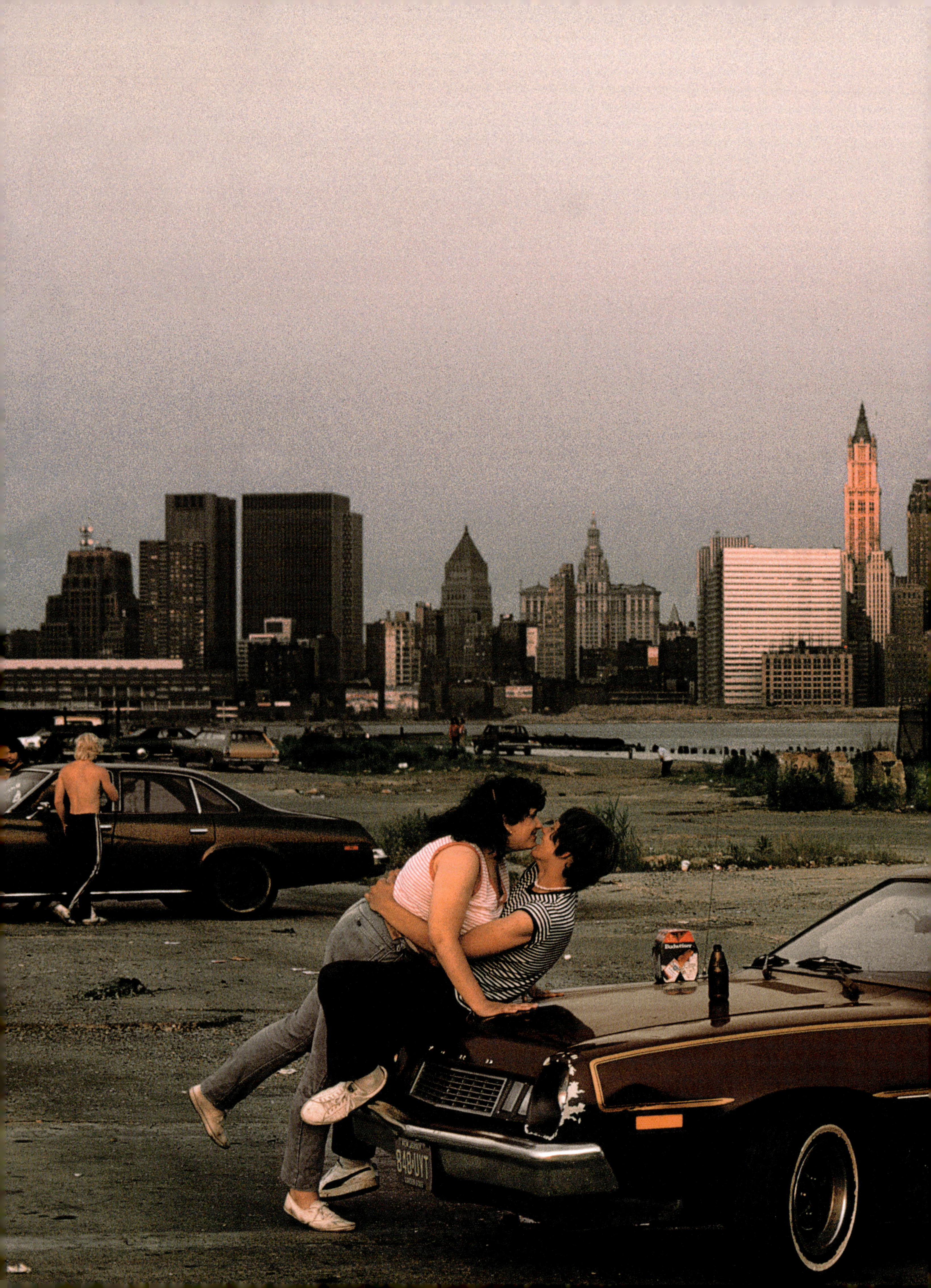

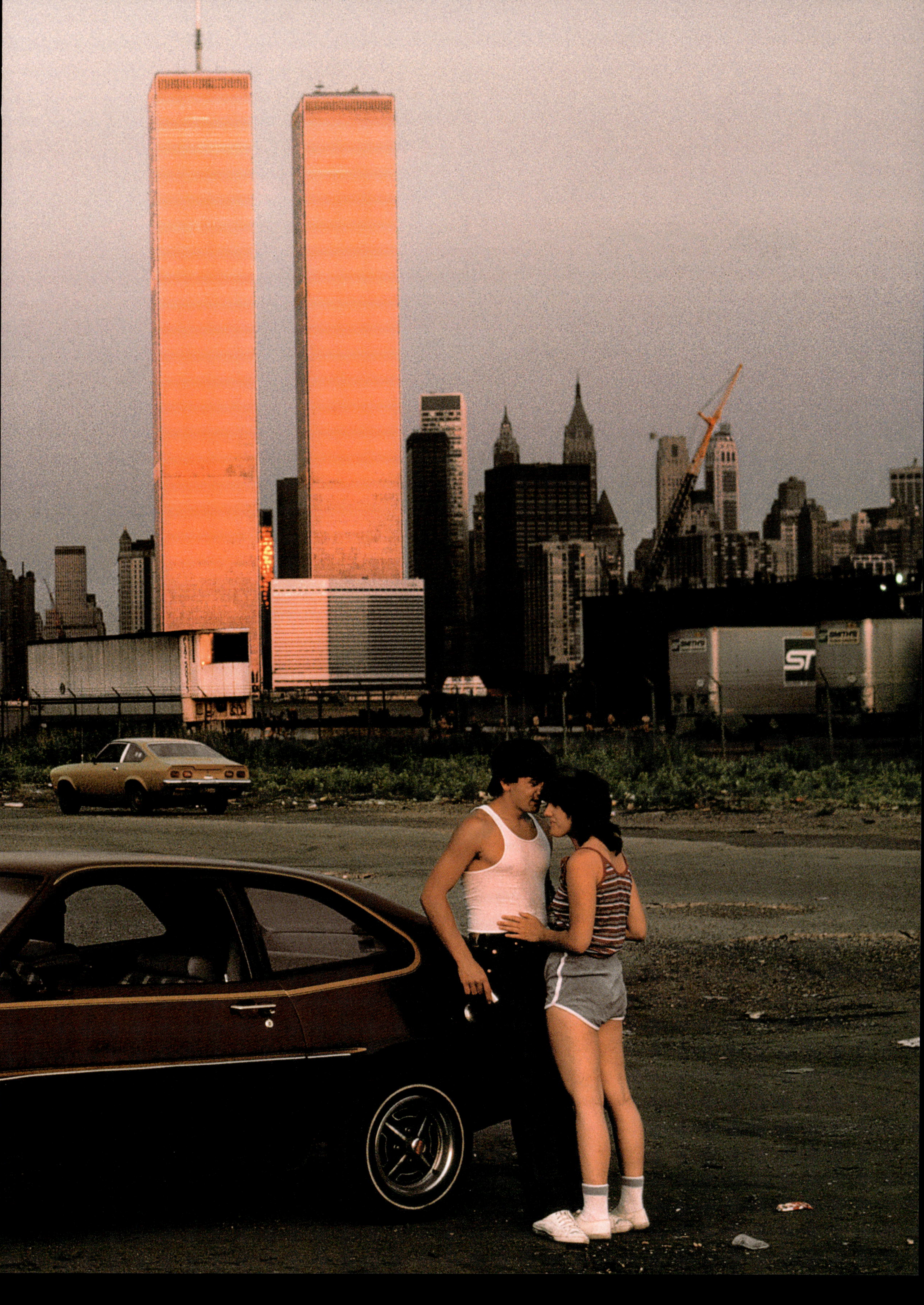

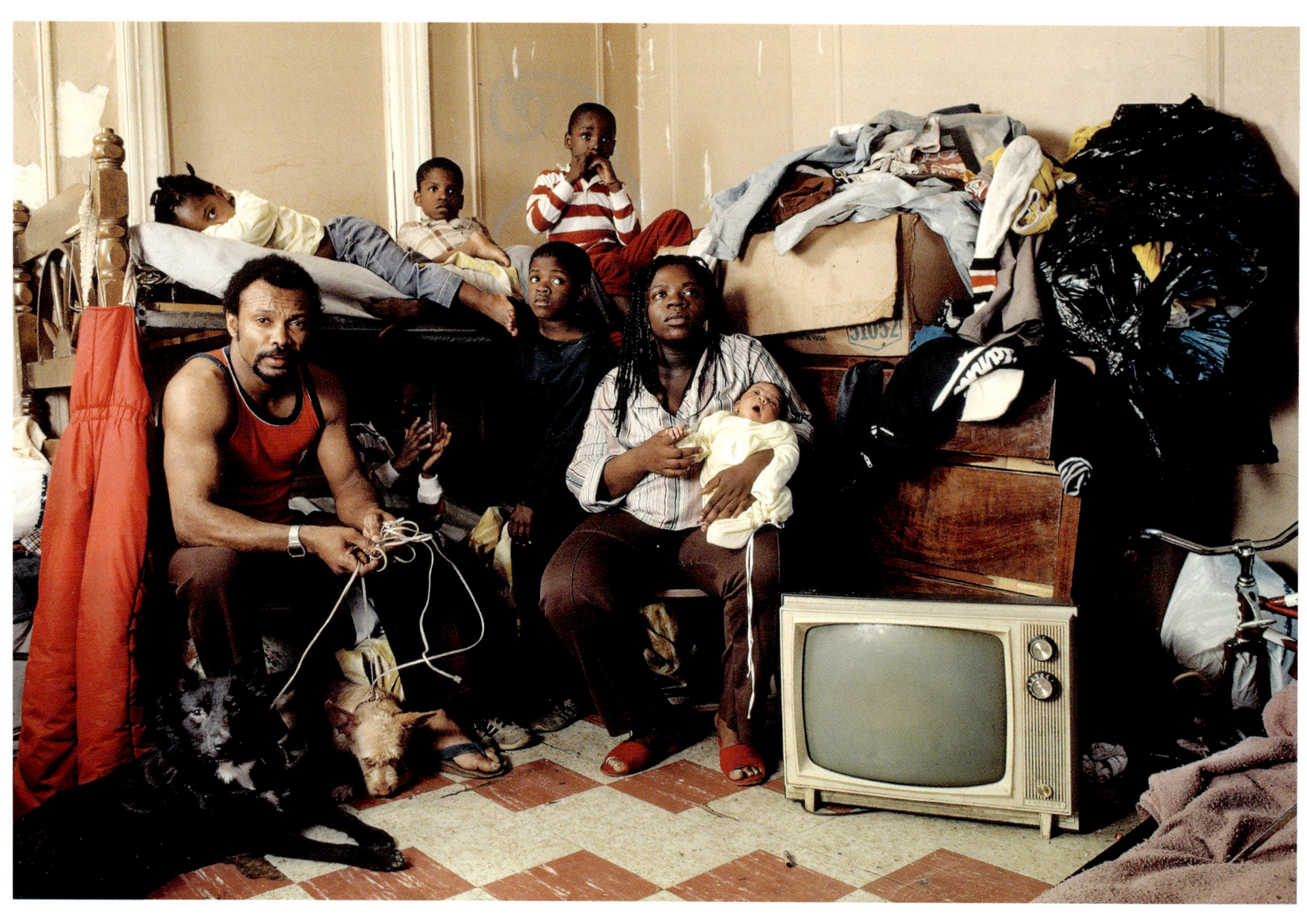

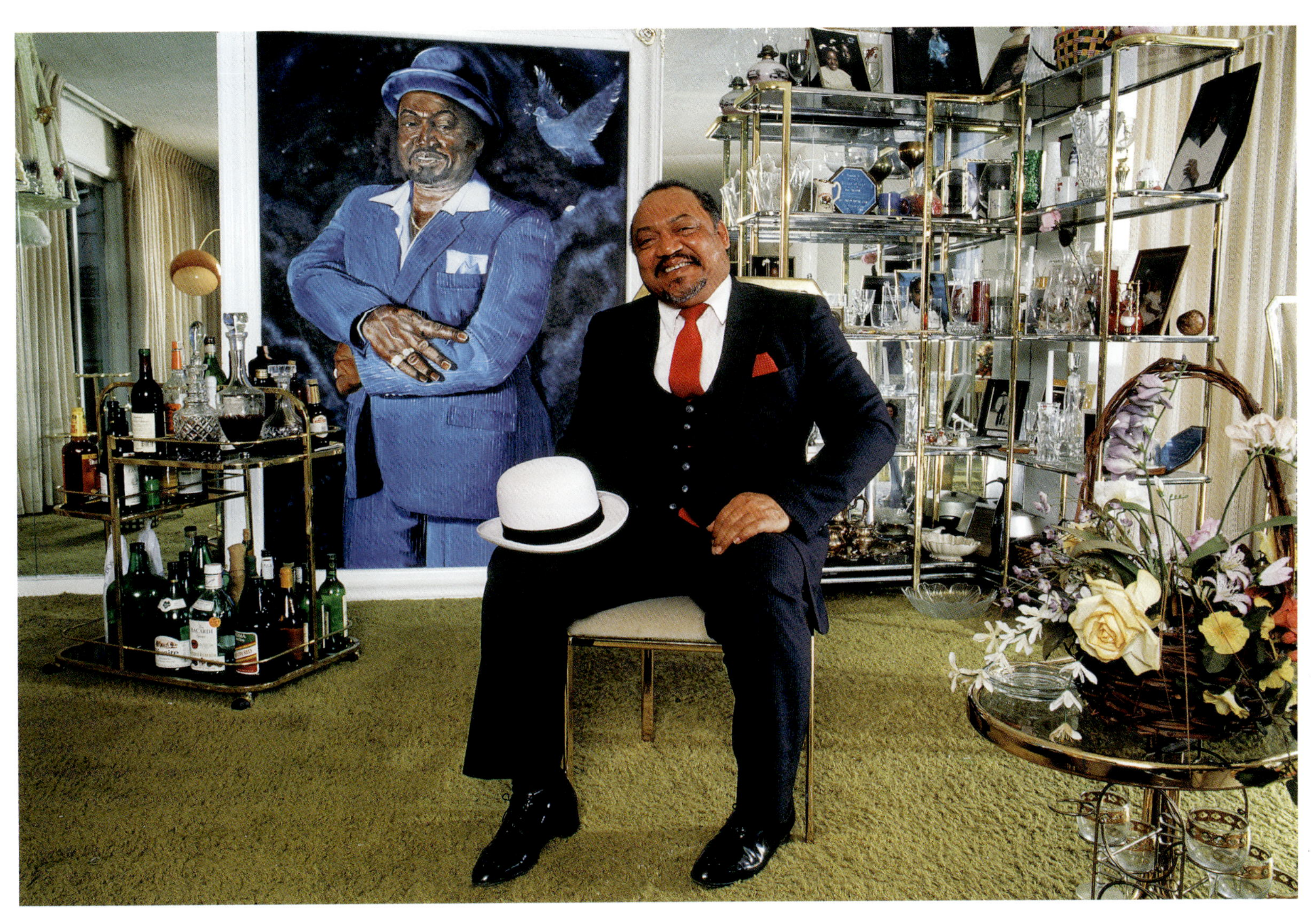

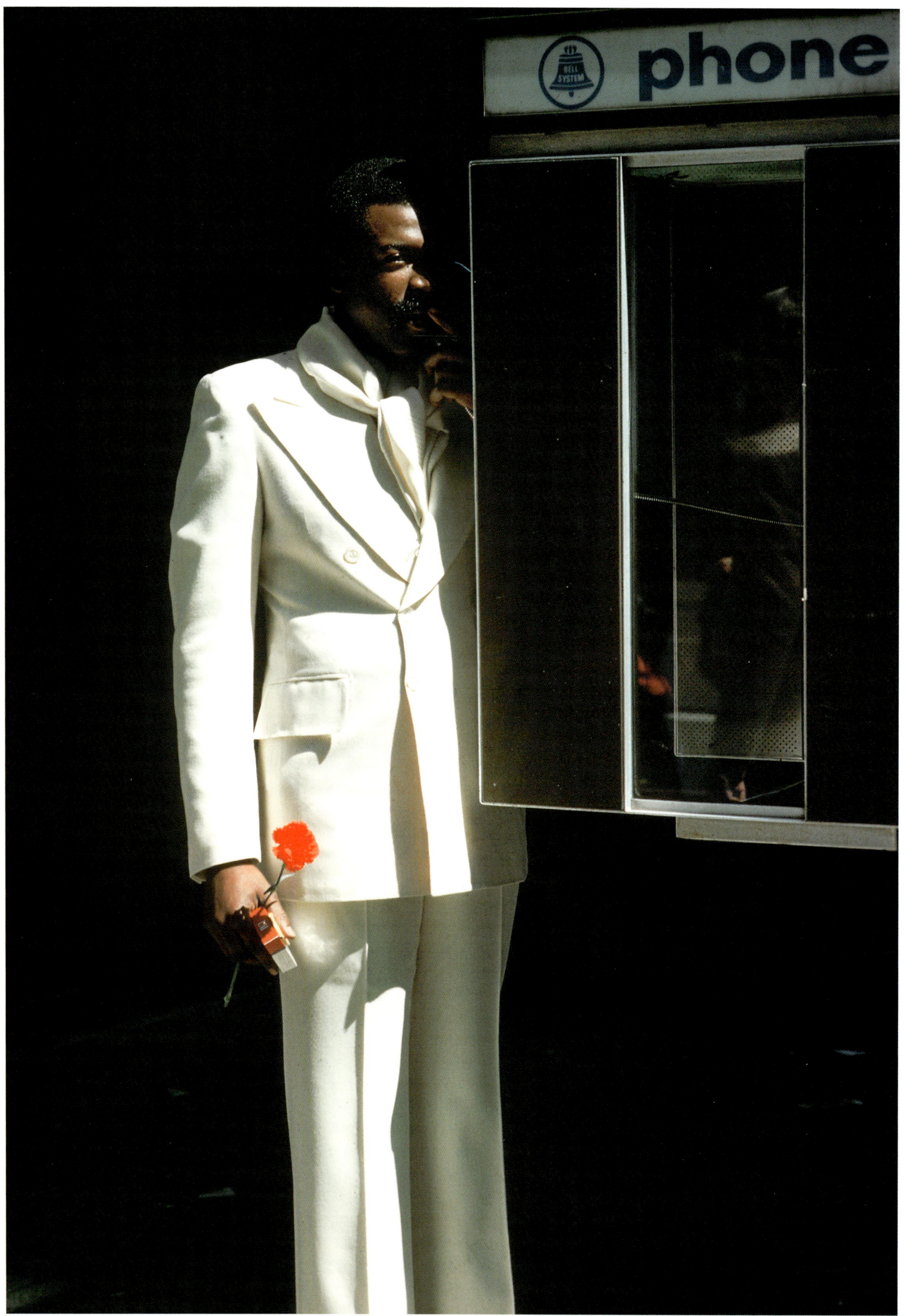

BELL SYSTEM
phone

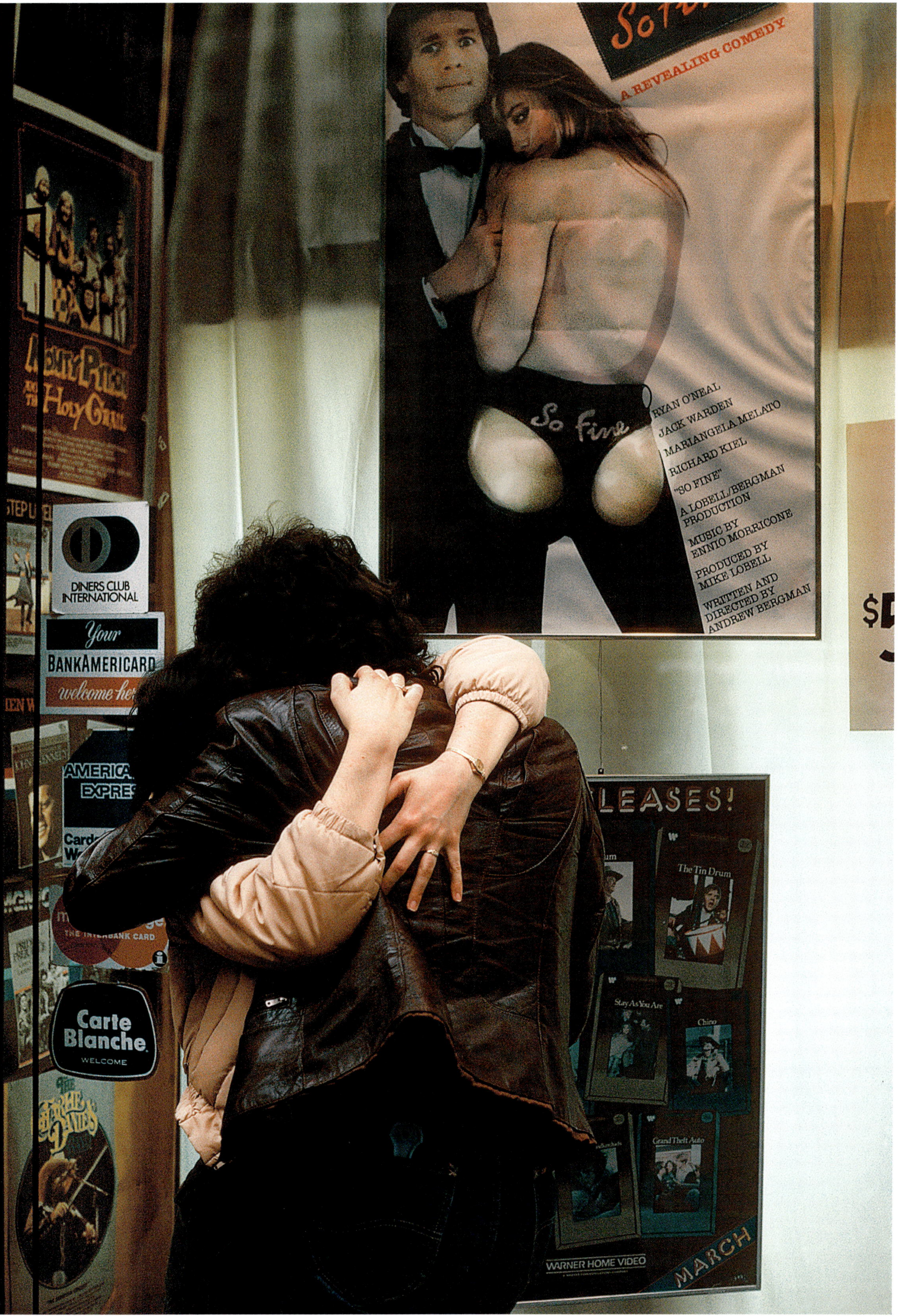
SO FINE
A REVEALING COMEDY
RYAN O'NEAL
JACK WARDEN
MARIANGELA MELATO
RICHARD KIEL
"SO FINE"
A LOBELL/BERGMAN PRODUCTION
MUSIC BY ENNIO MORRICONE
PRODUCED BY MIKE LOBELL
WRITTEN AND DIRECTED BY ANDREW BERGMAN
So Fine
DINERS CLUB INTERNATIONAL
Your BankAmericard welcome here
AMERICAN EXPRESS
THE INTERBANK CARD
Carte Blanche
WELCOME
MONTY PYTHON AND THE HOLY GRAIL
RELEASES!
The Tin Drum
Stay As You Are
Chino
Grand Theft Auto
WARNER HOME VIDEO
MARCH
$

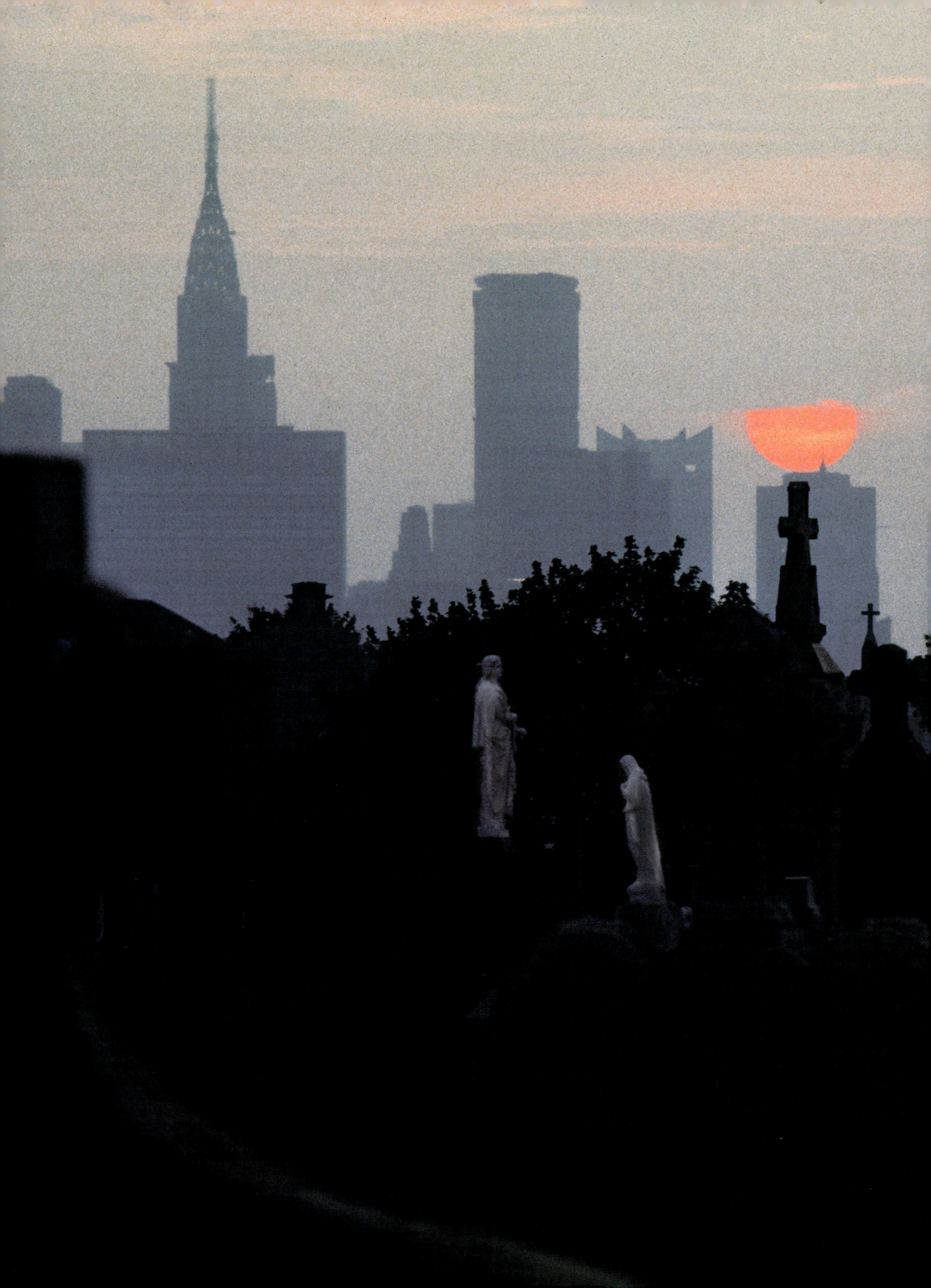

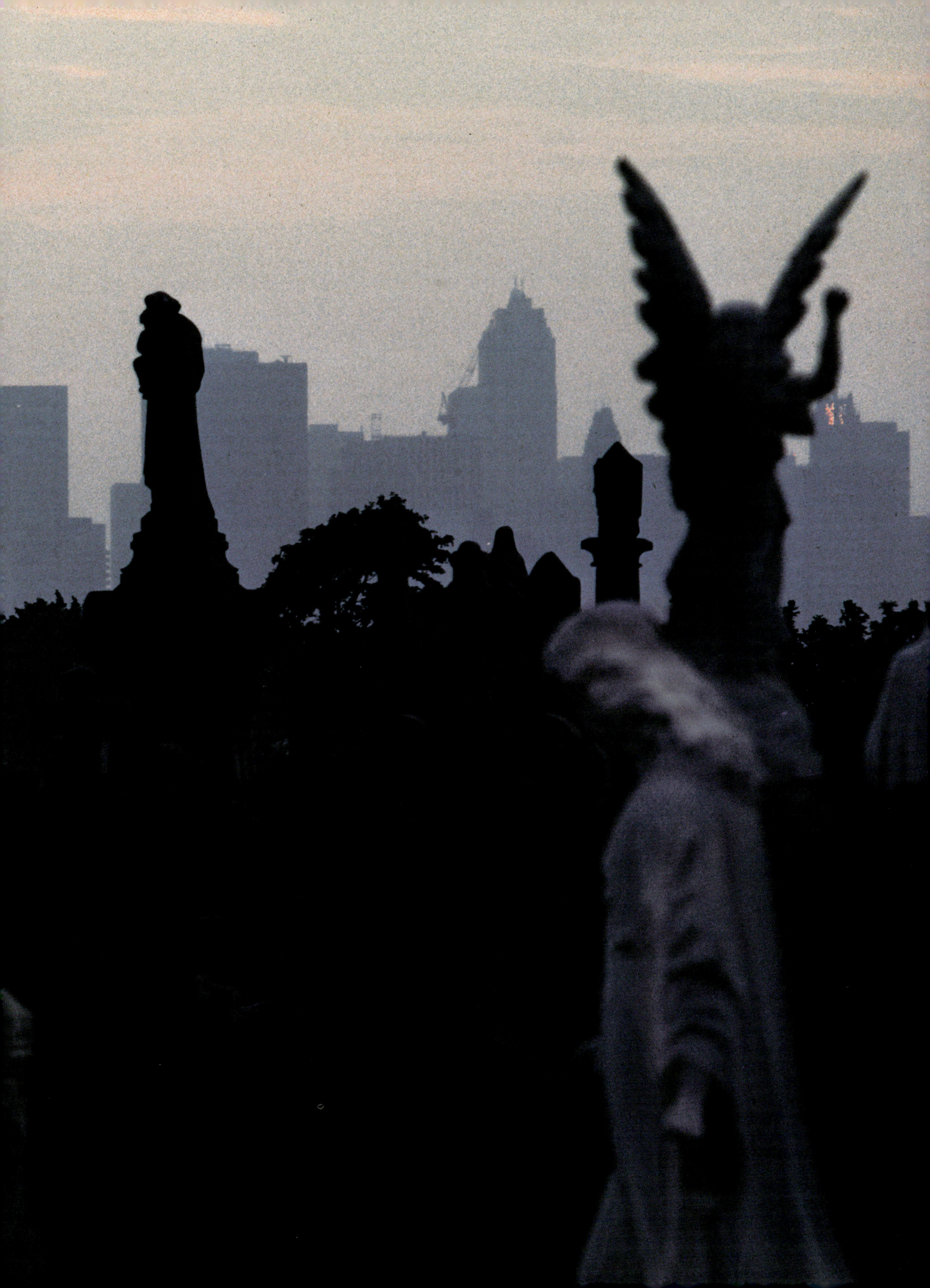

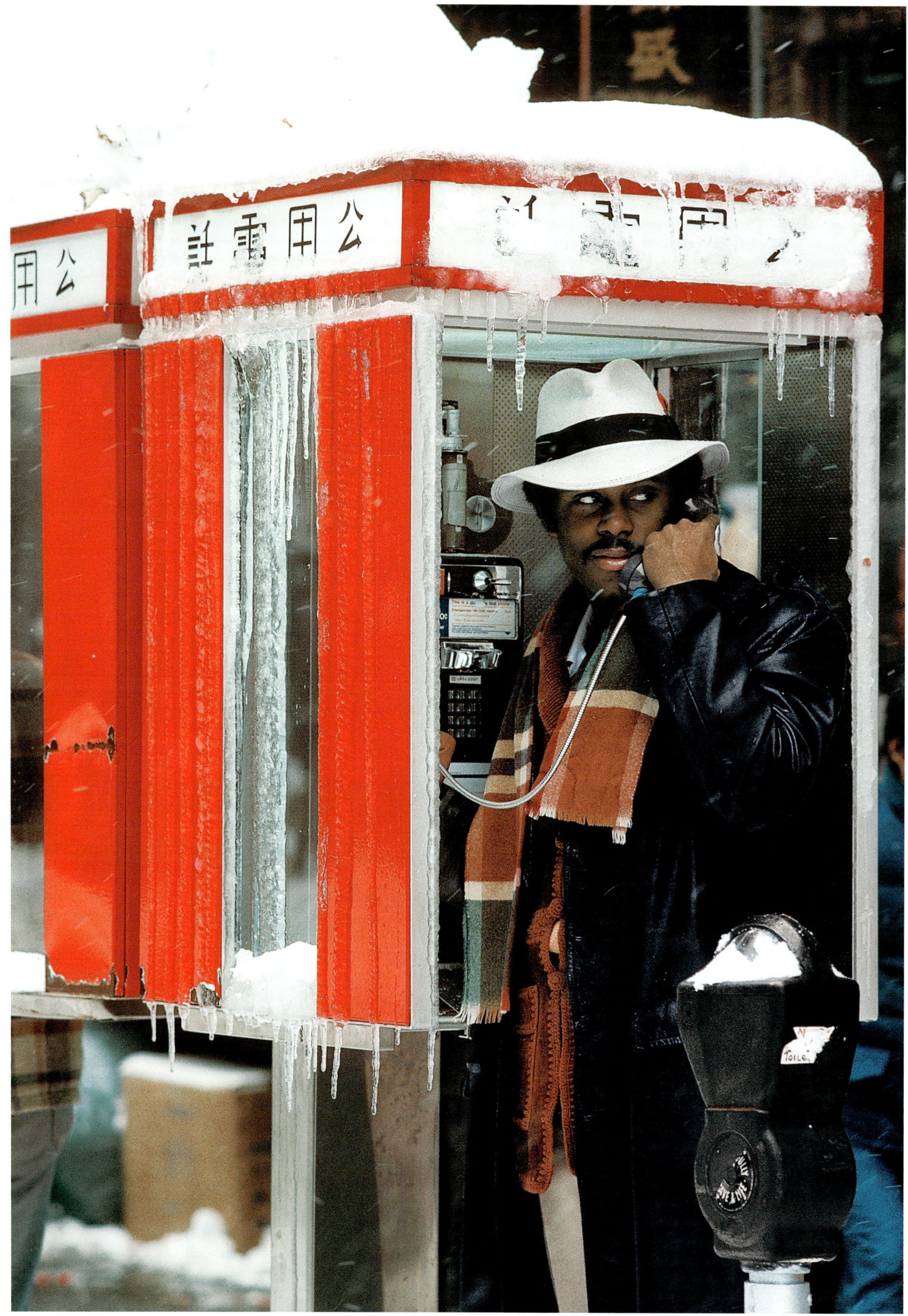

公用電話

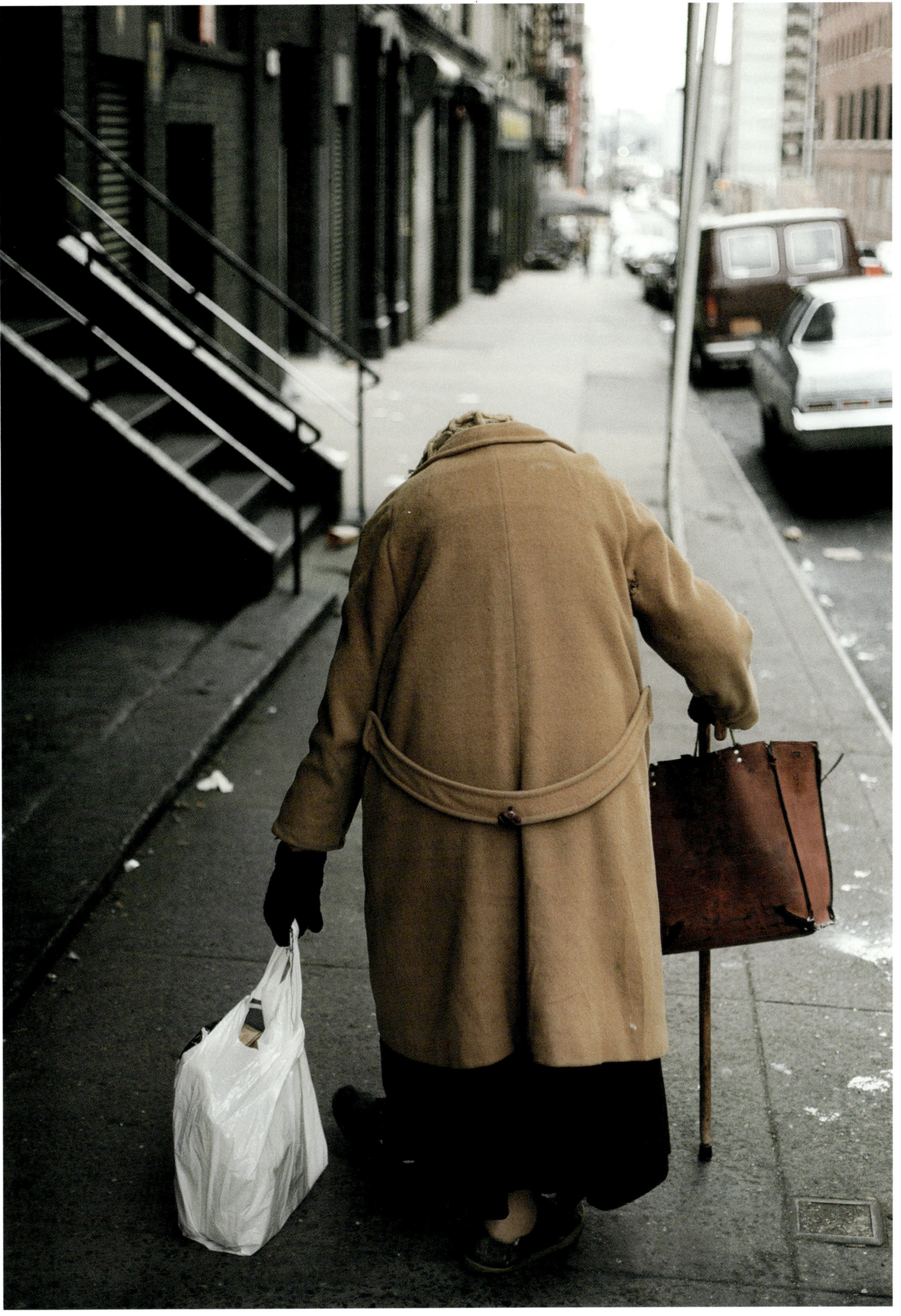

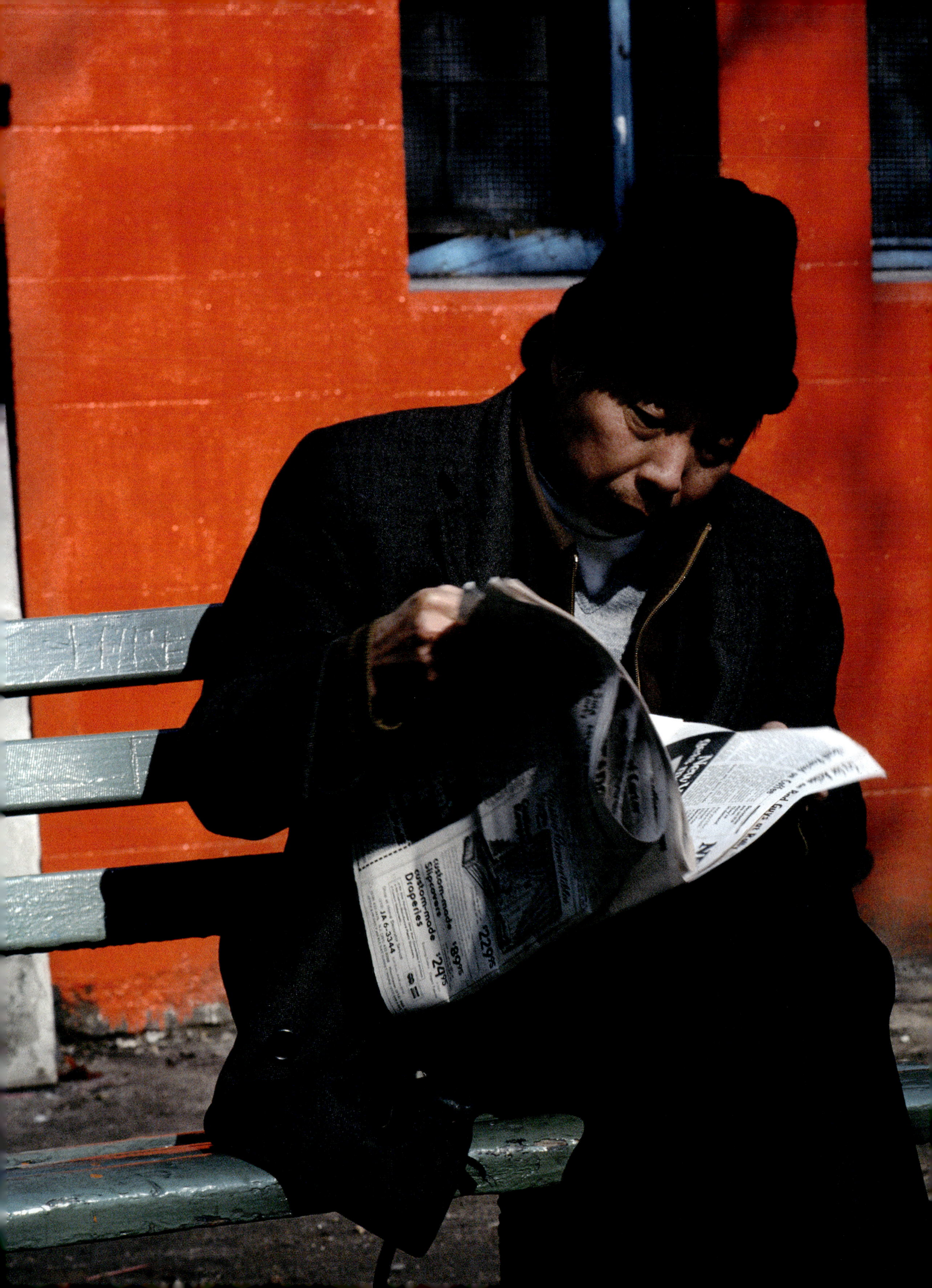

custom-made
Slipcovers
$24.95
custom-made
Draperies
$189.95
$229.95
JA 6-3344

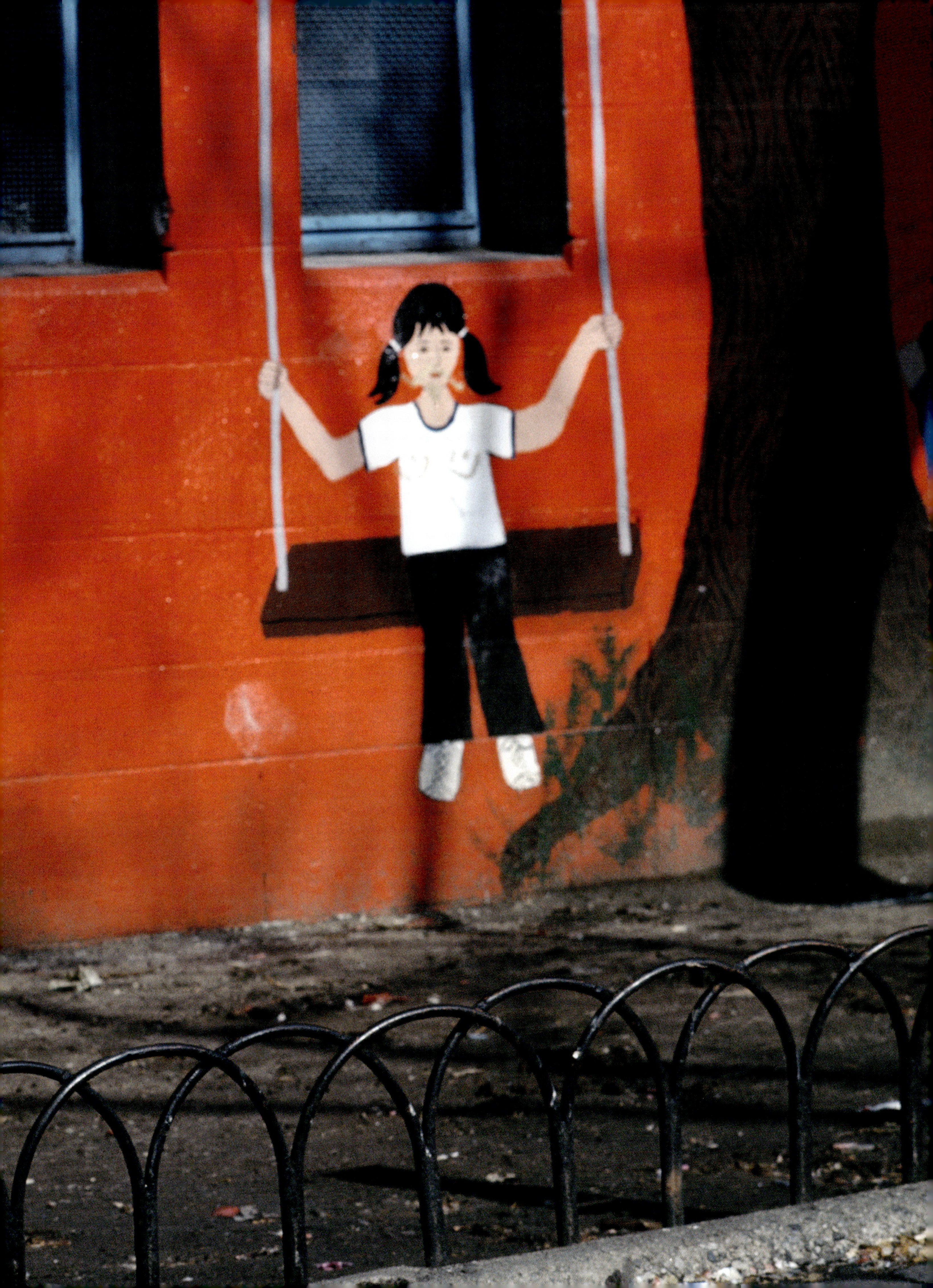

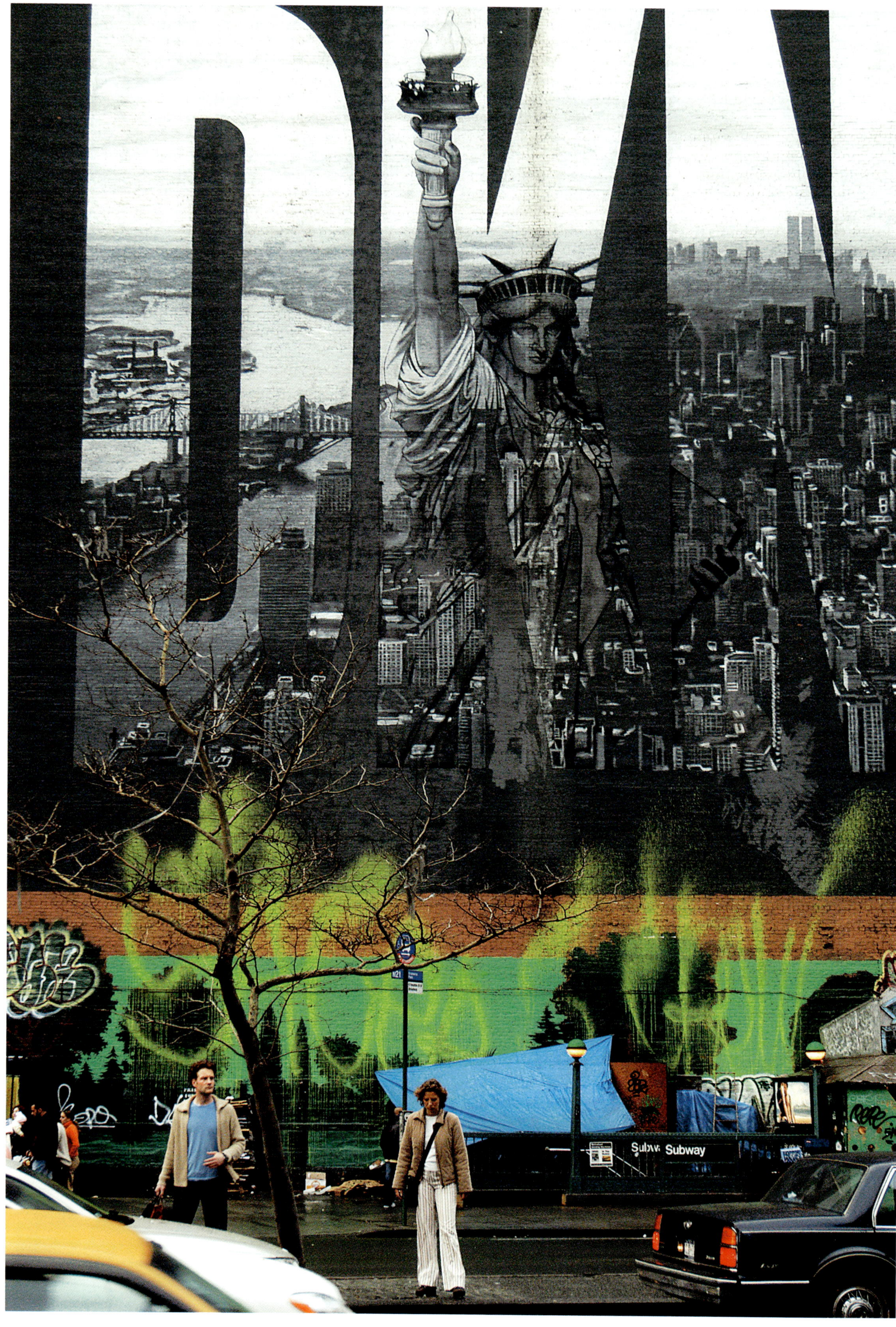

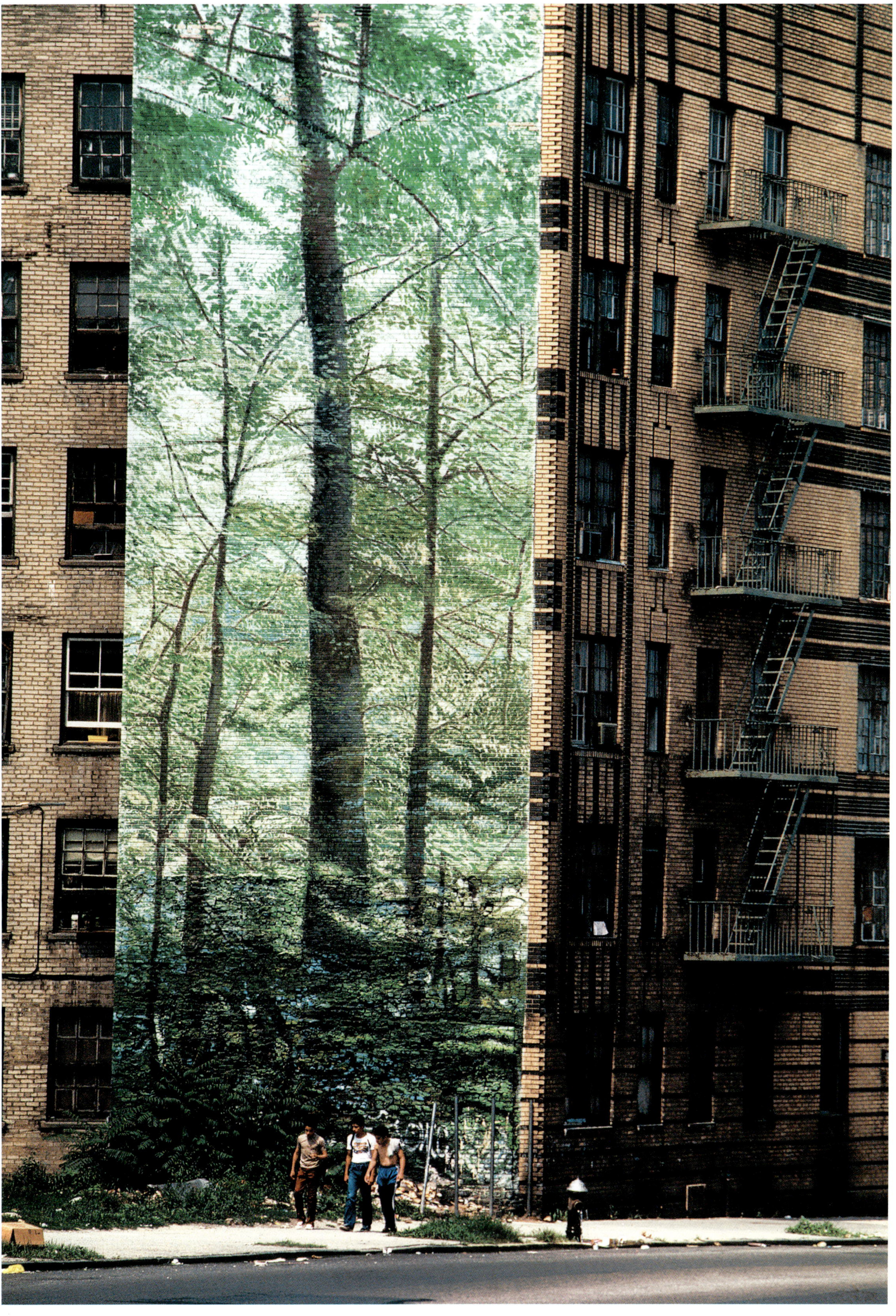

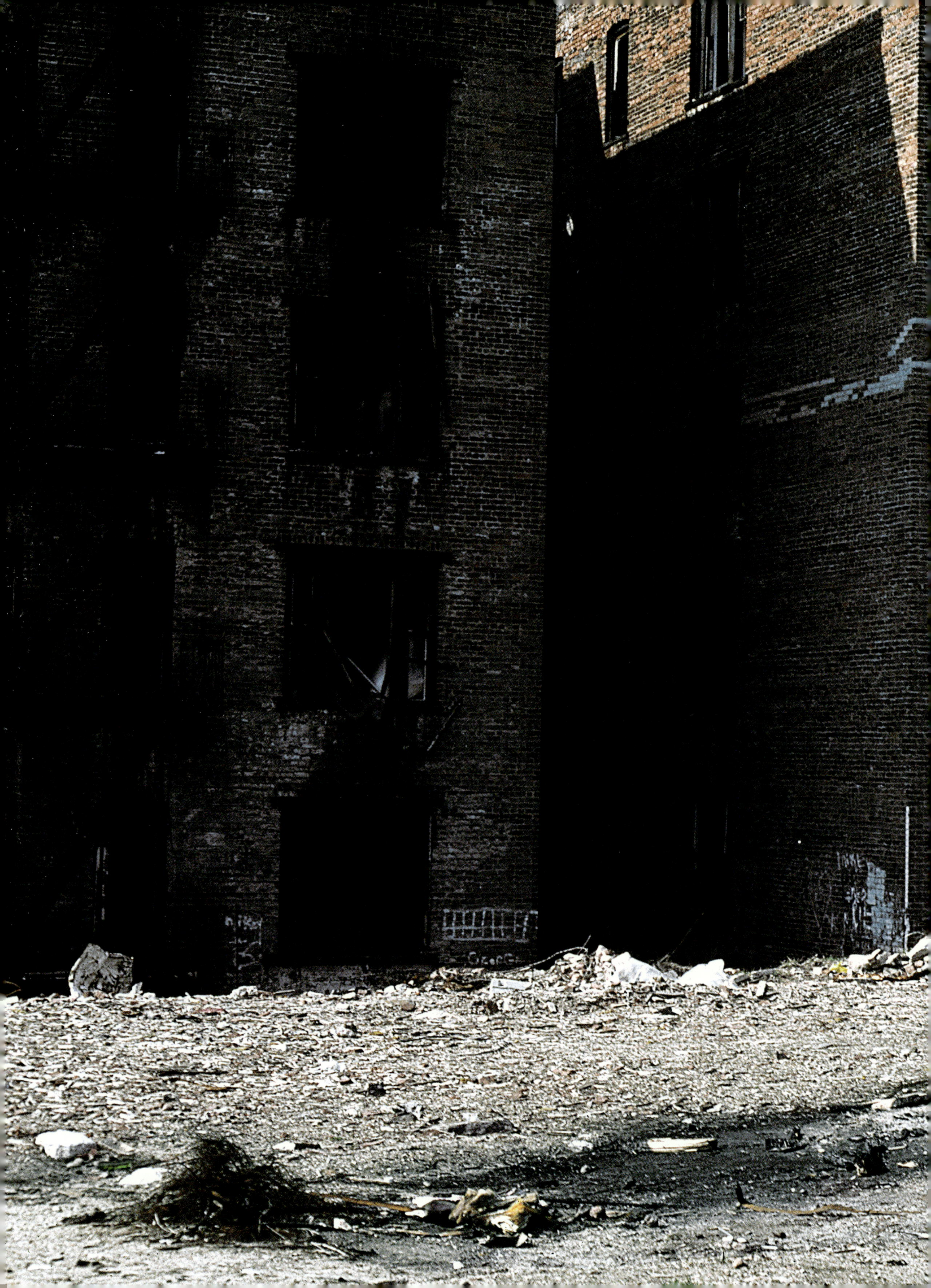

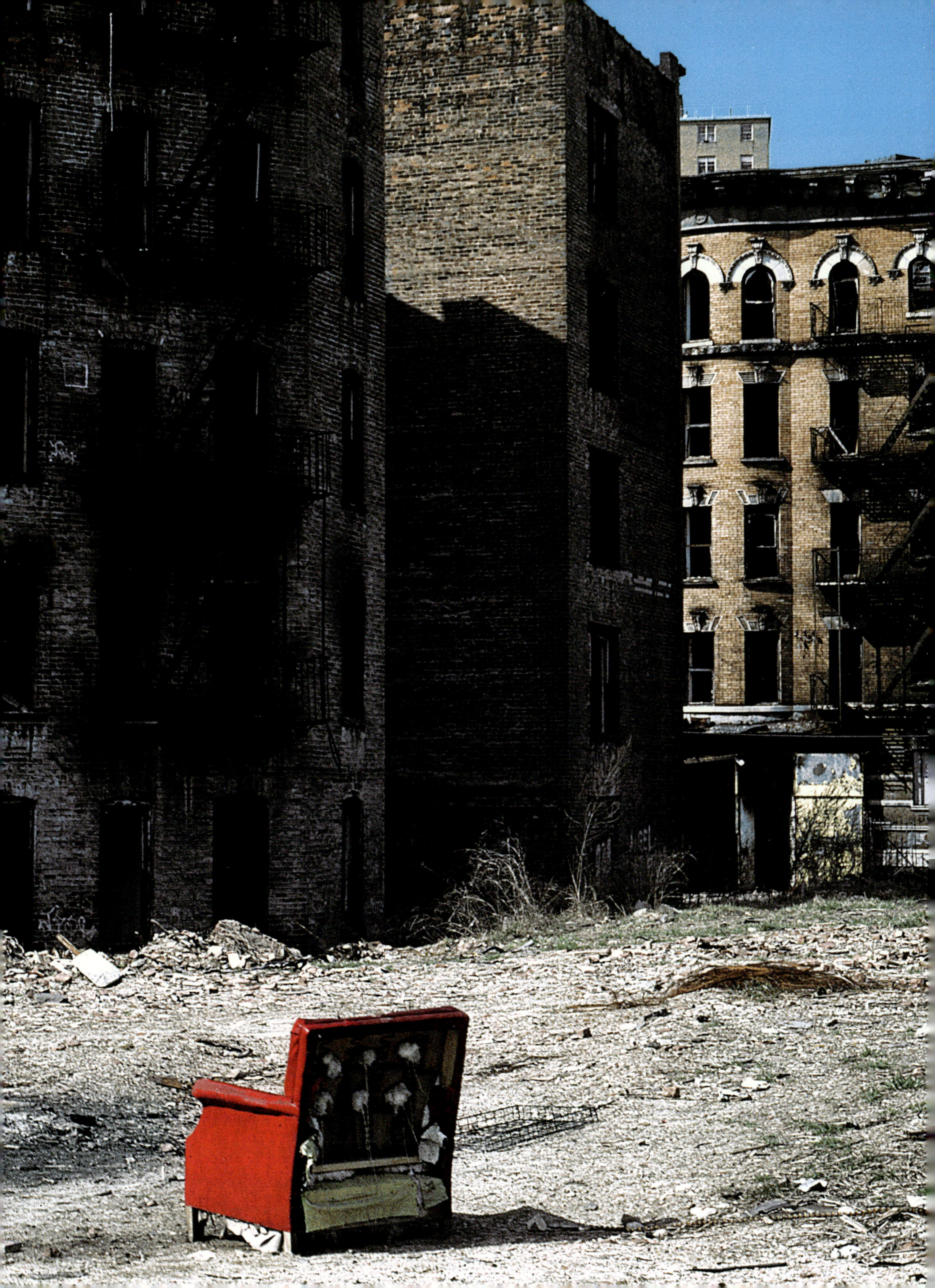

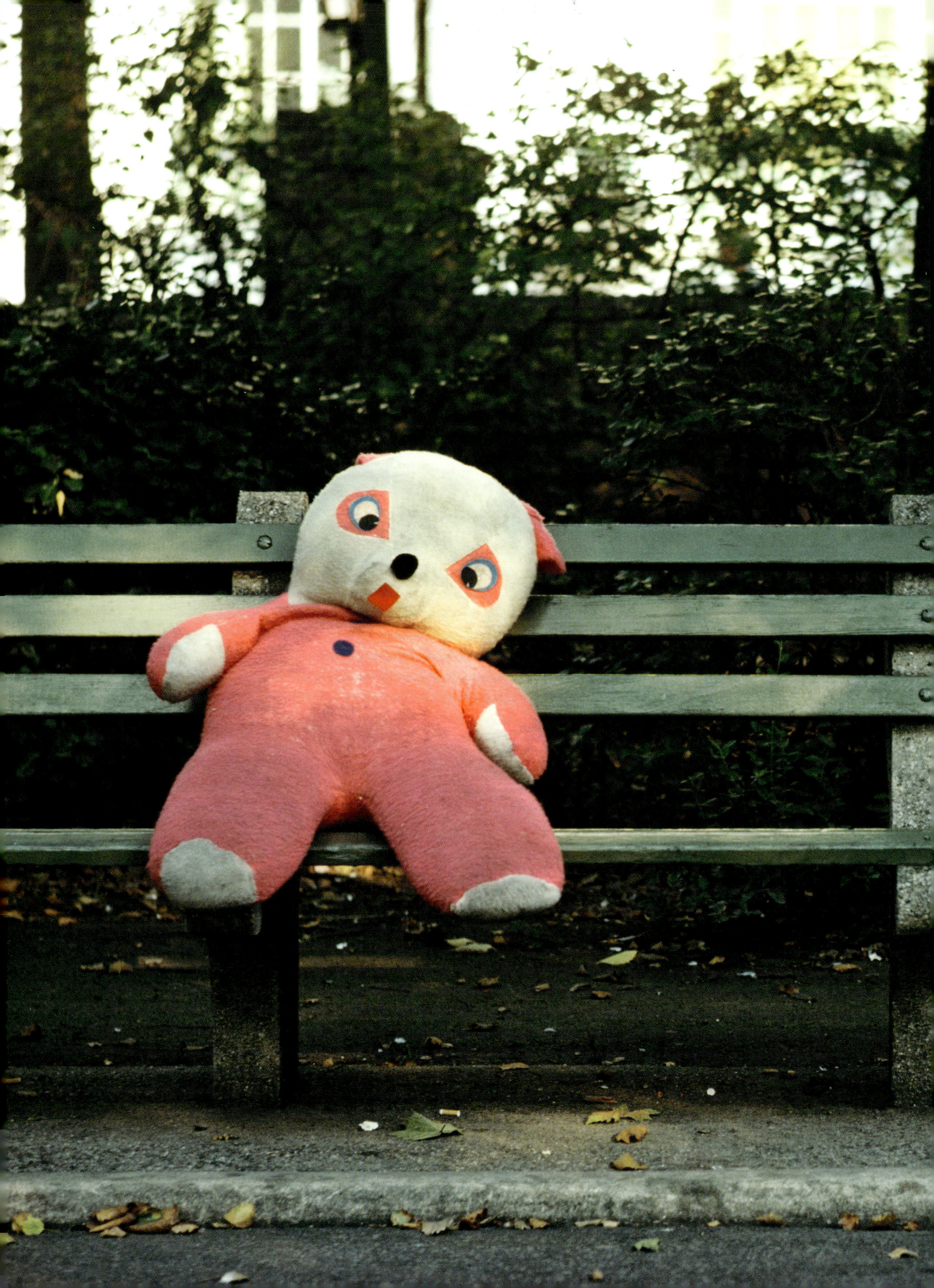

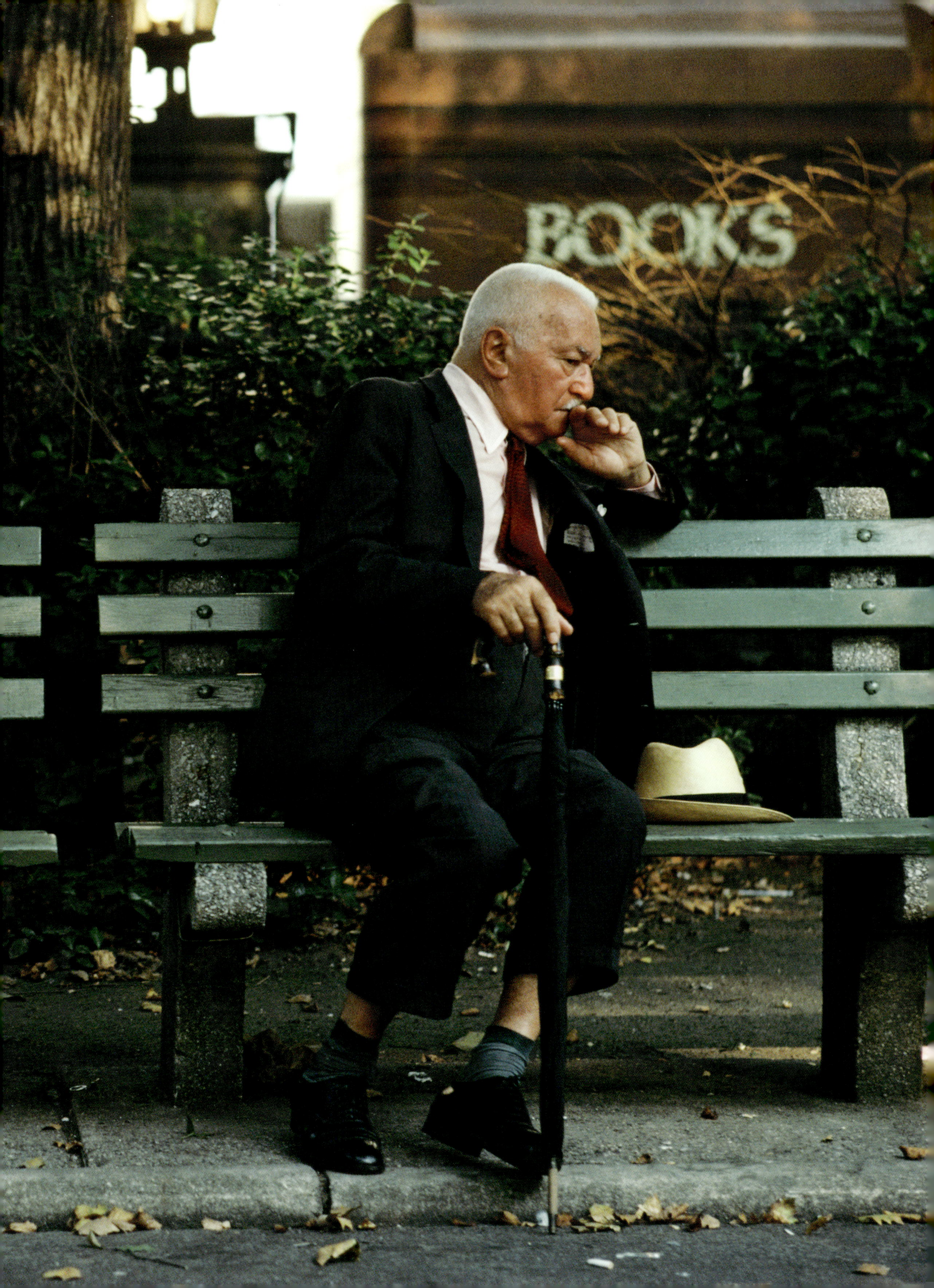

BOOKS

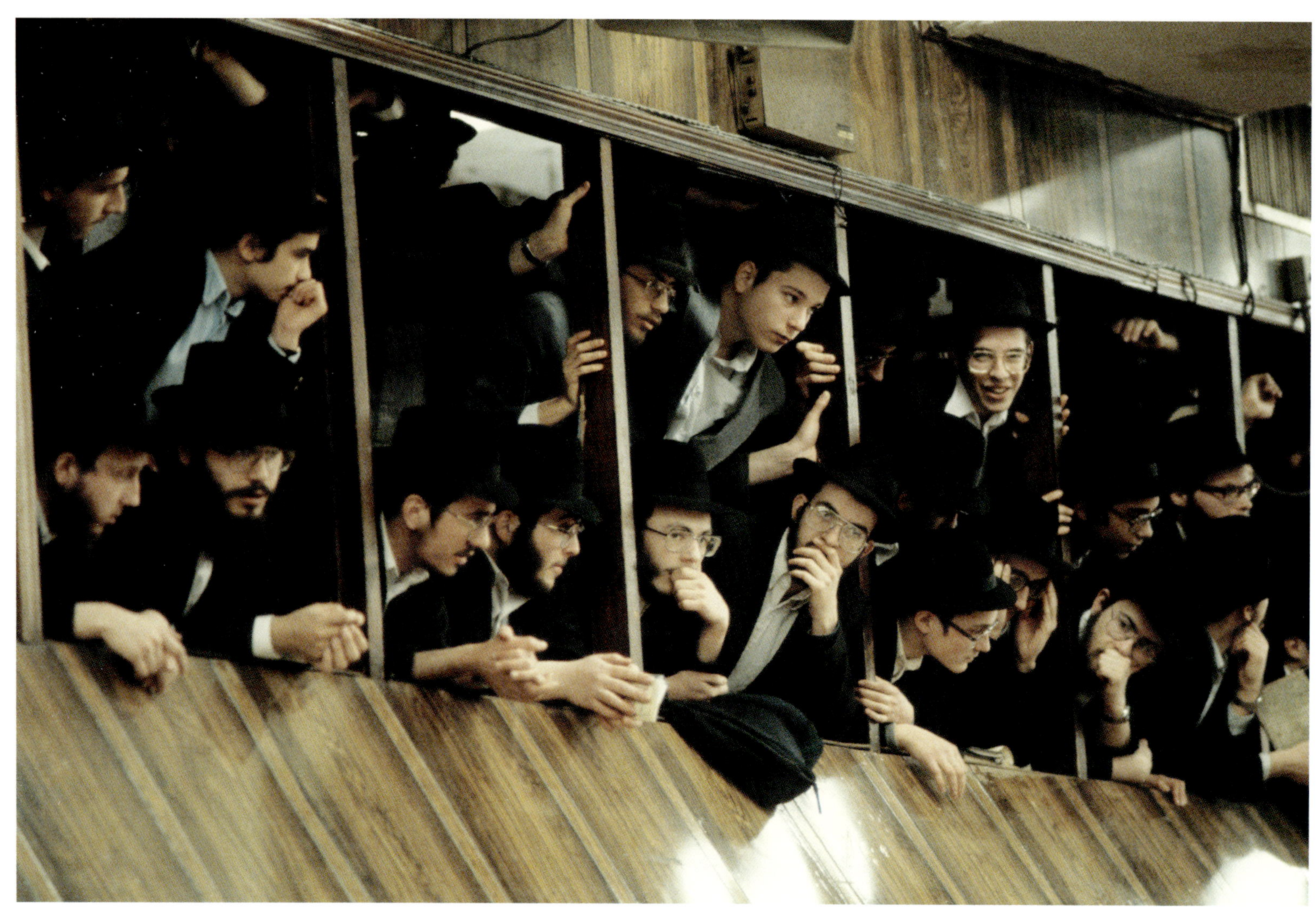

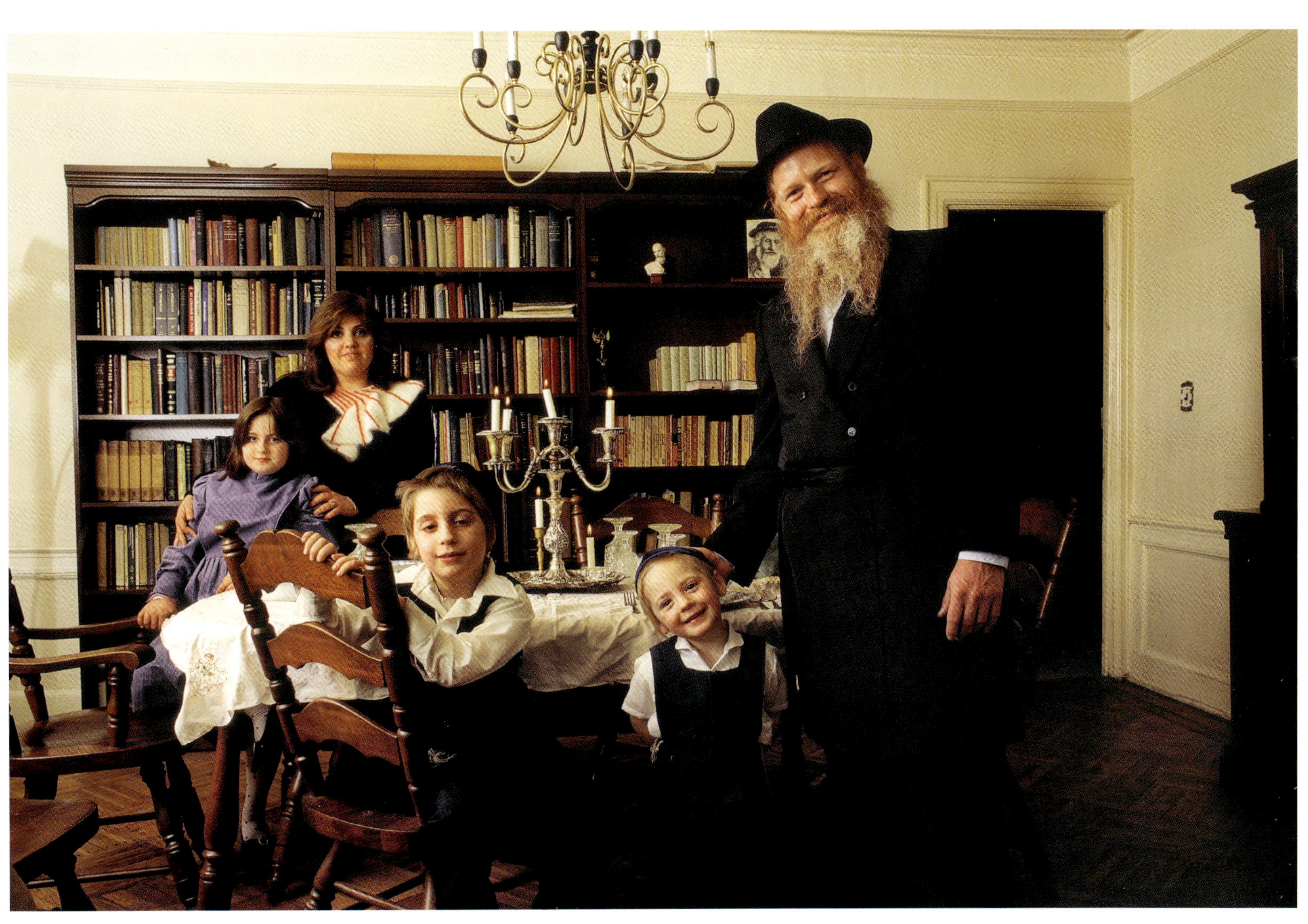

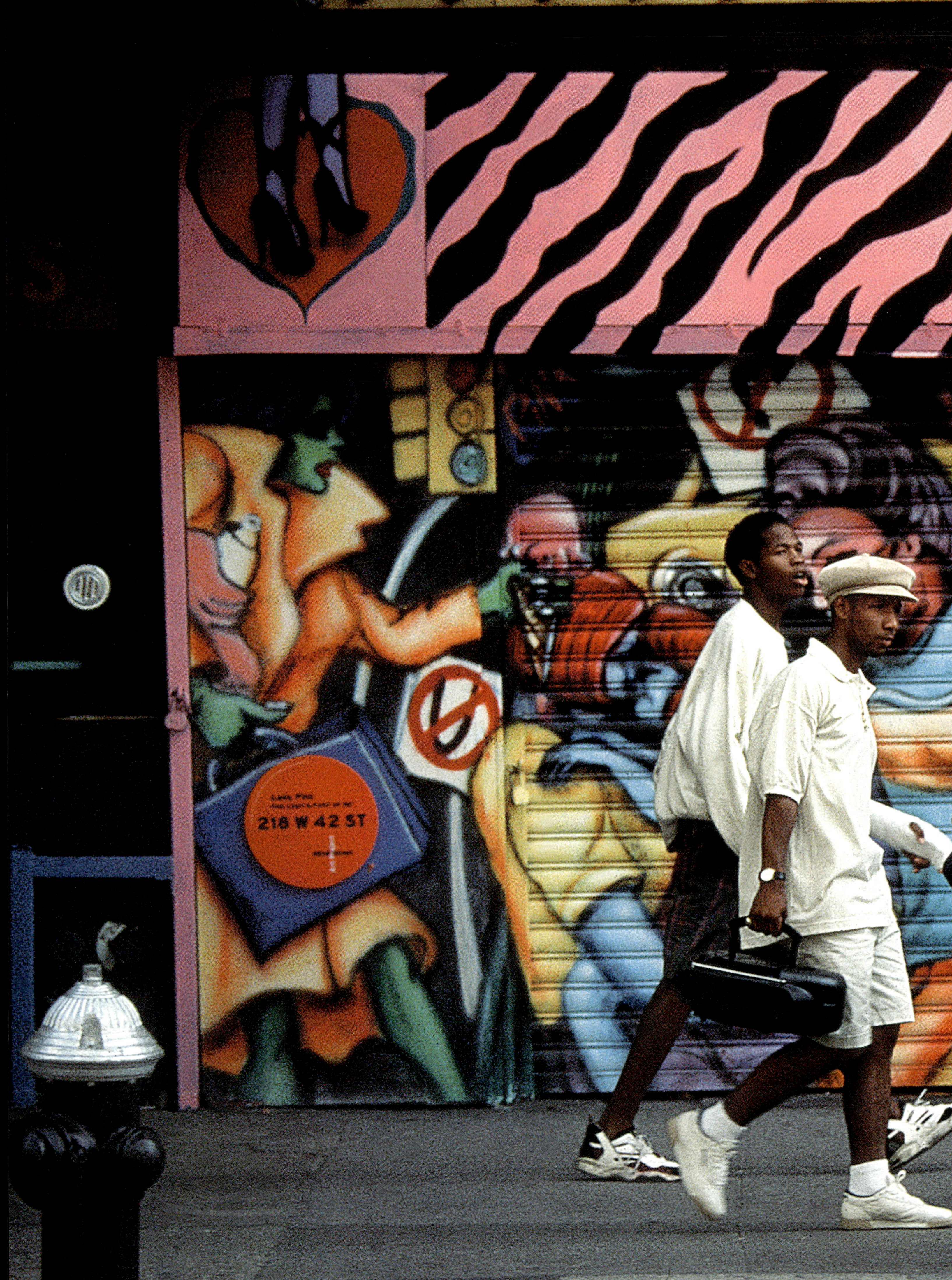
218 W 42 ST

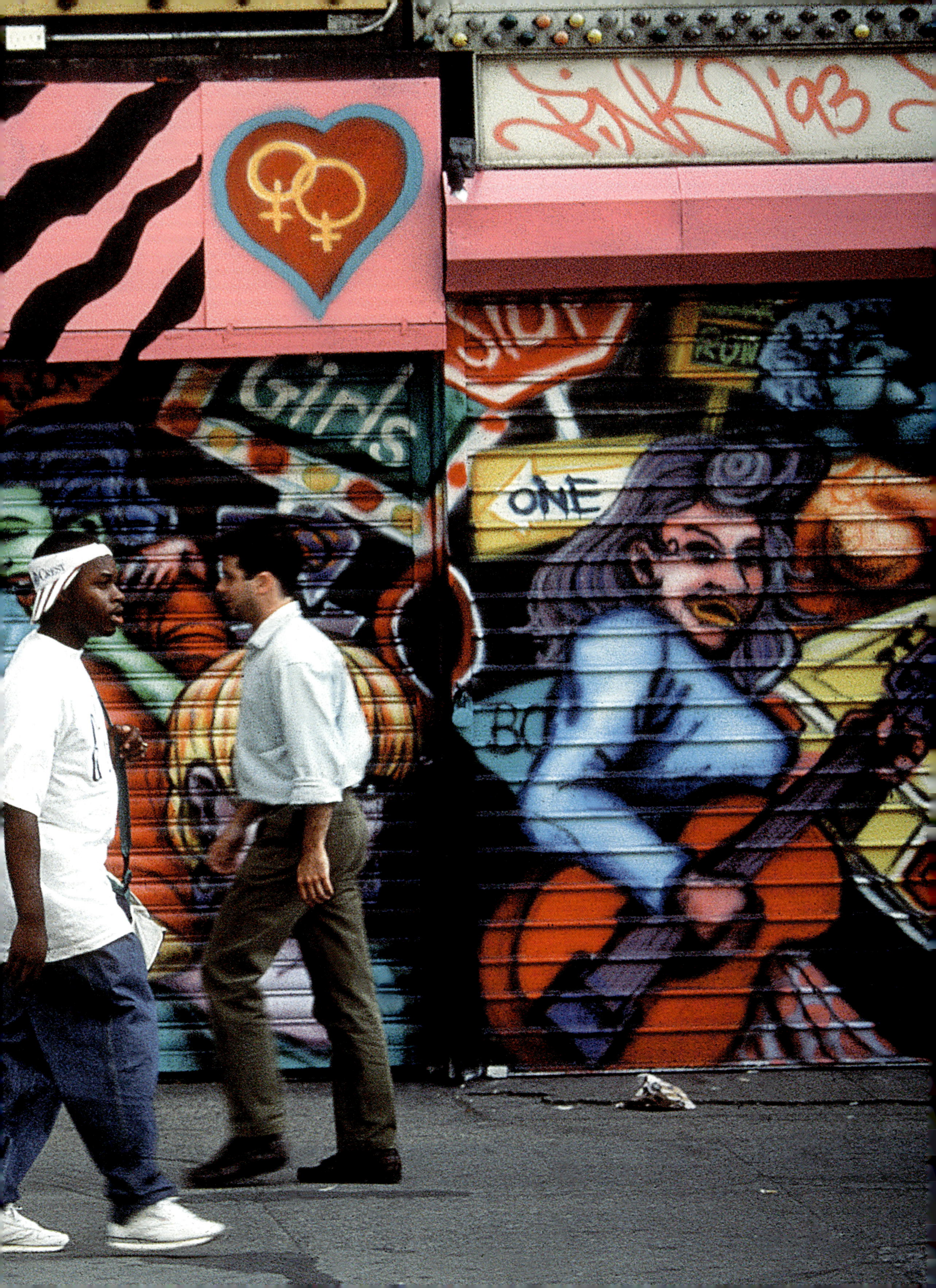

SILK '03
Girls
ONE

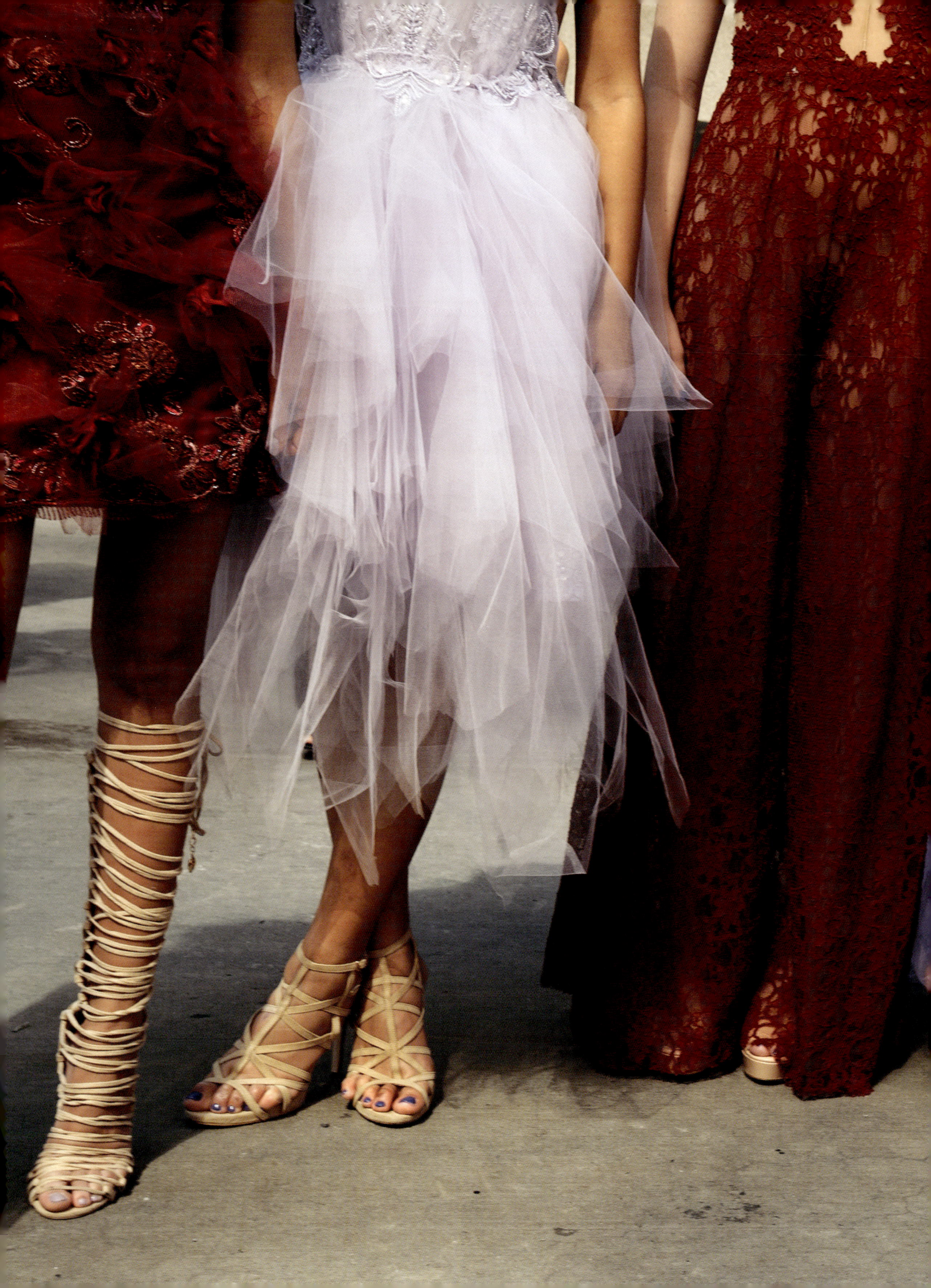

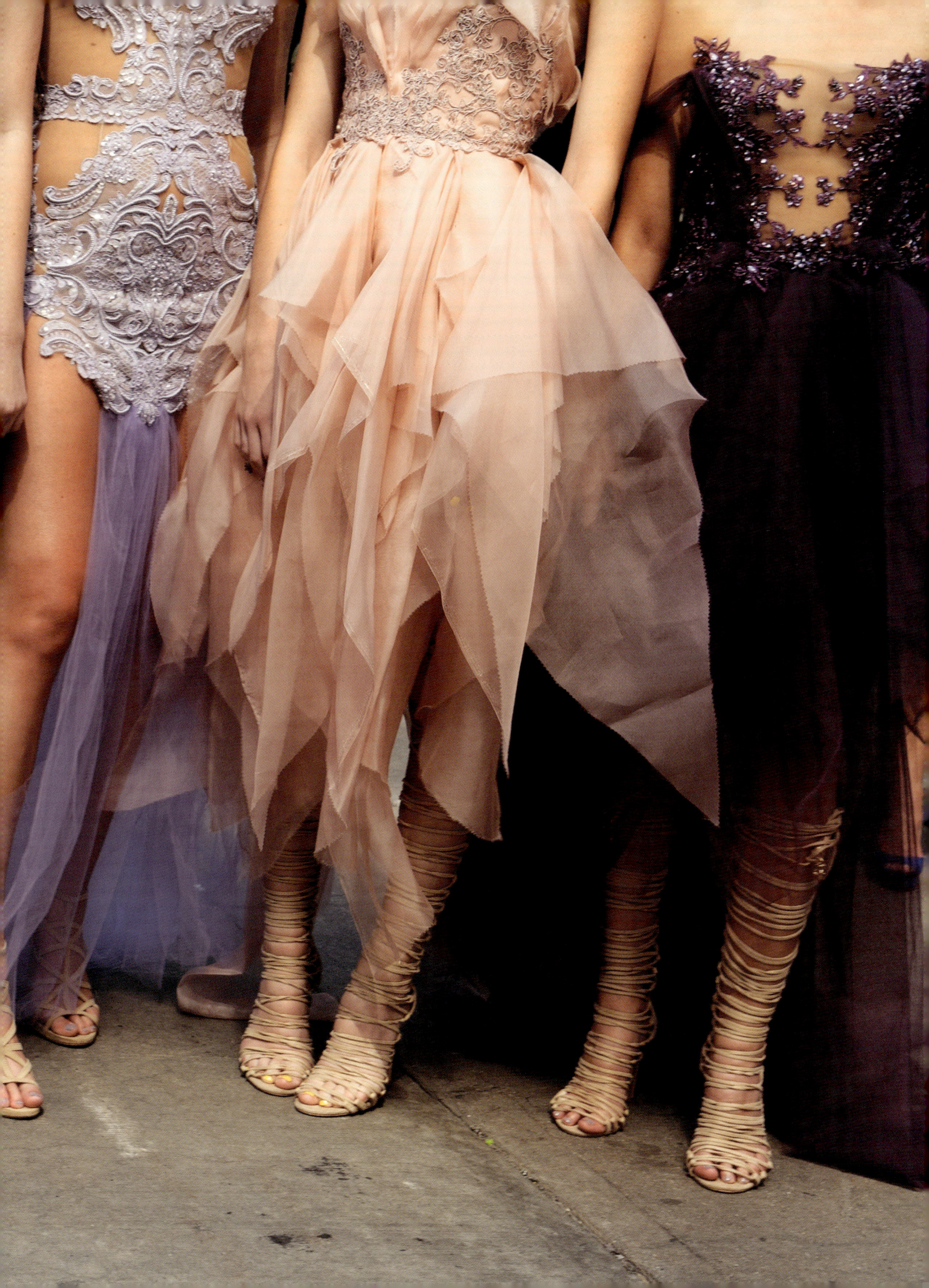

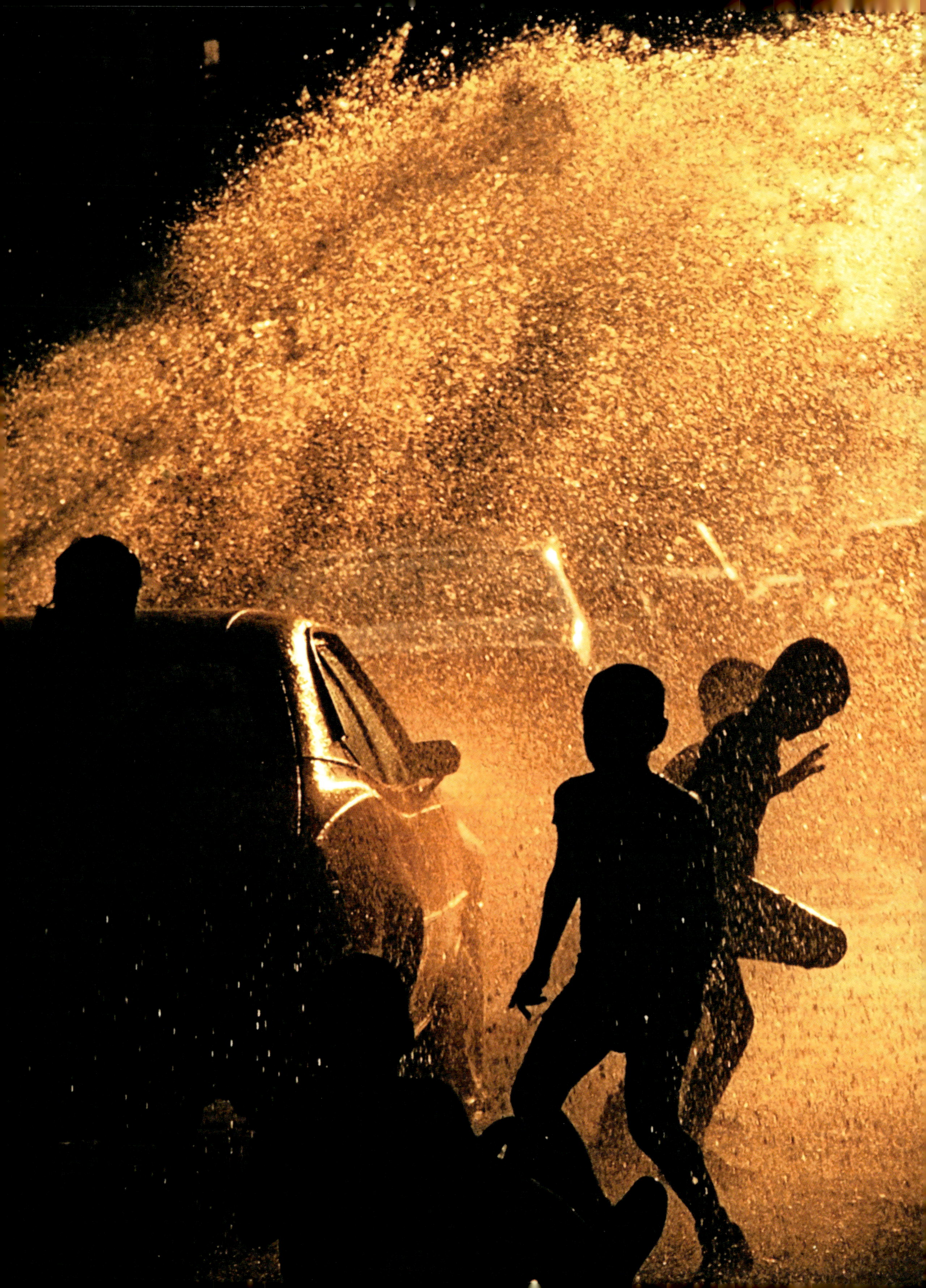

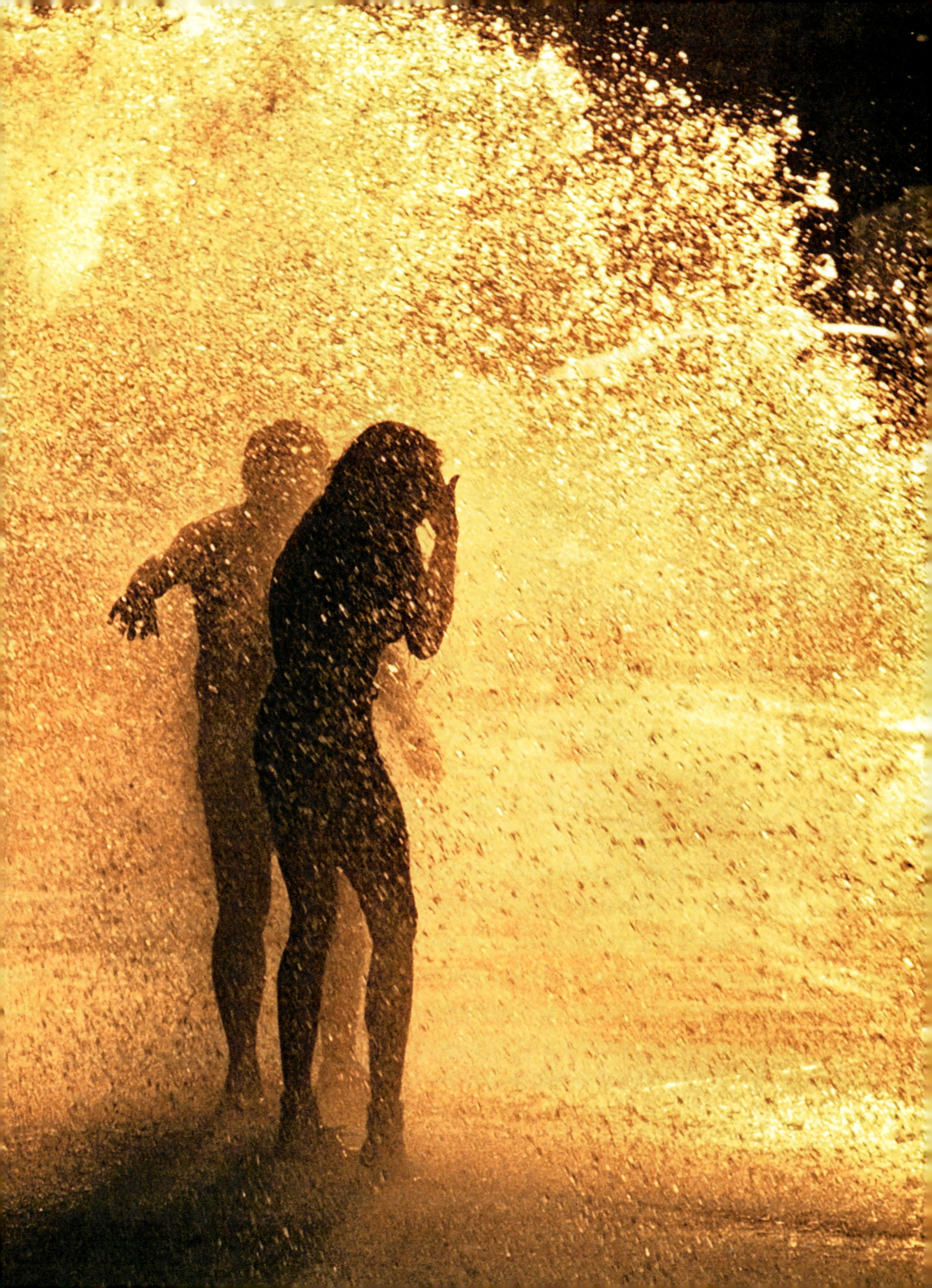

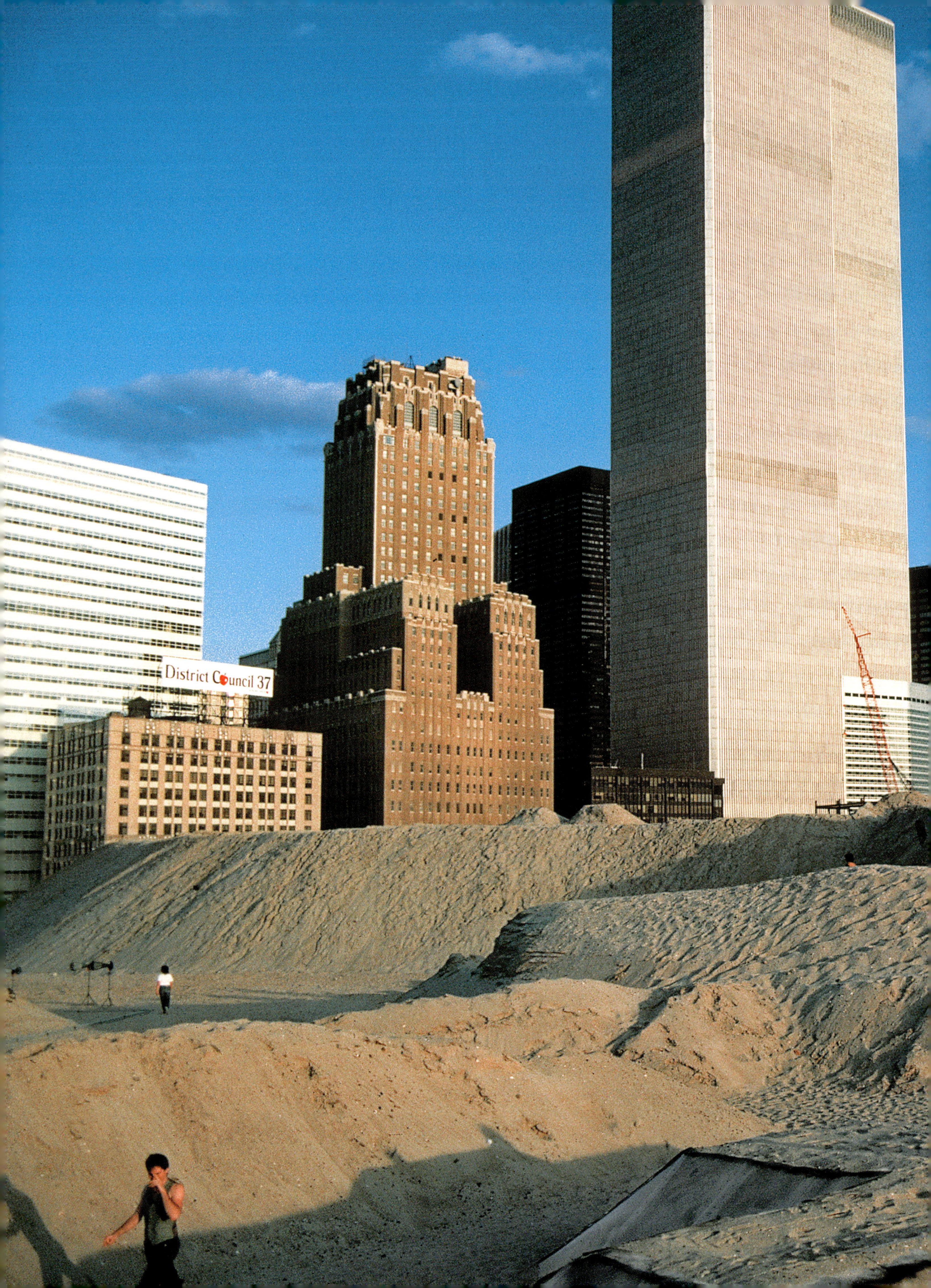

District Council 37

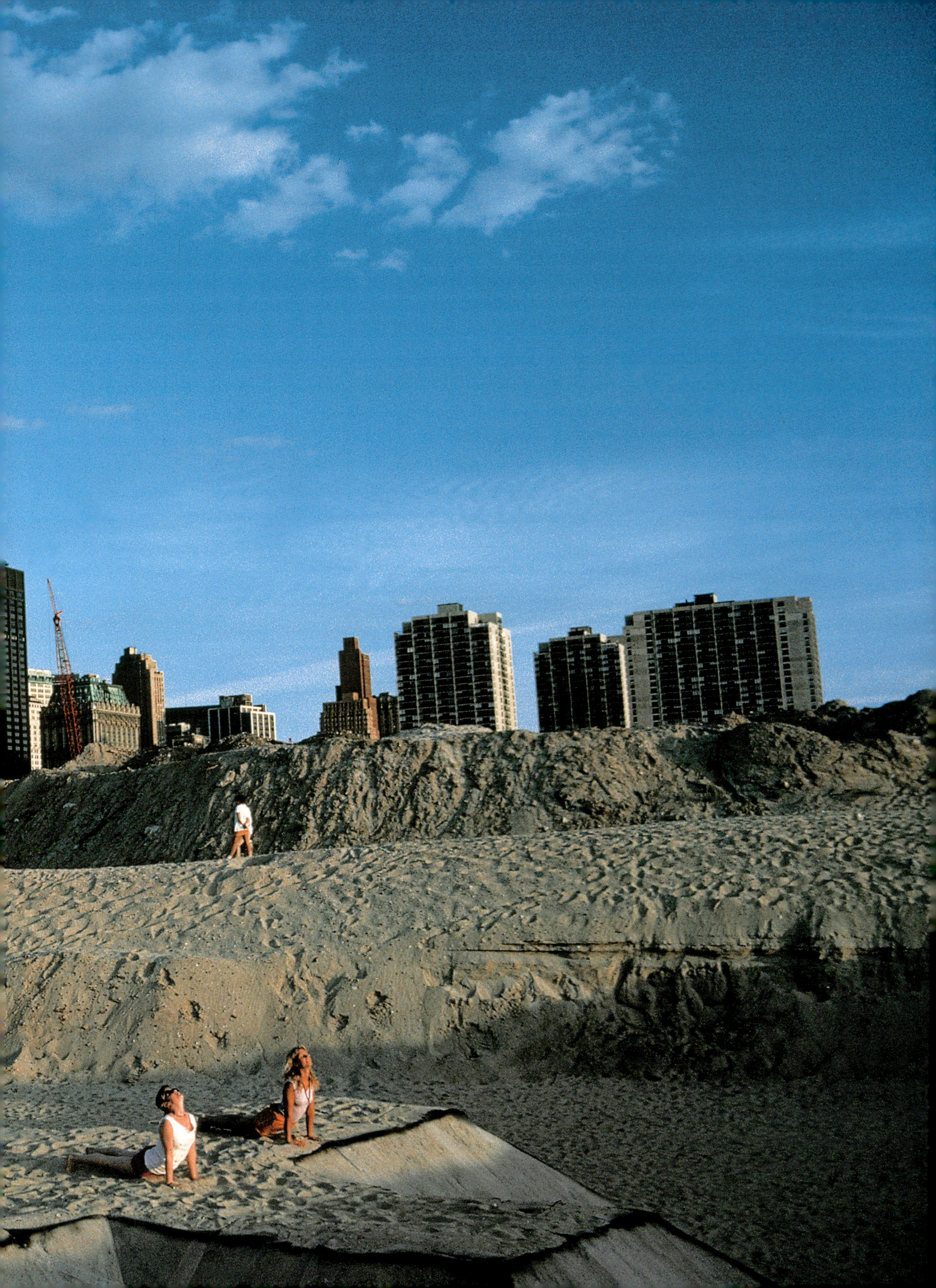

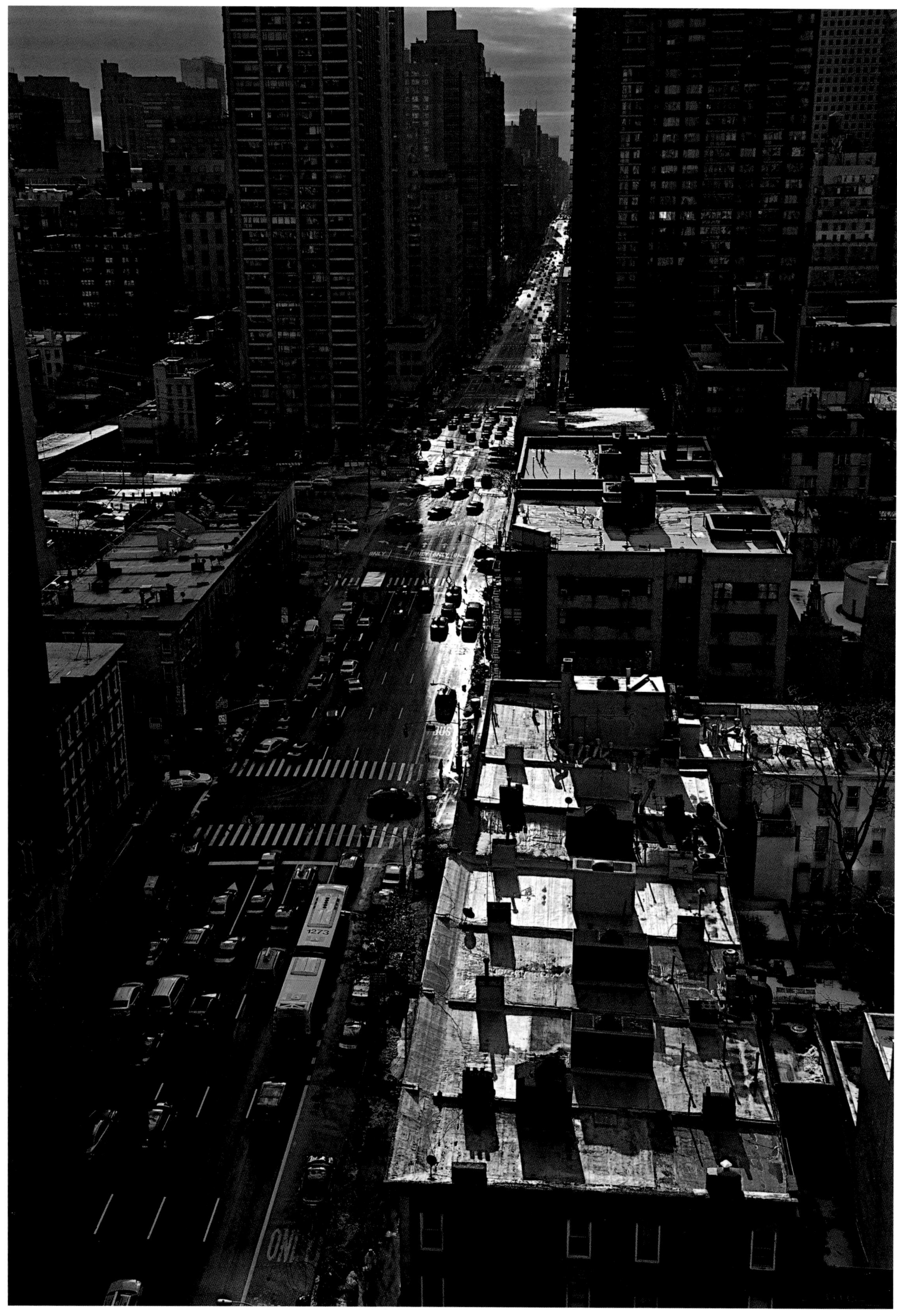

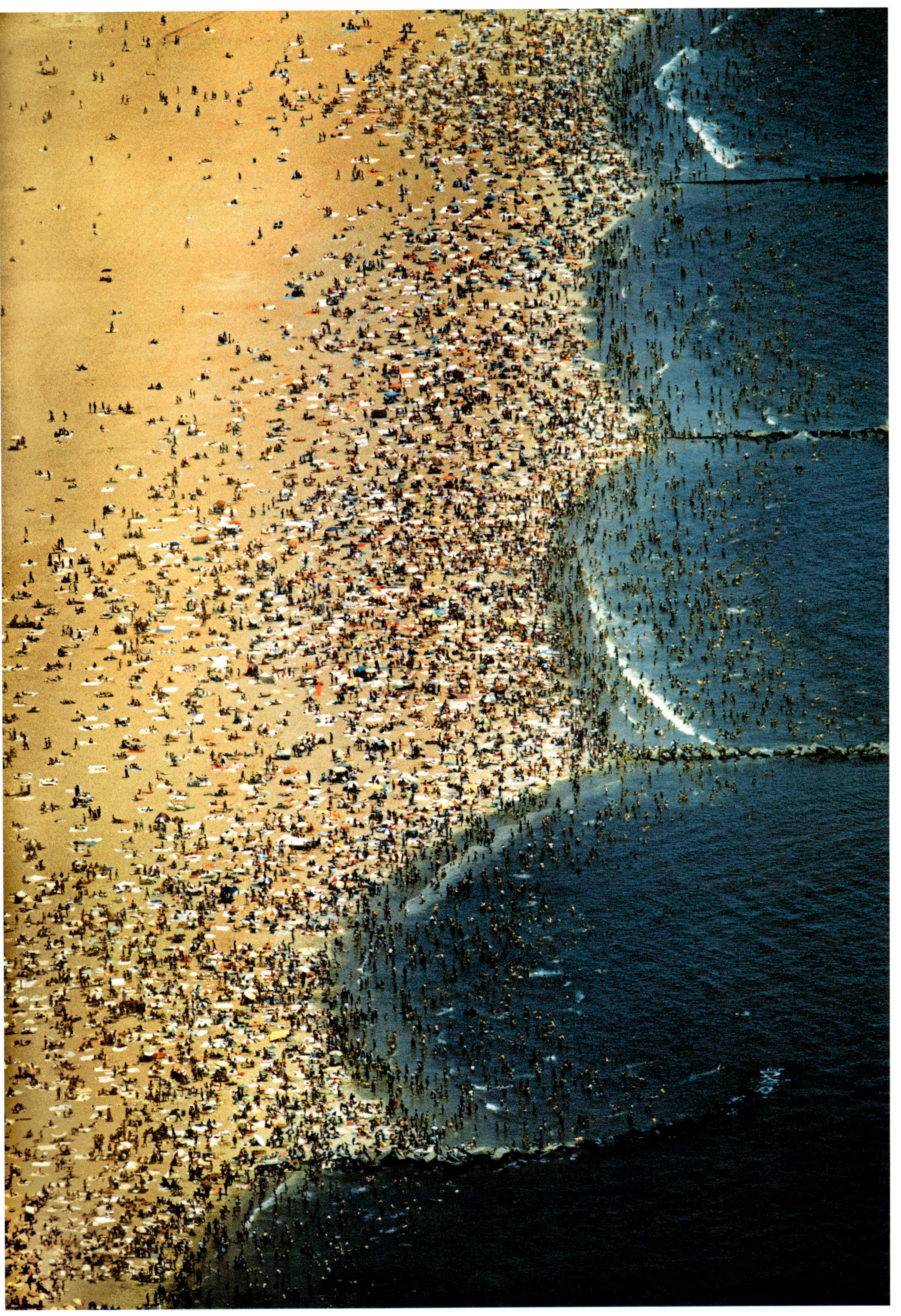

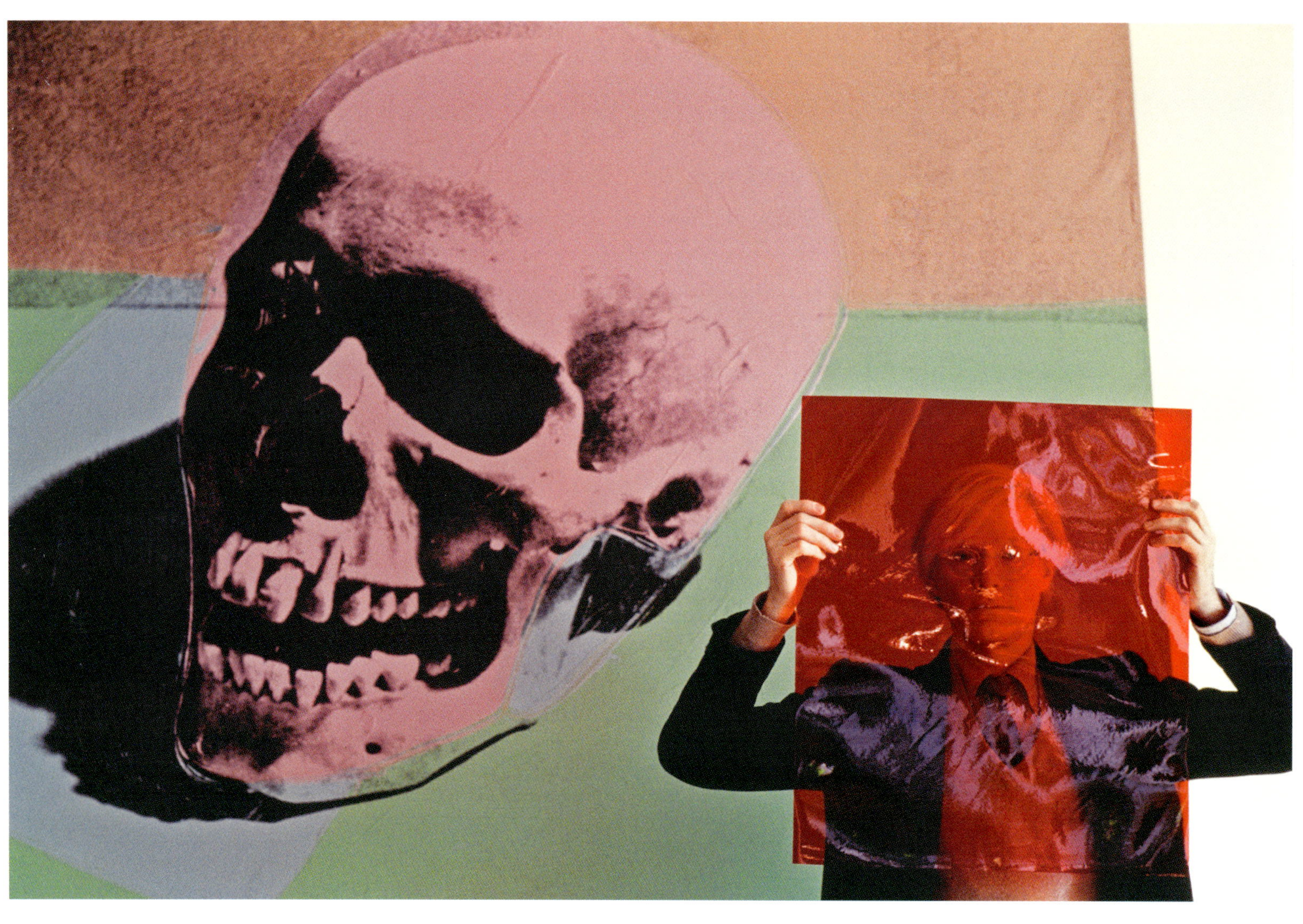

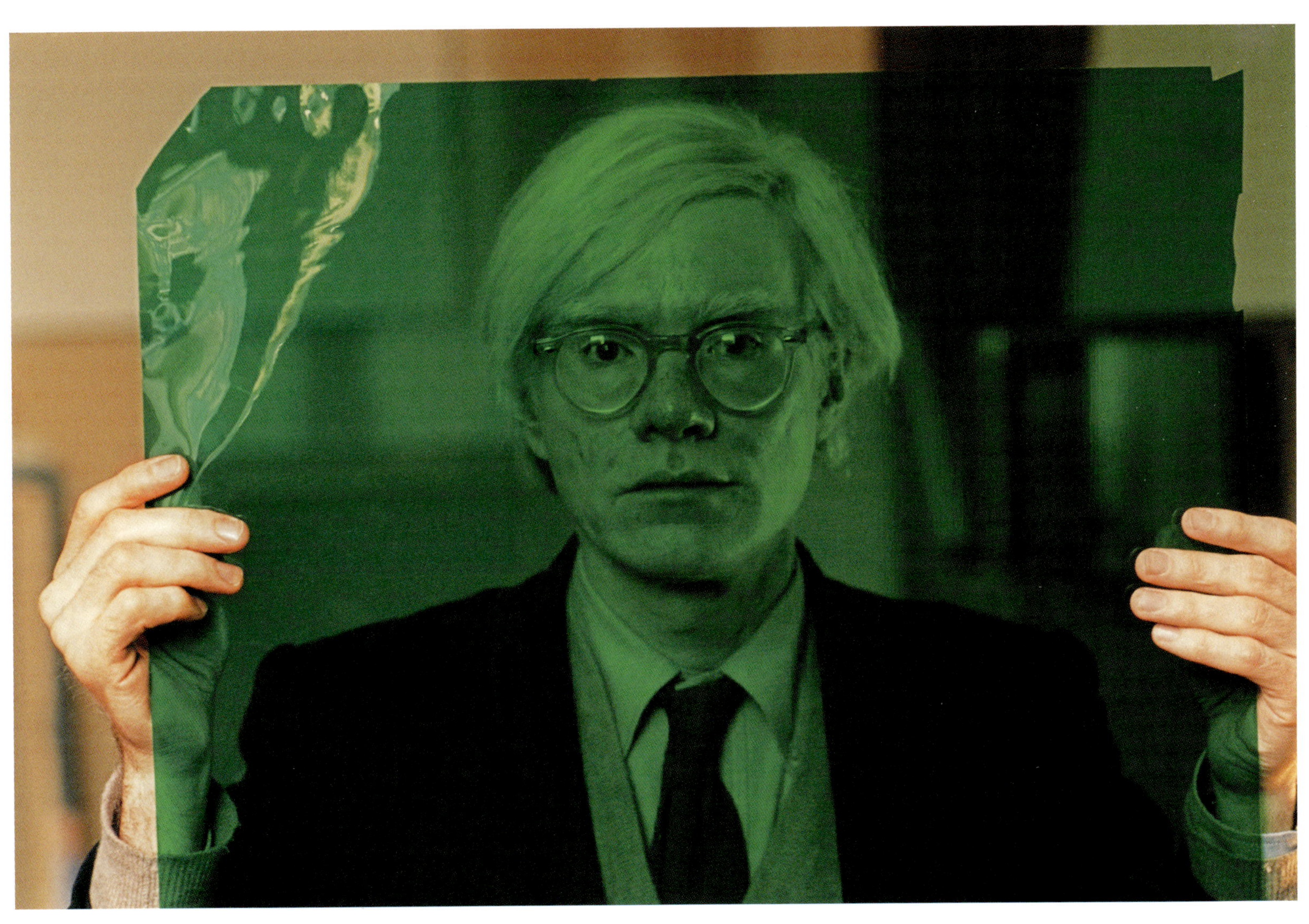

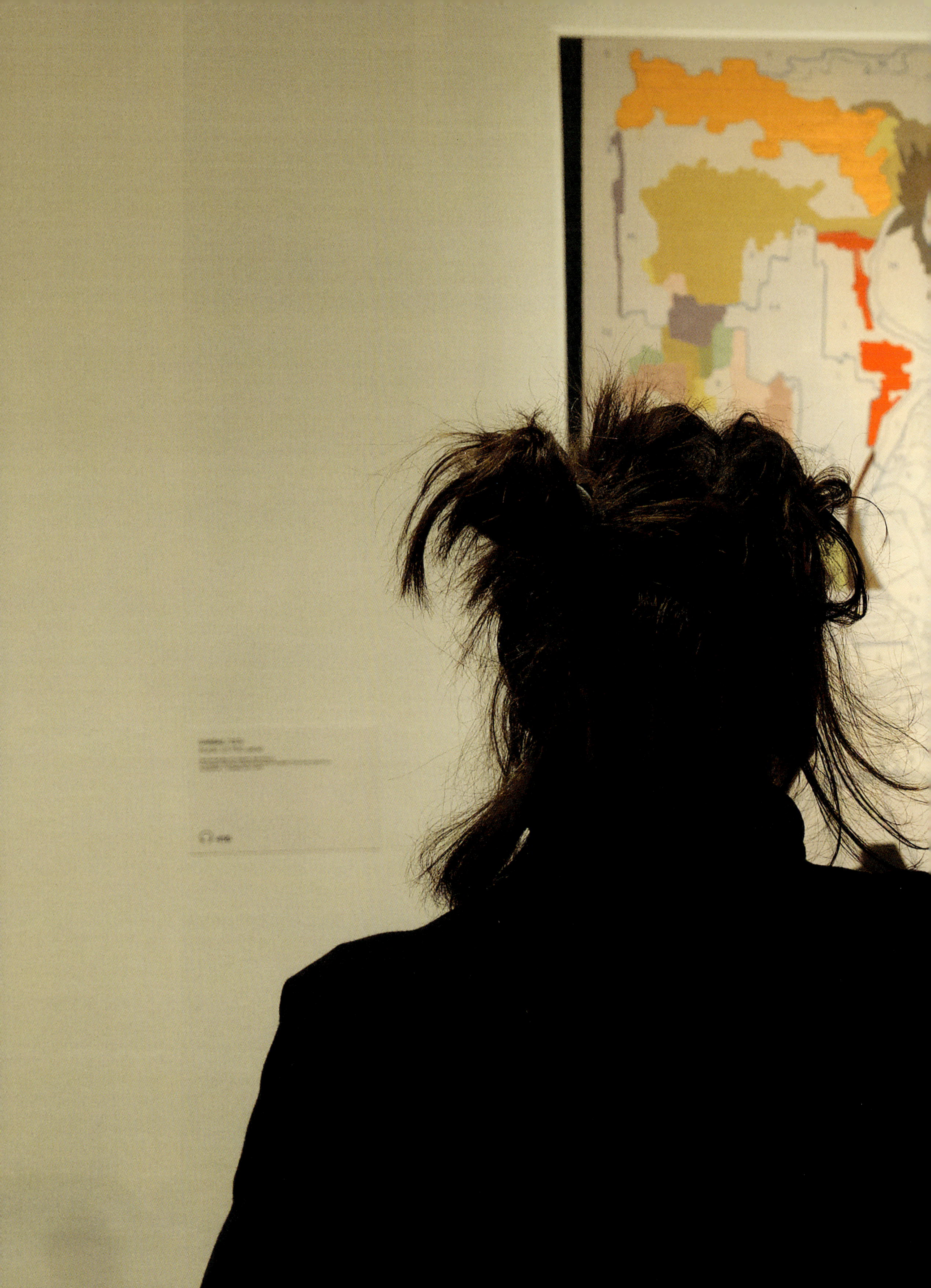

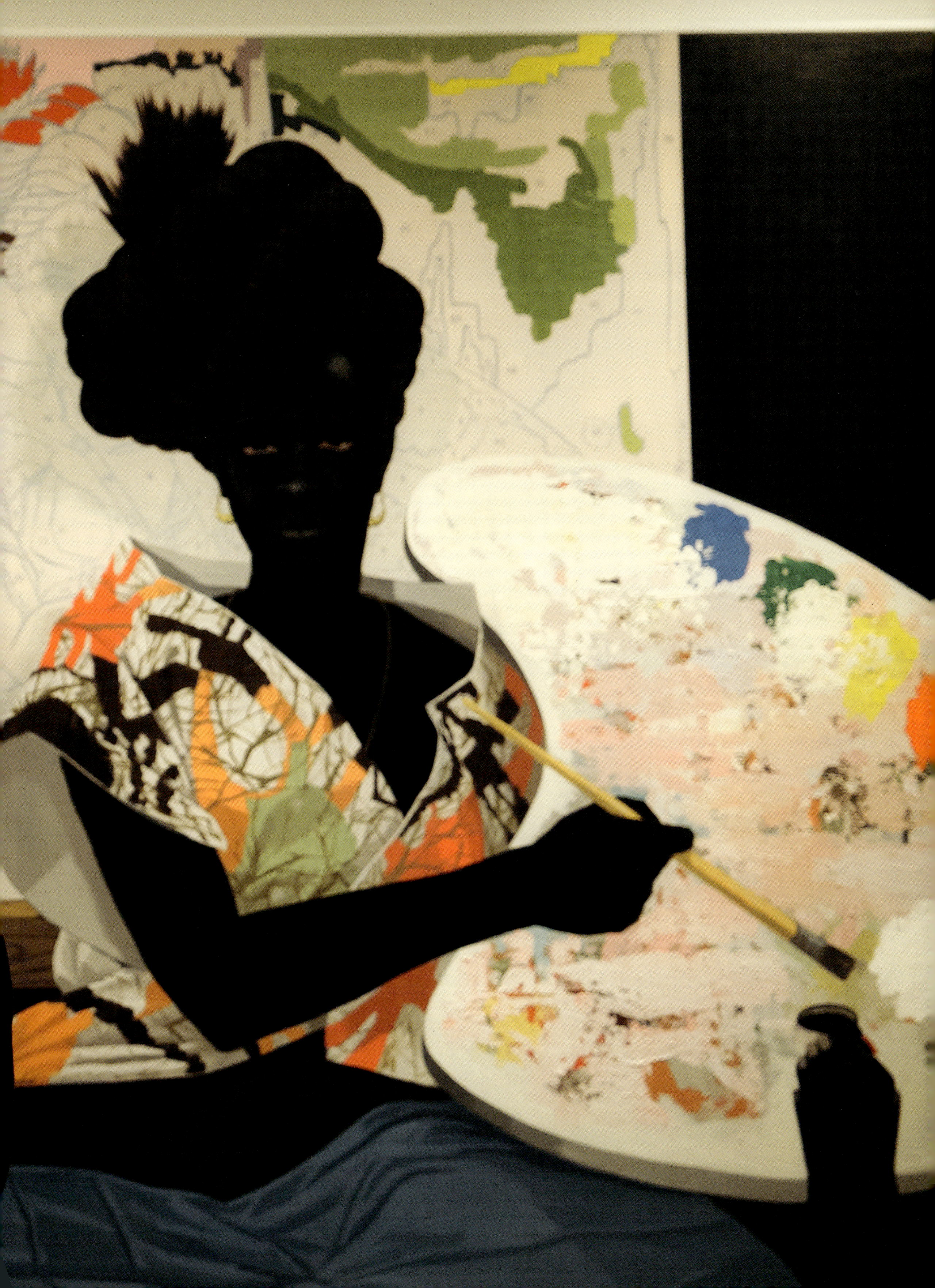

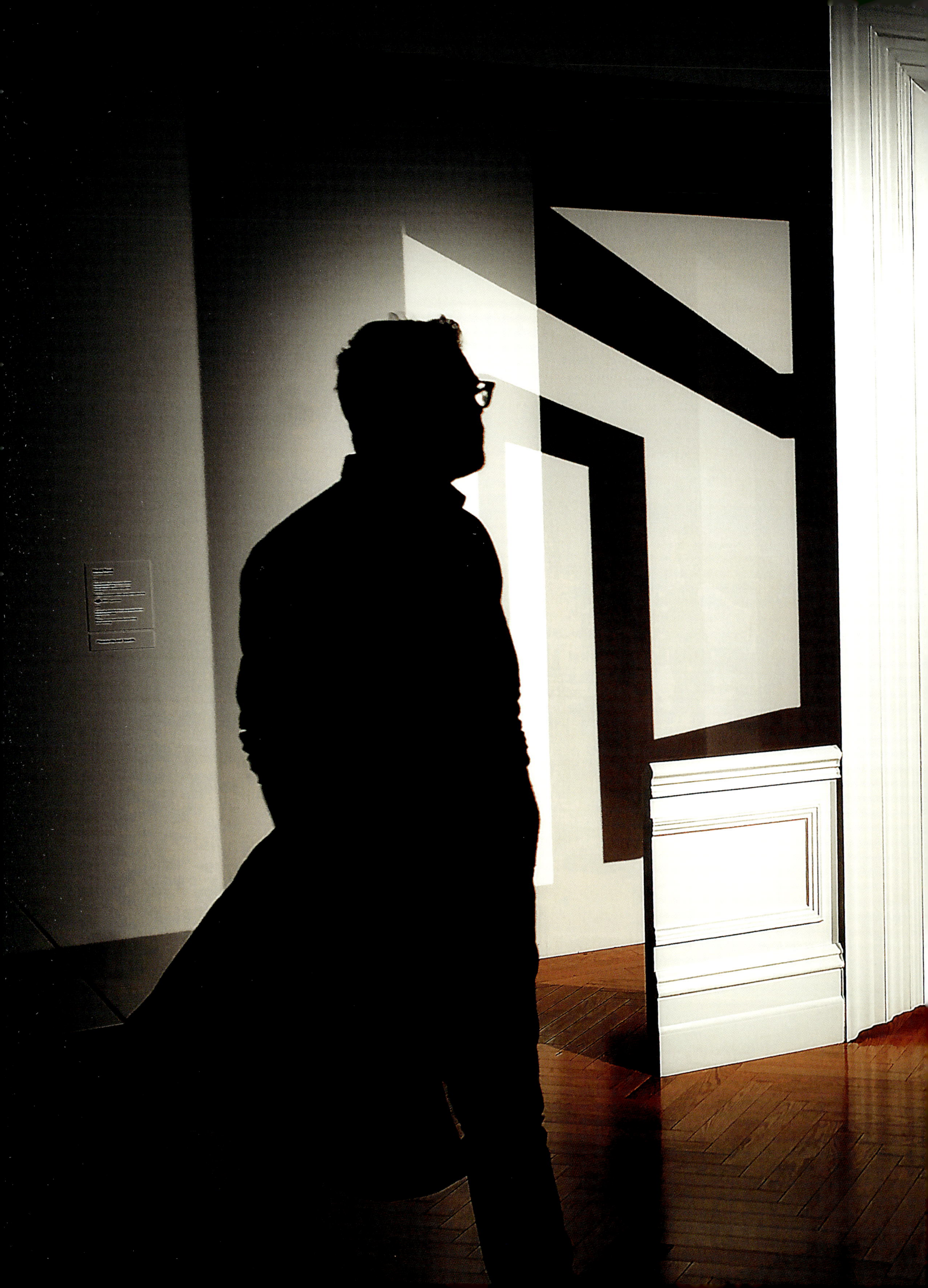

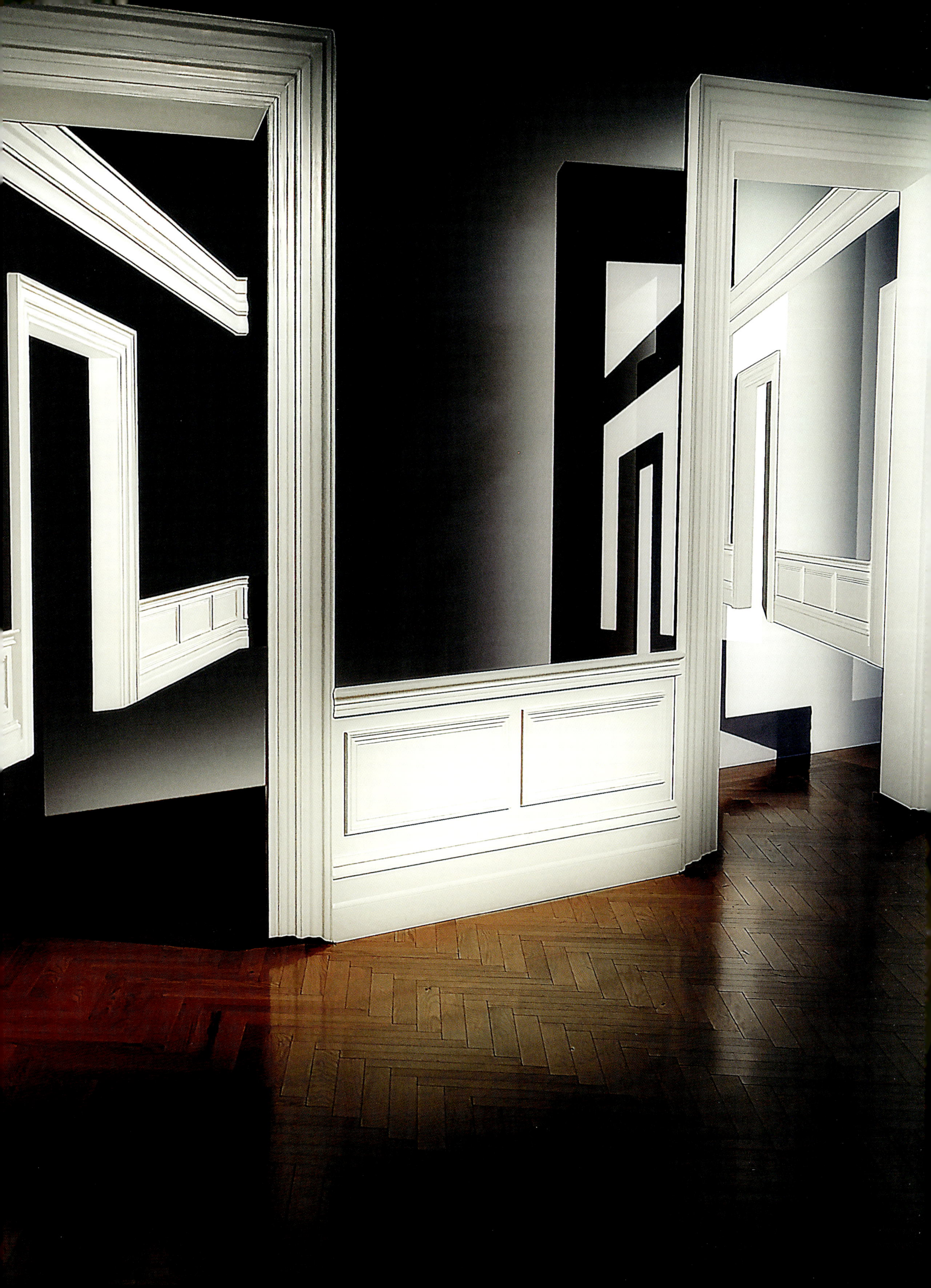

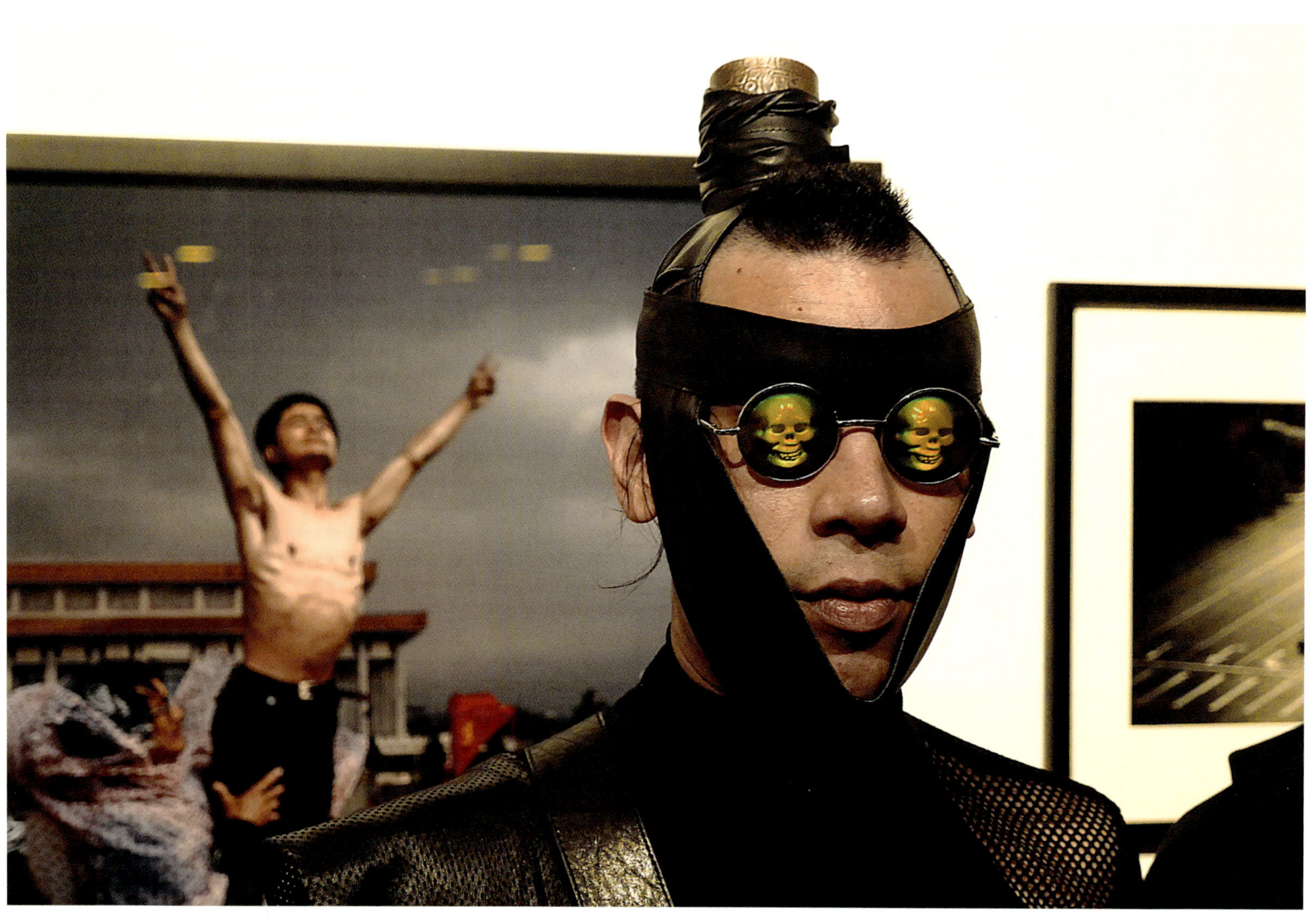

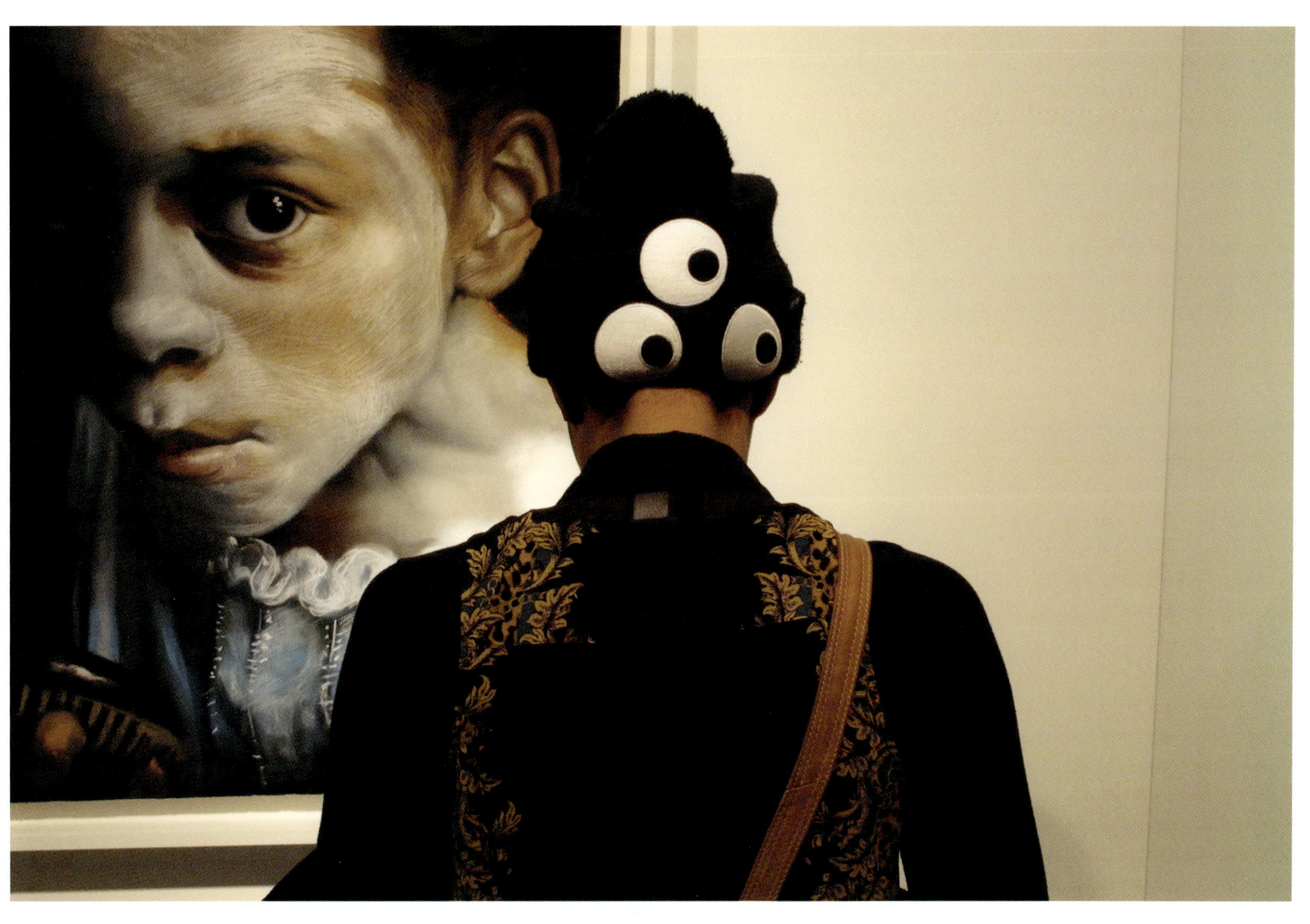

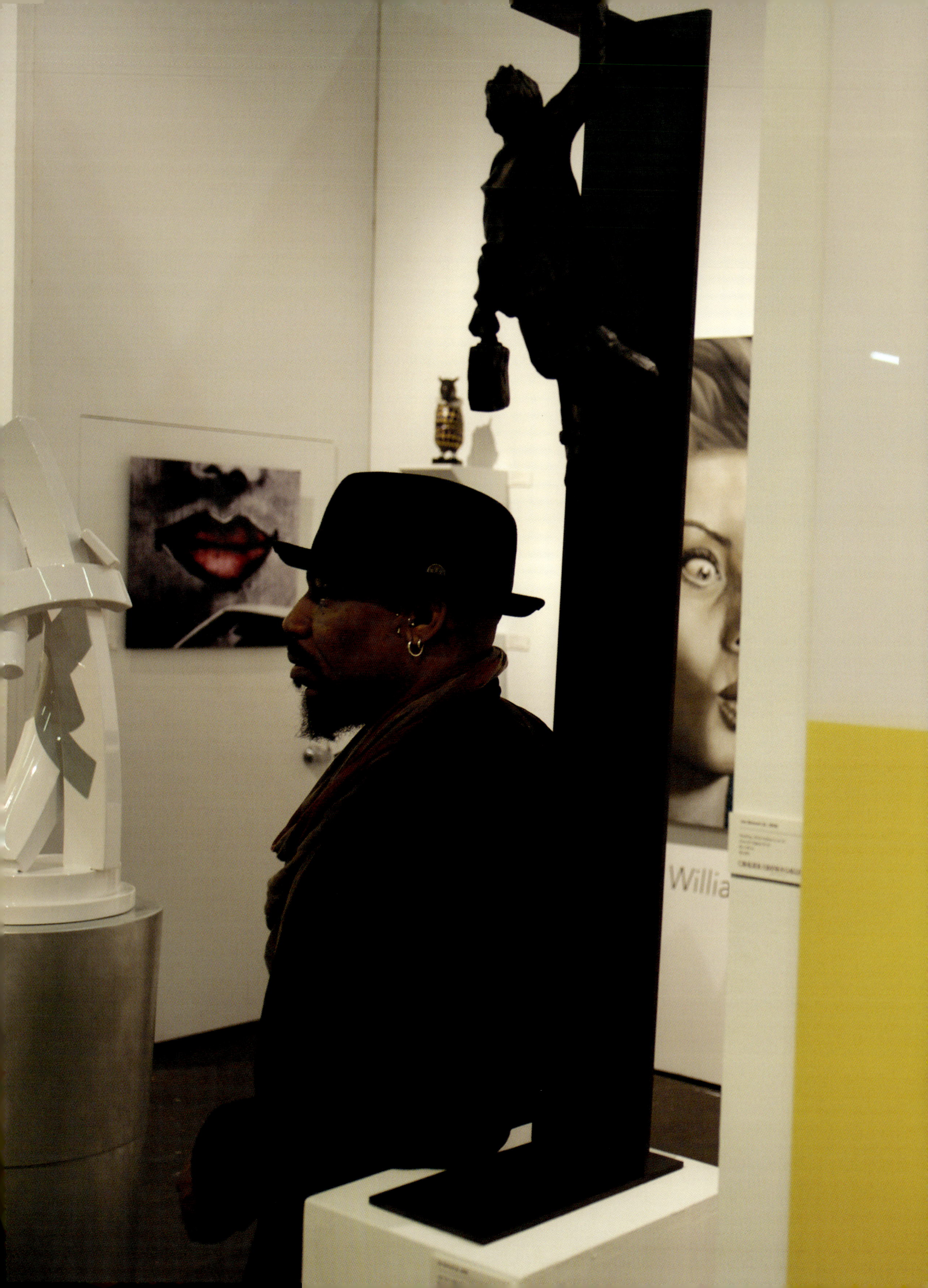

Willia

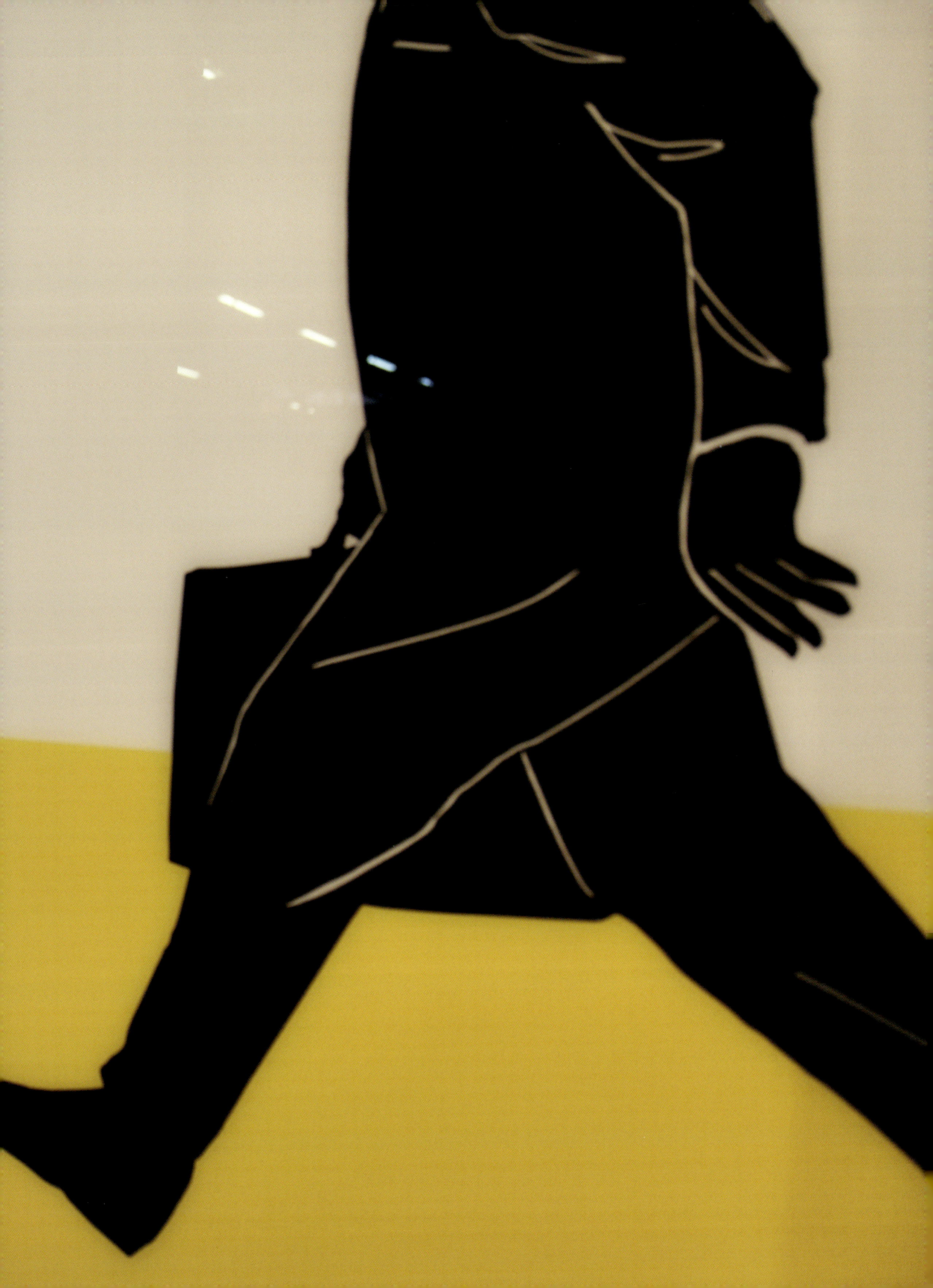

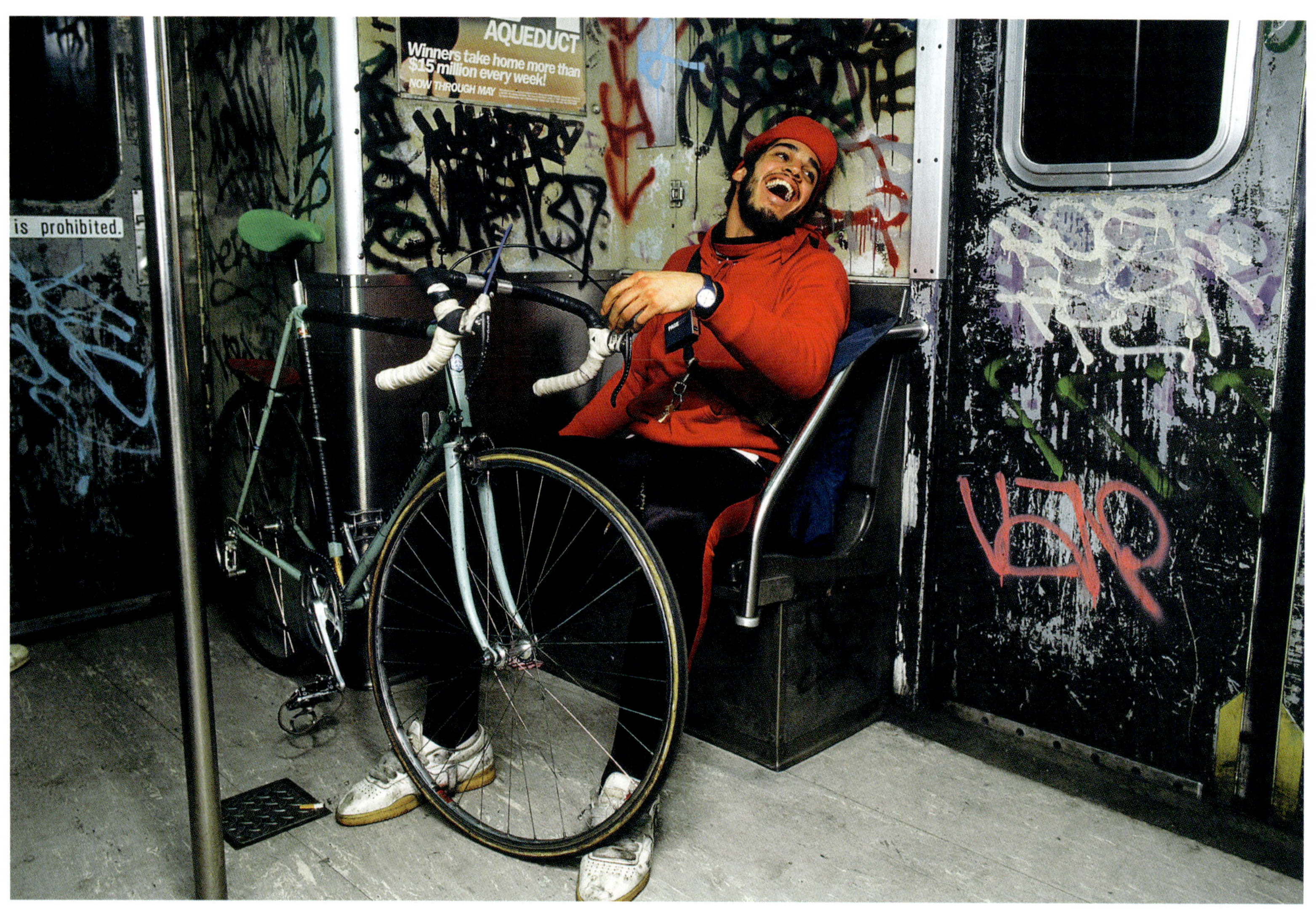

AQUEDUCT
Winners take home more than
$15 million every week!
NOW THROUGH MAY
is prohibited.

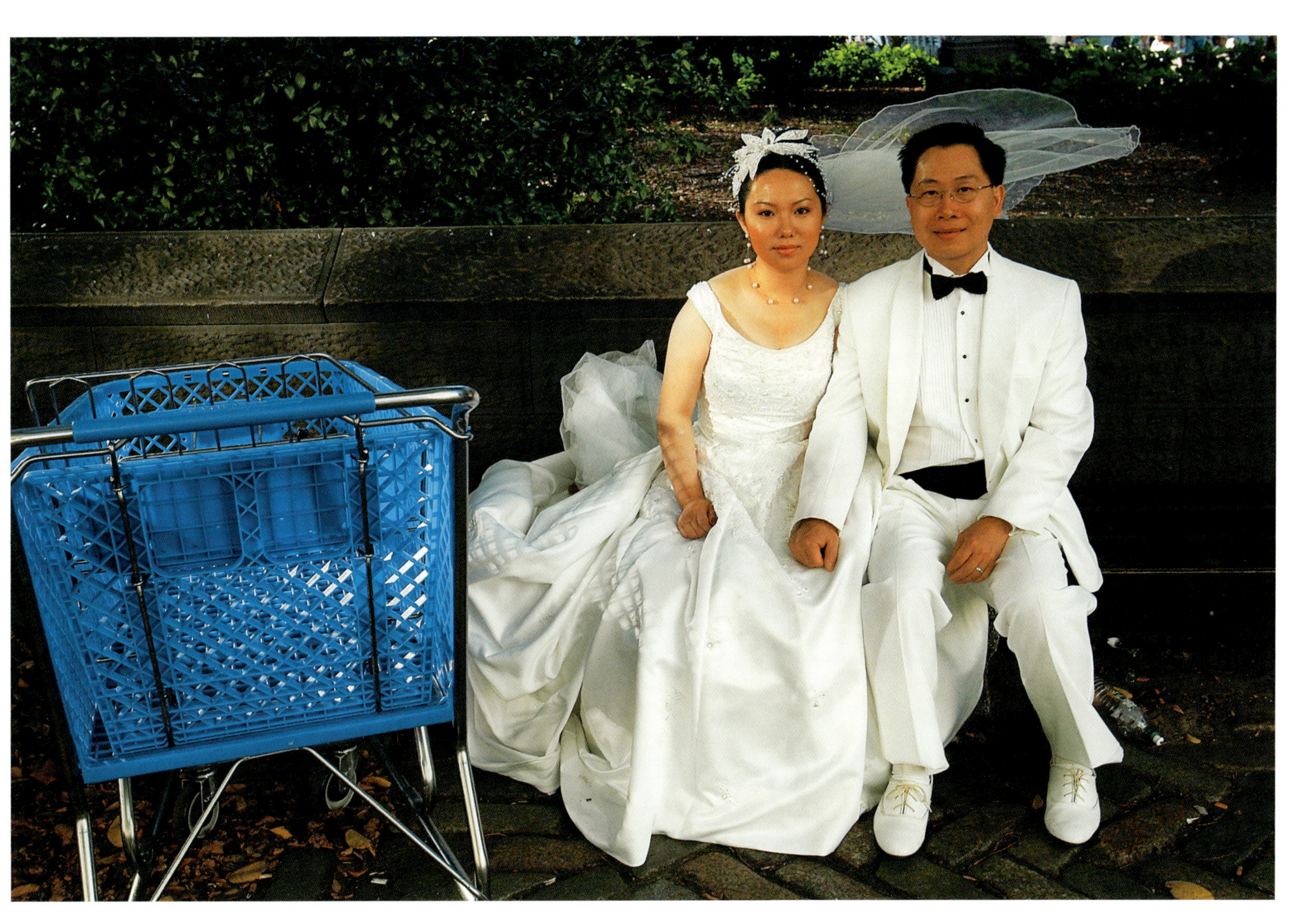

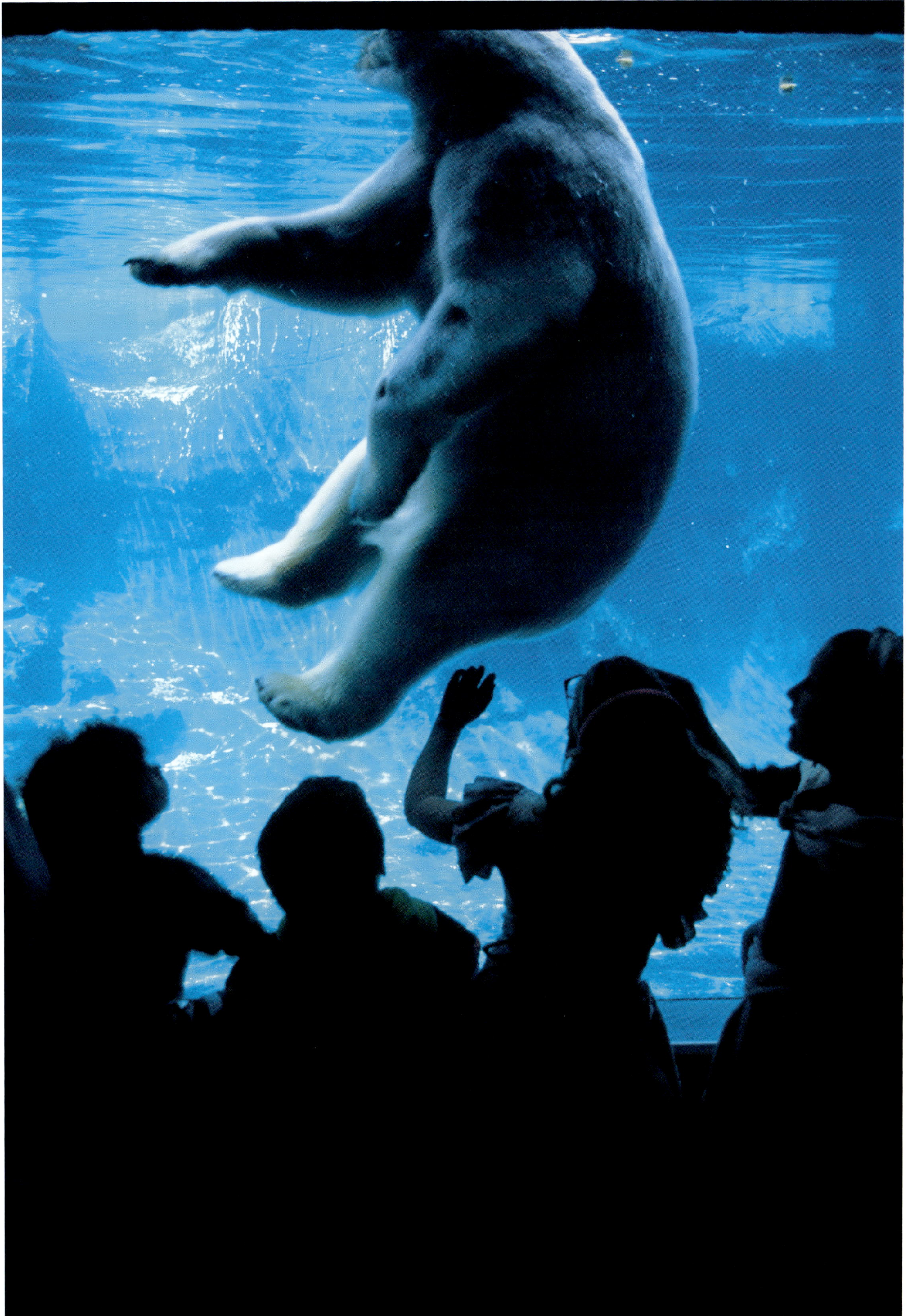

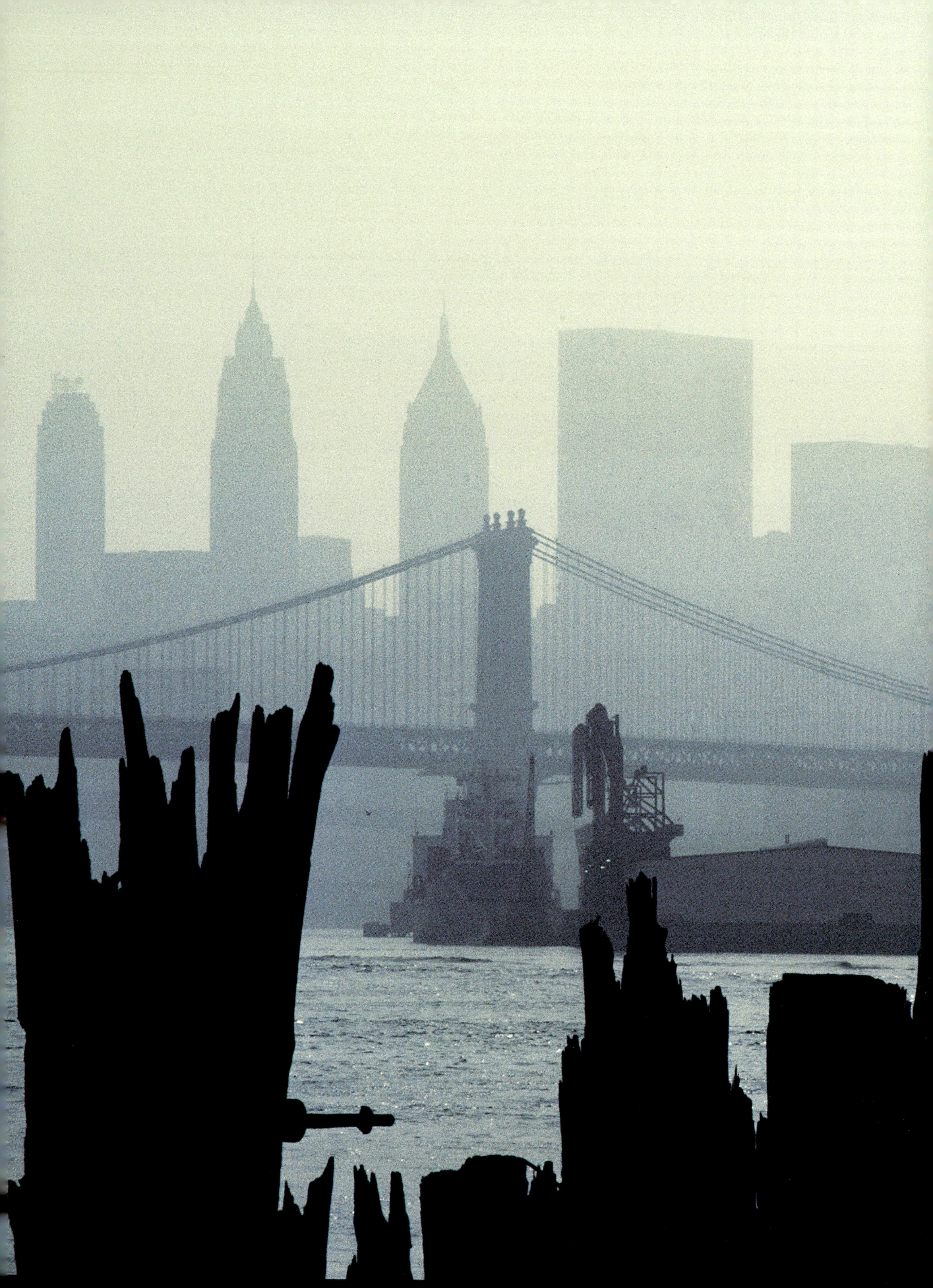

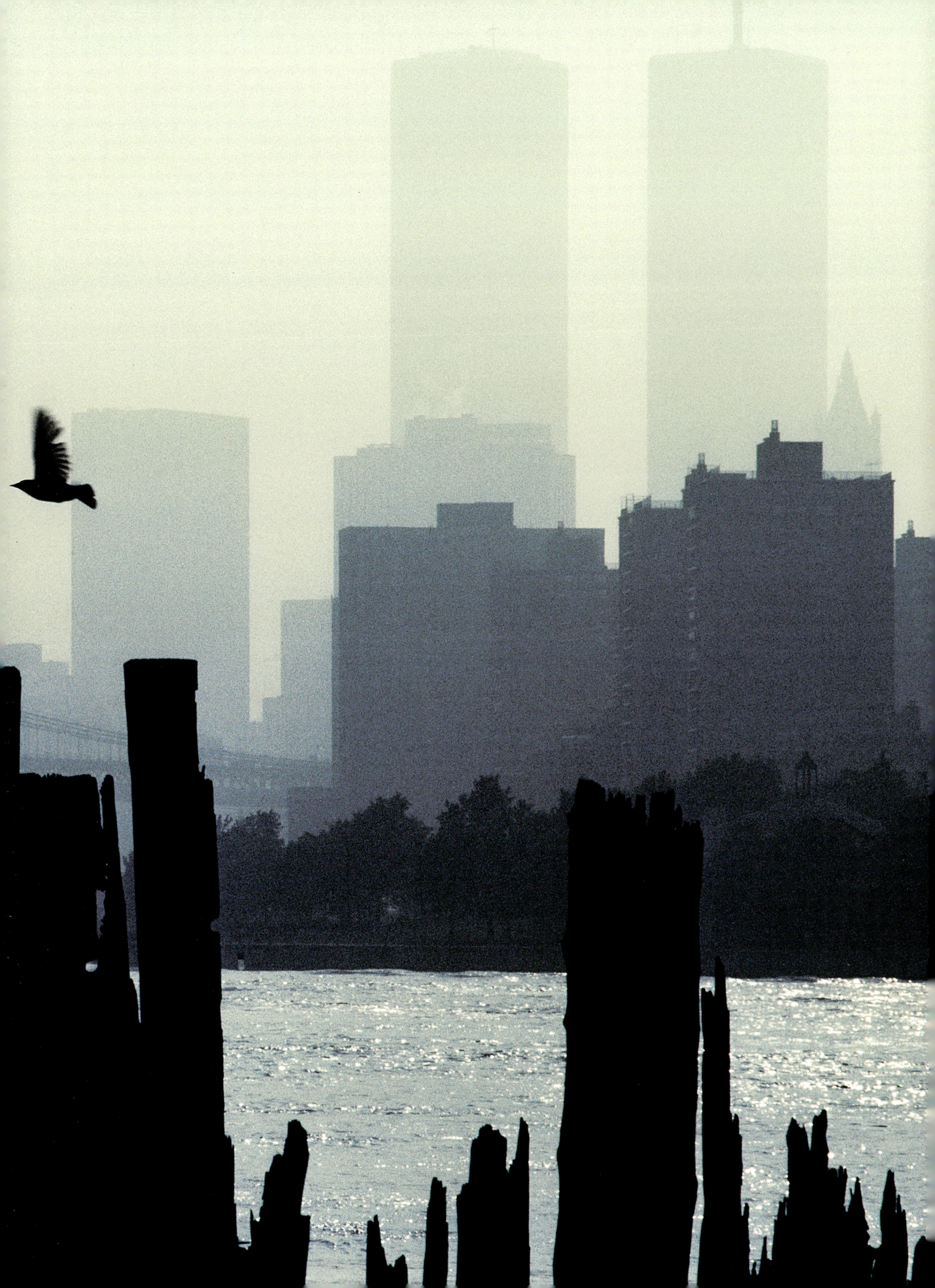

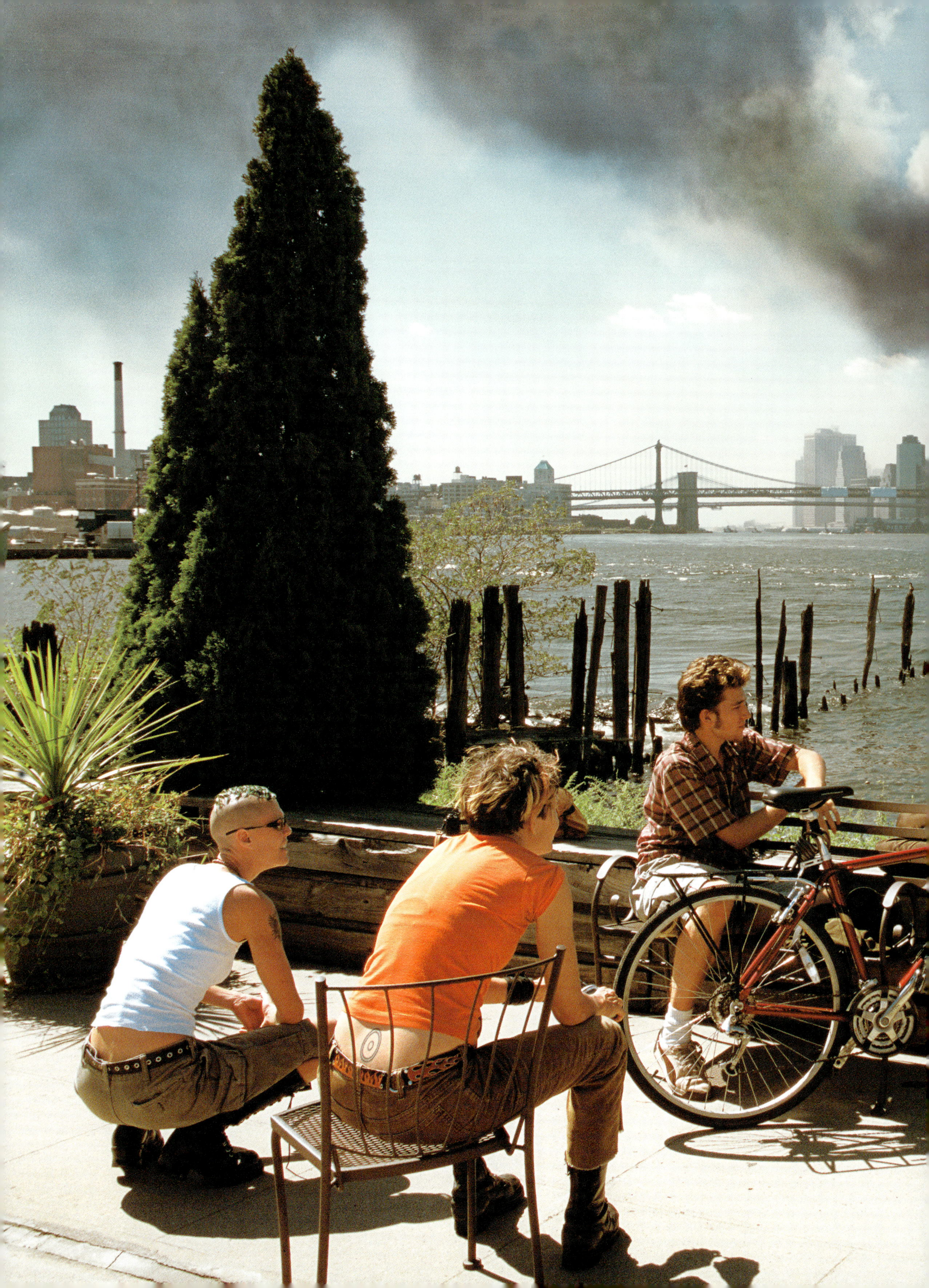

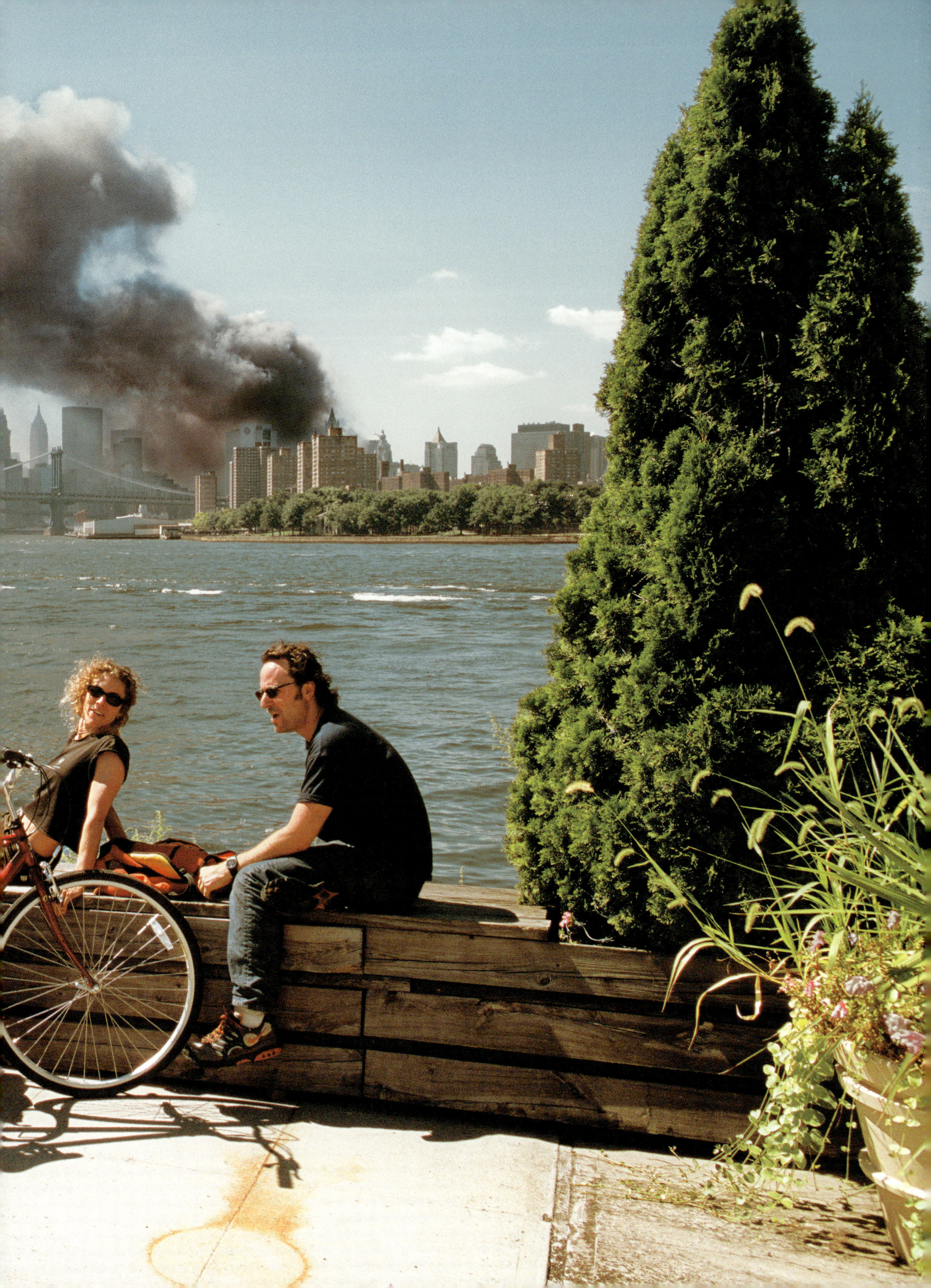

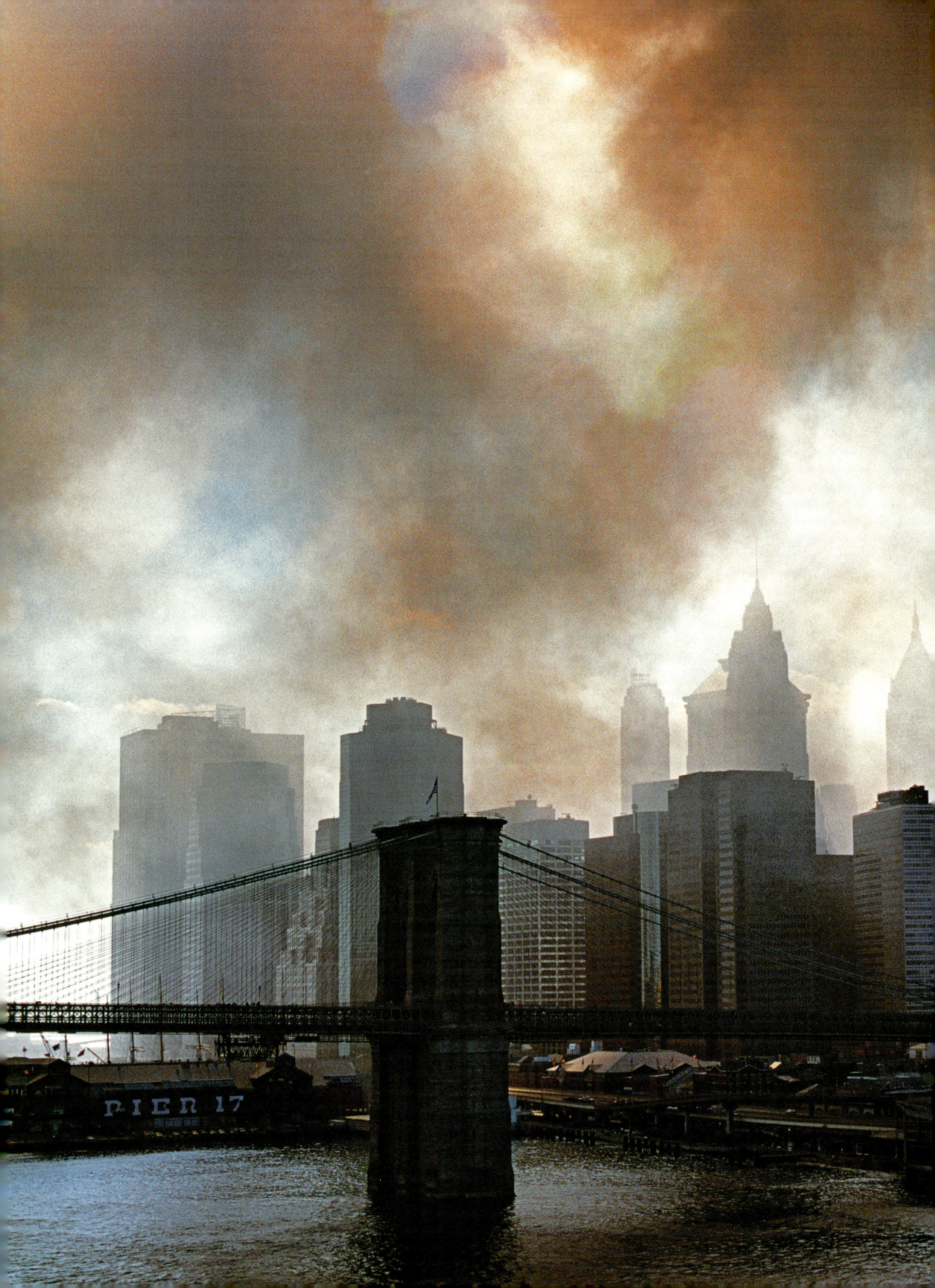

PIER 17

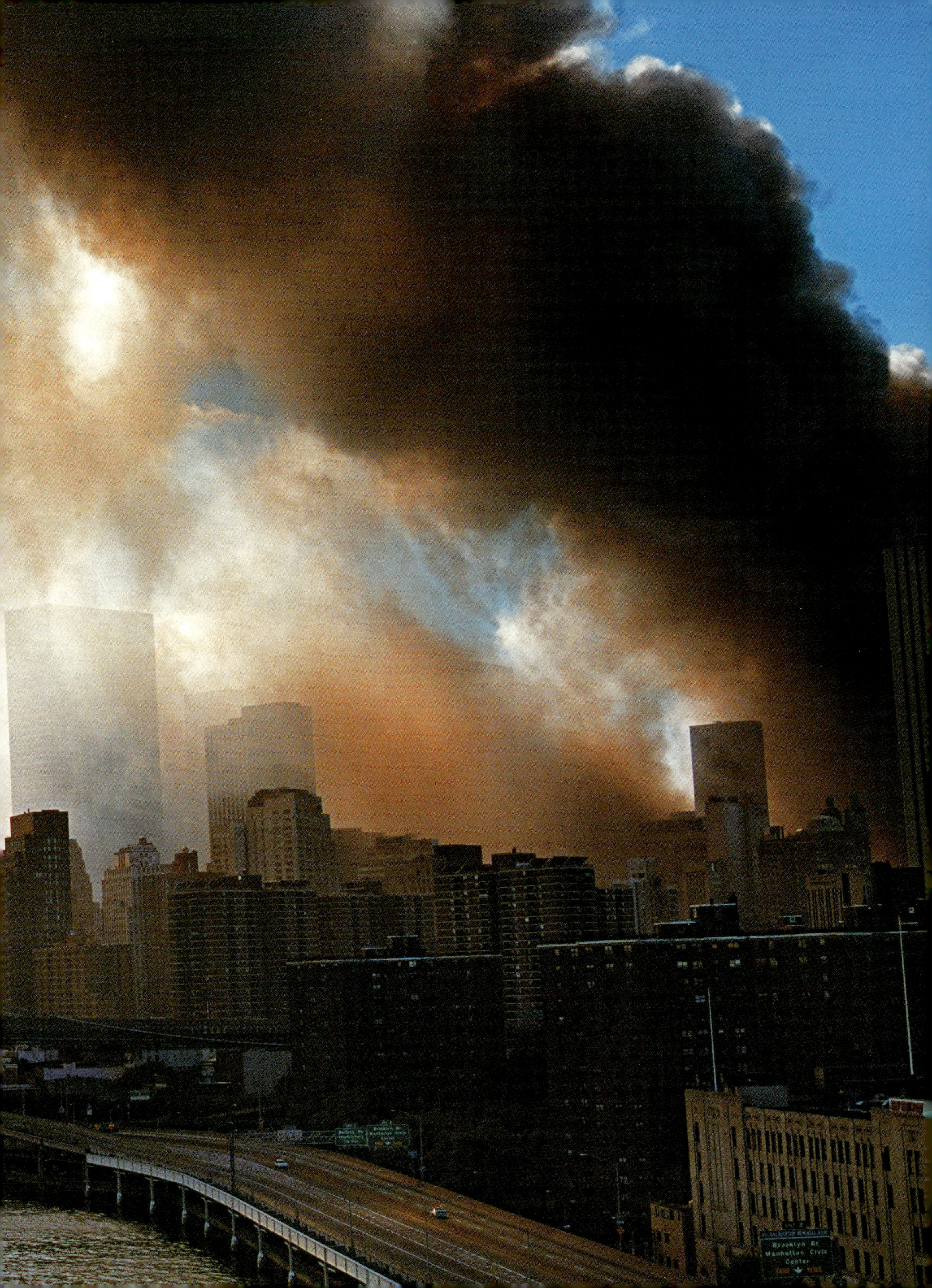

Brooklyn Br
Manhattan Civic
Center

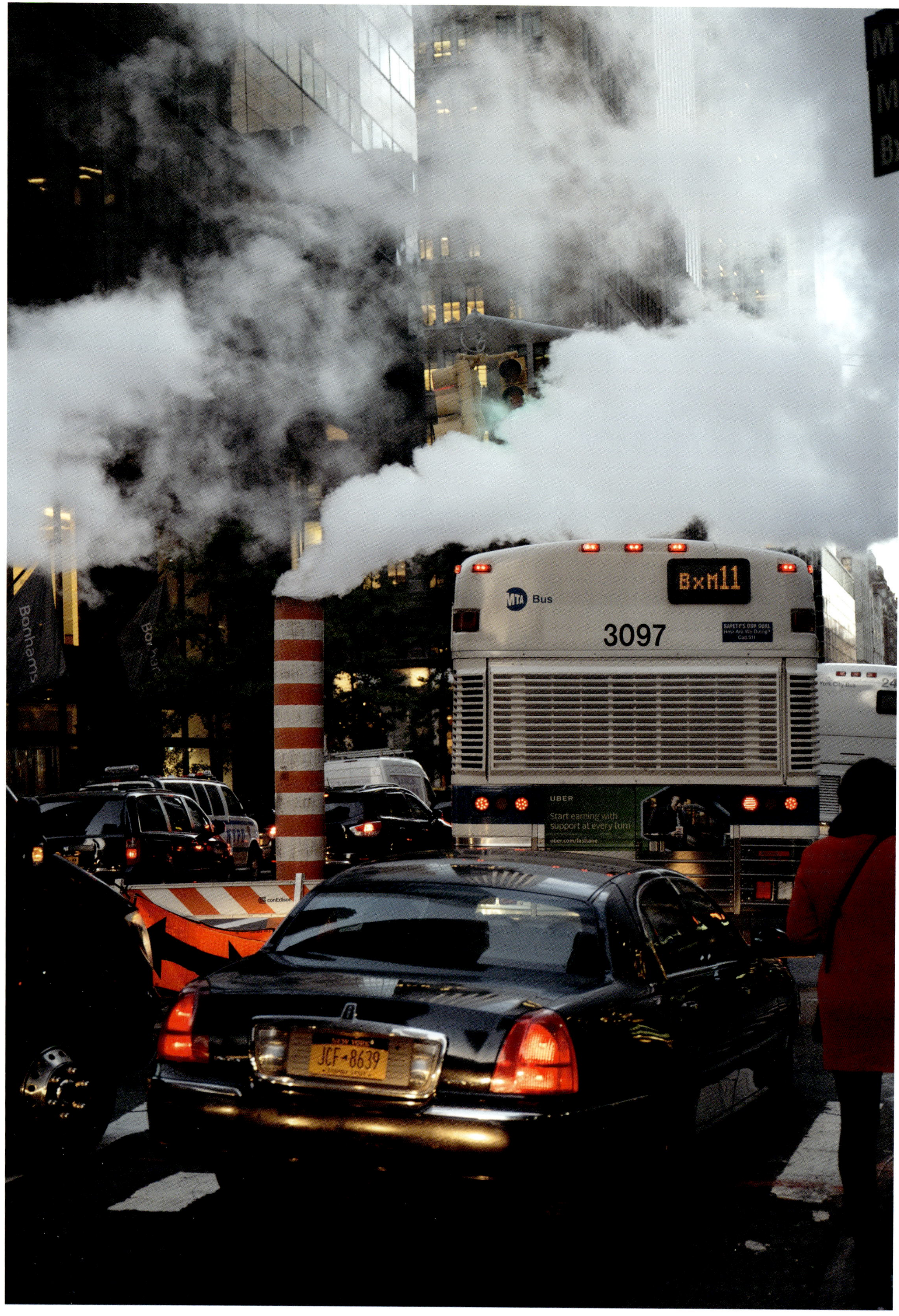

BxM11
MTA Bus
3097
SAFETY'S OUR GOAL
How Are We Doing?
Call 511
New York City Bus
24
UBER
Start earning with
support at every turn
uber.com/lastlane
NEW YORK
JCF·8639
conEdison
Bonhams
M
M
B

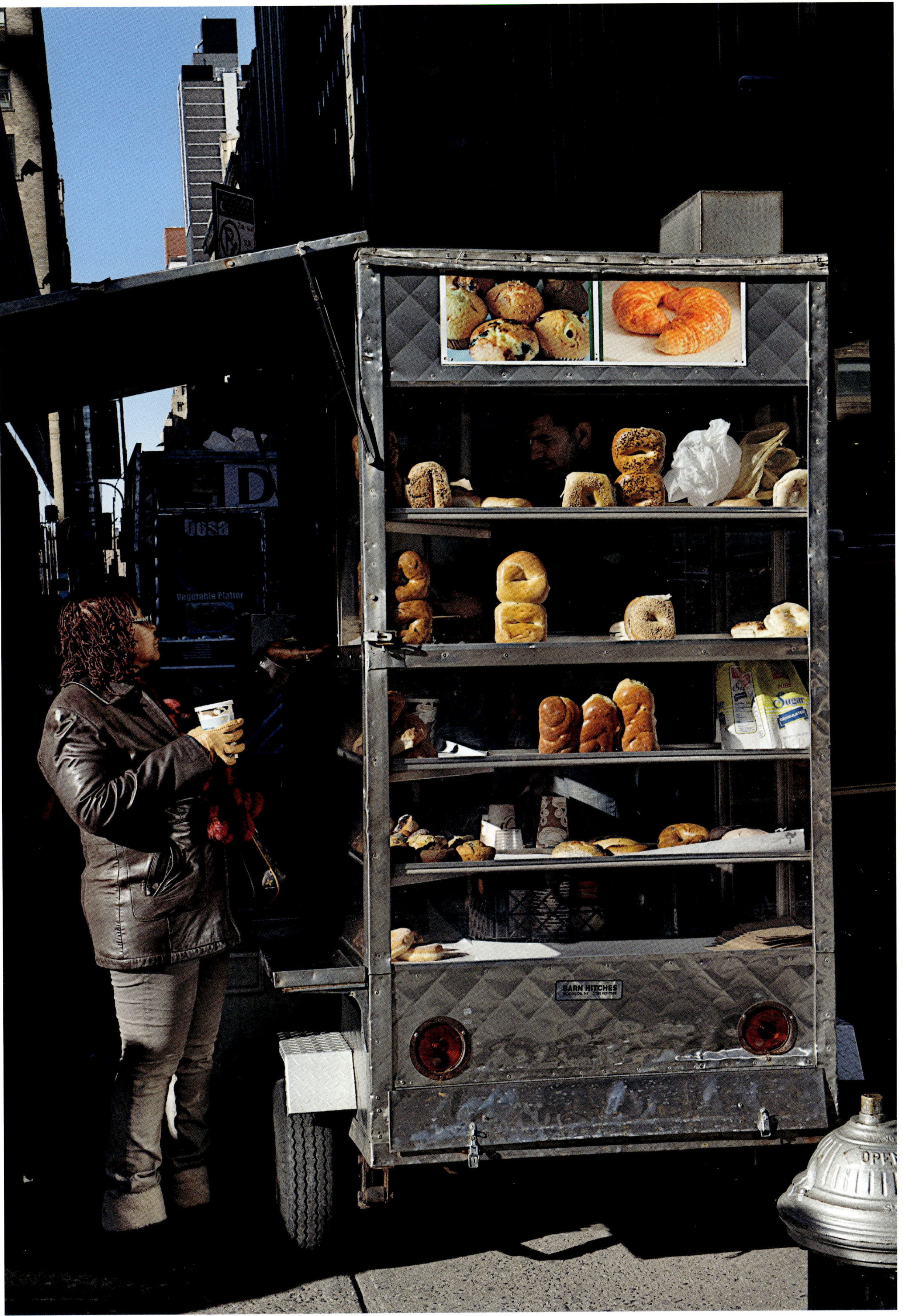
Dosa
Vegetable Platter
Sugar
BARN HITCHES
OPEN

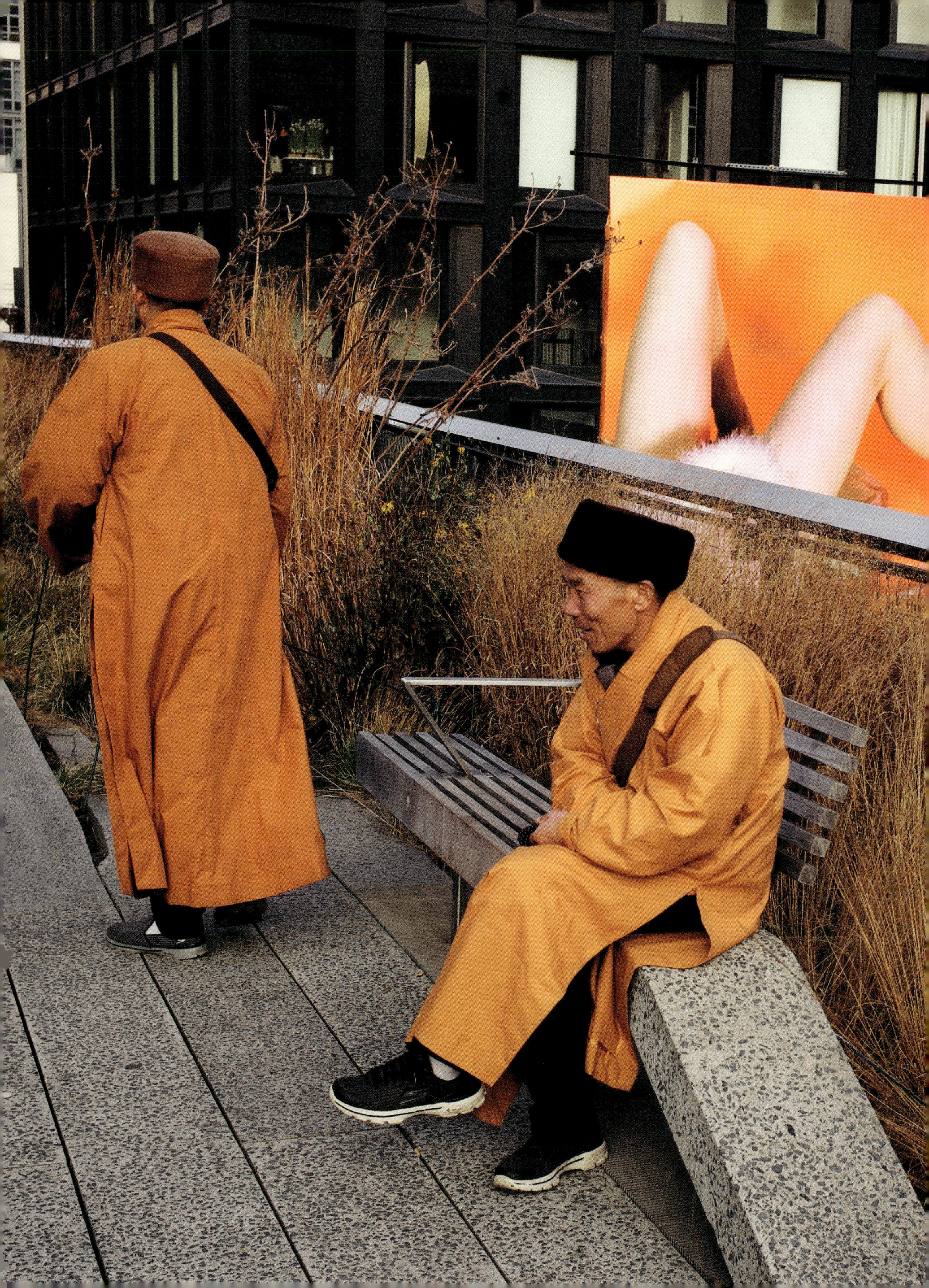

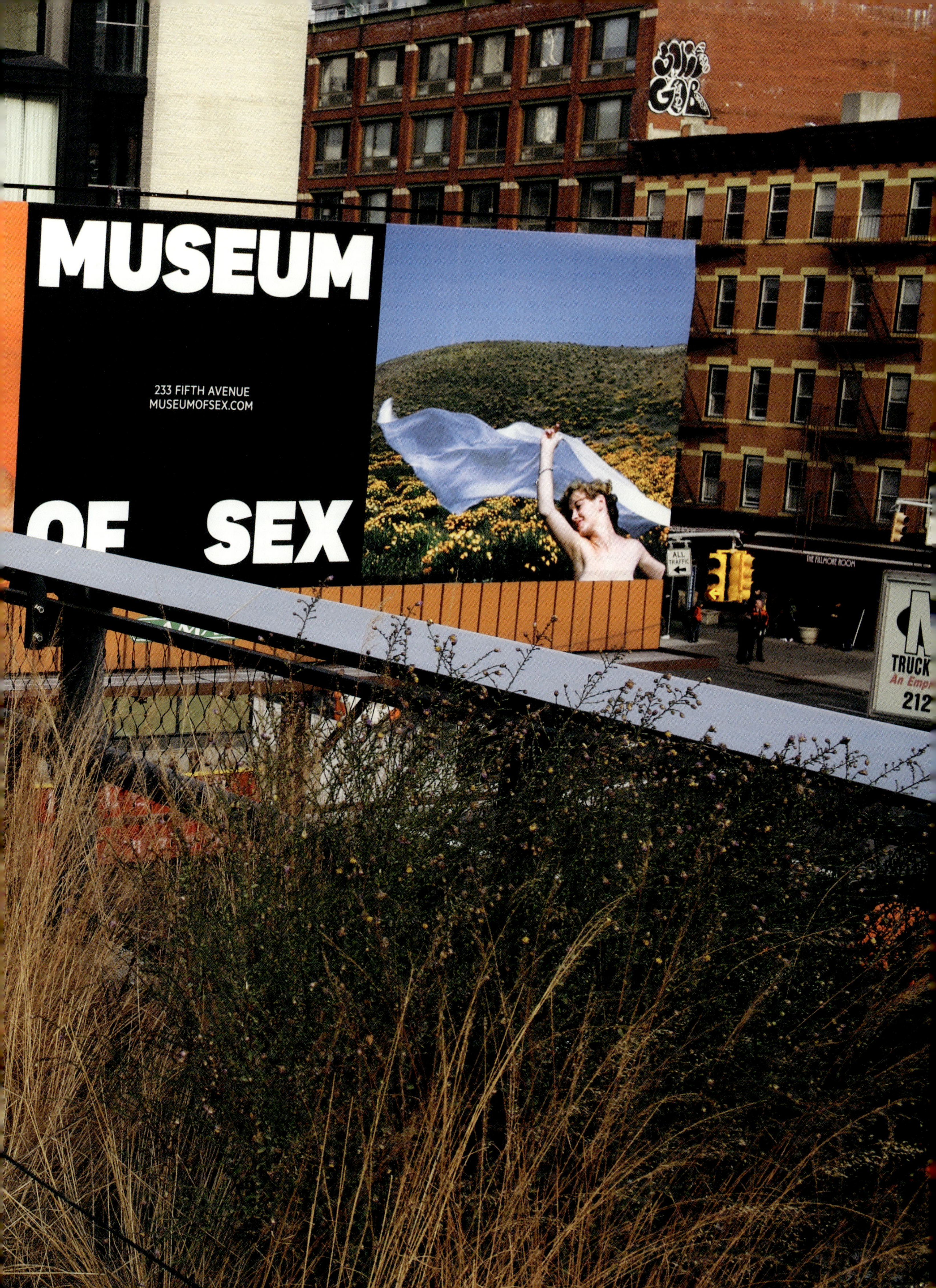

MUSEUM
OF SEX
233 FIFTH AVENUE
MUSEUMOFSEX.COM
ALL TRAFFIC
THE FILLMORE ROOM
TRUCK
An Emp
212

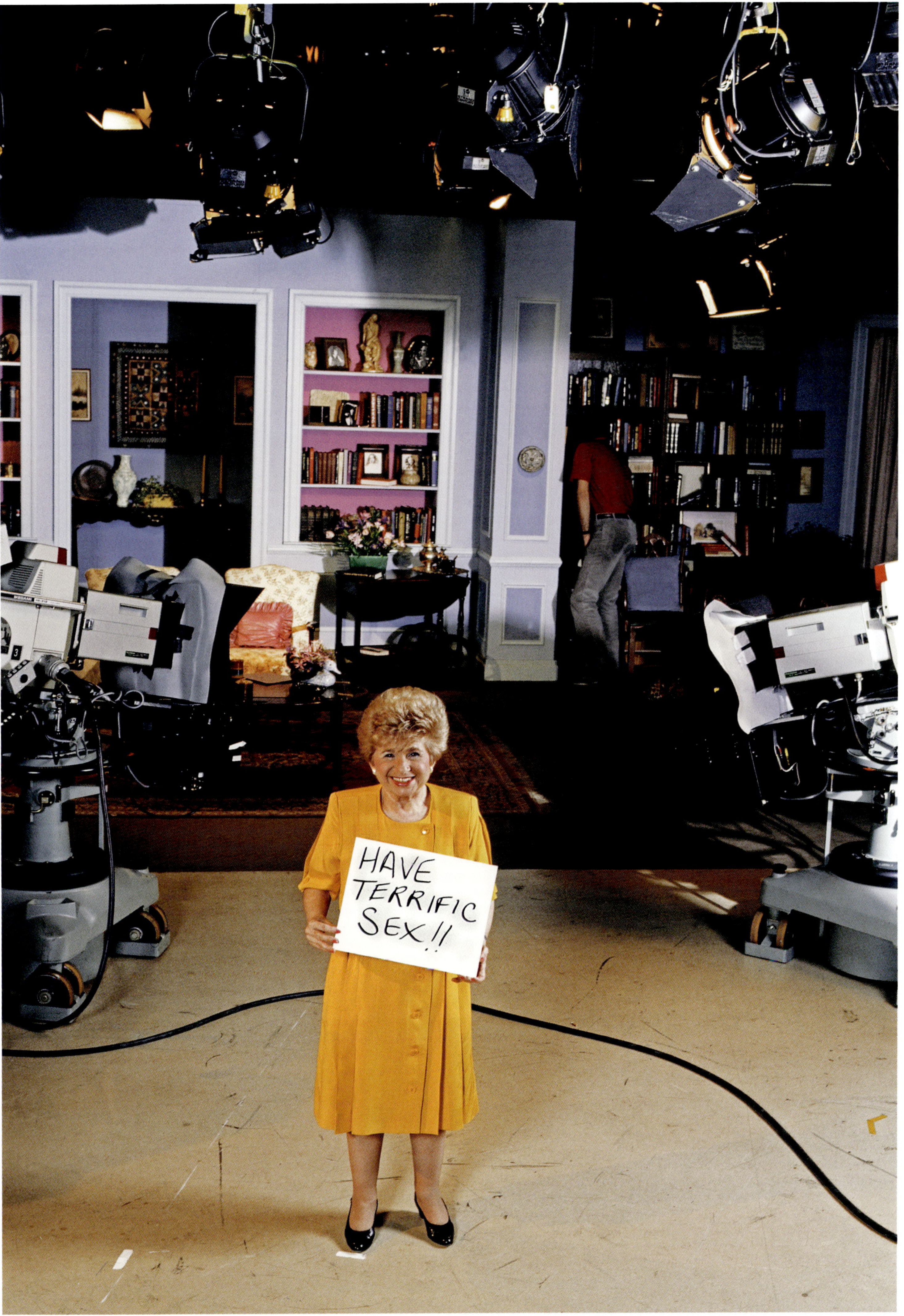

HAVE
TERRIFIC
SEX!!

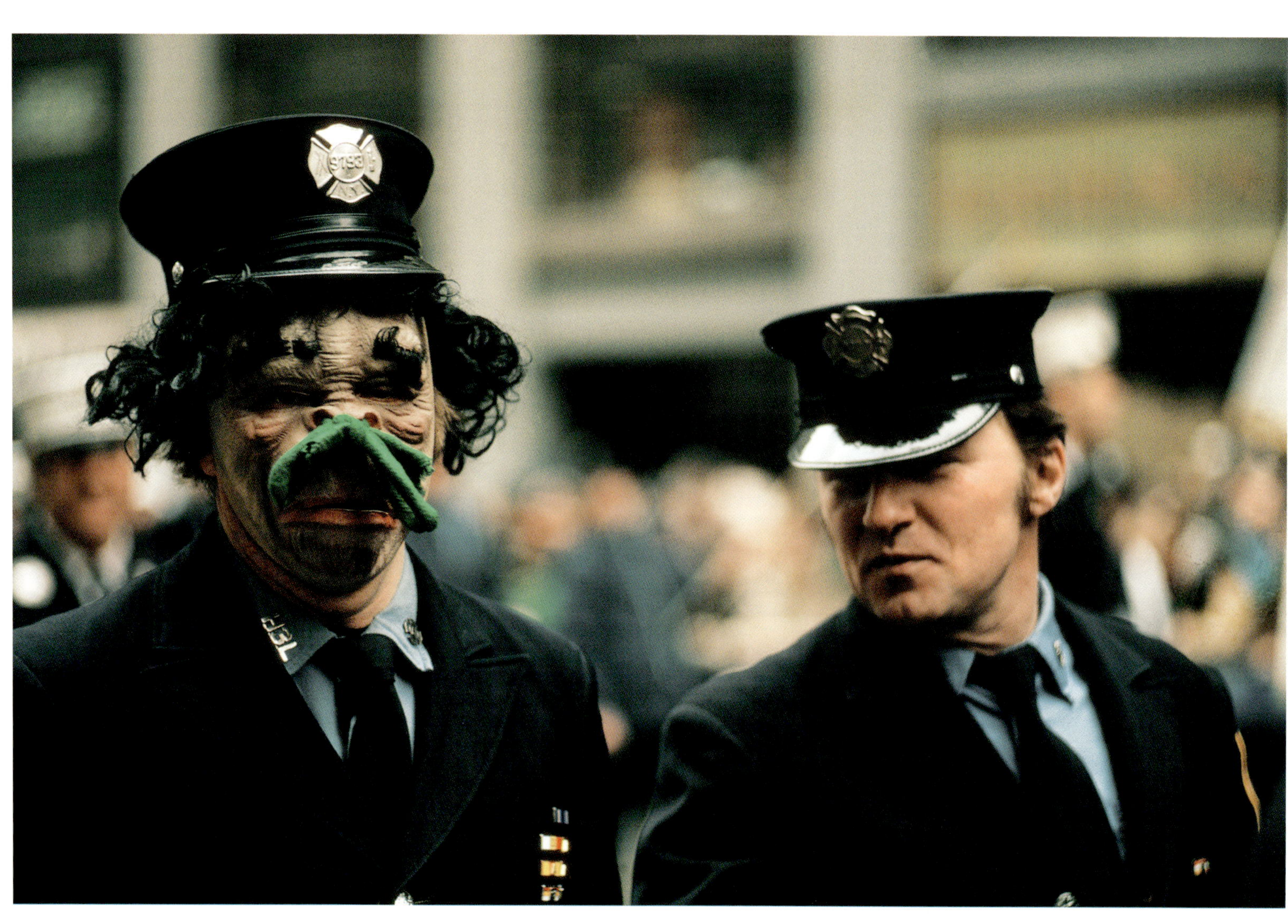

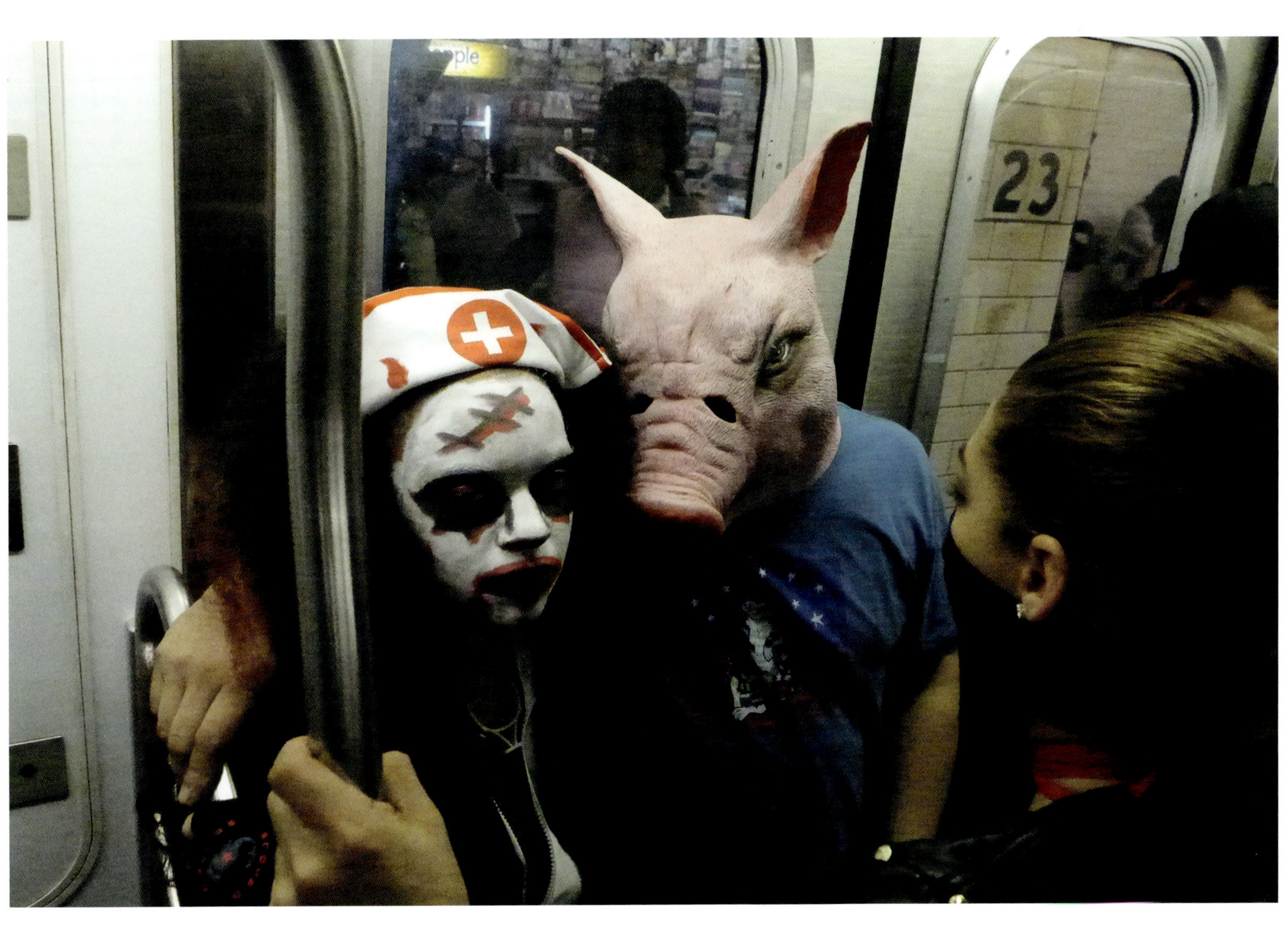

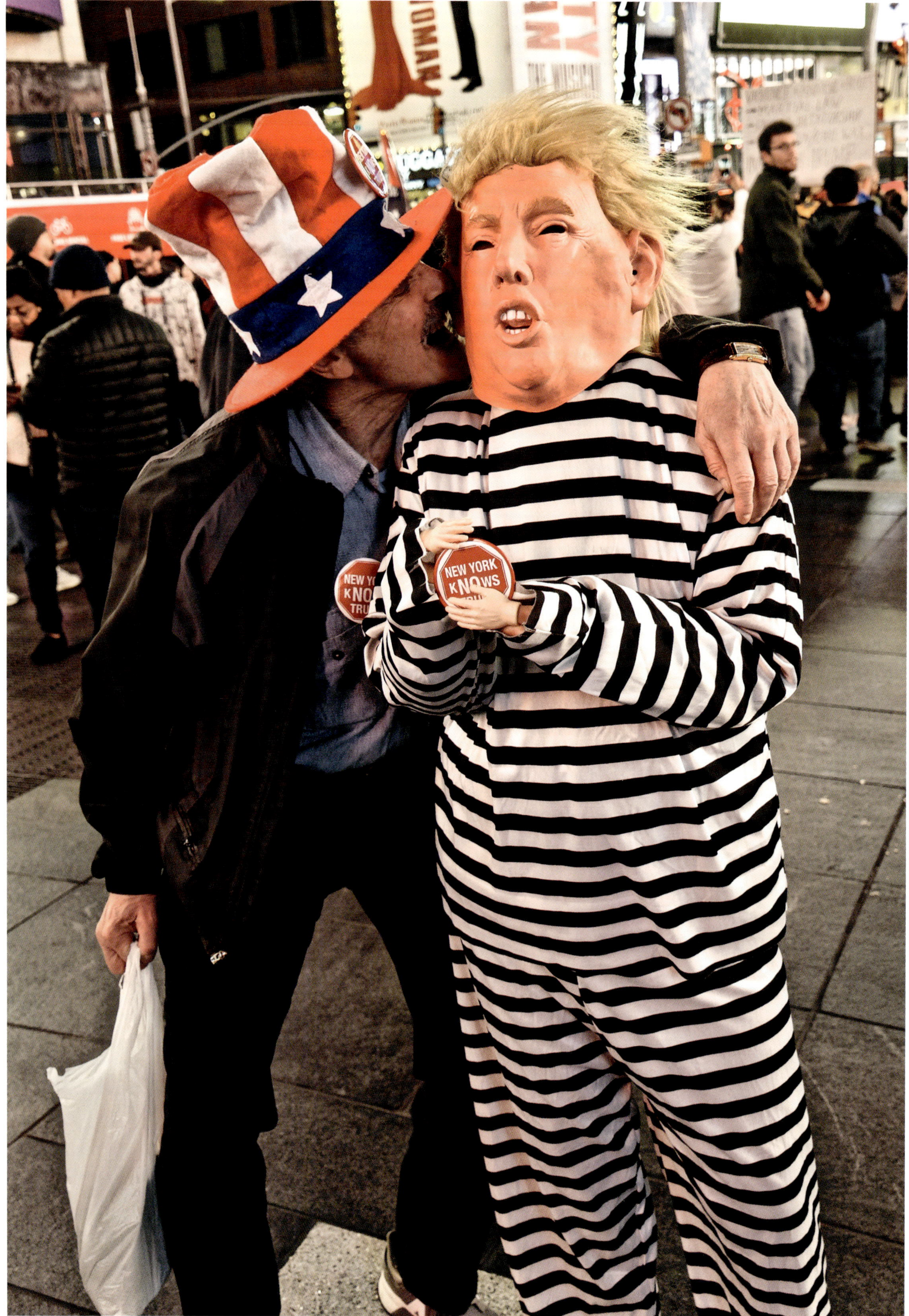

NEW YORK kNOws TRU
NEW YORK kNOws

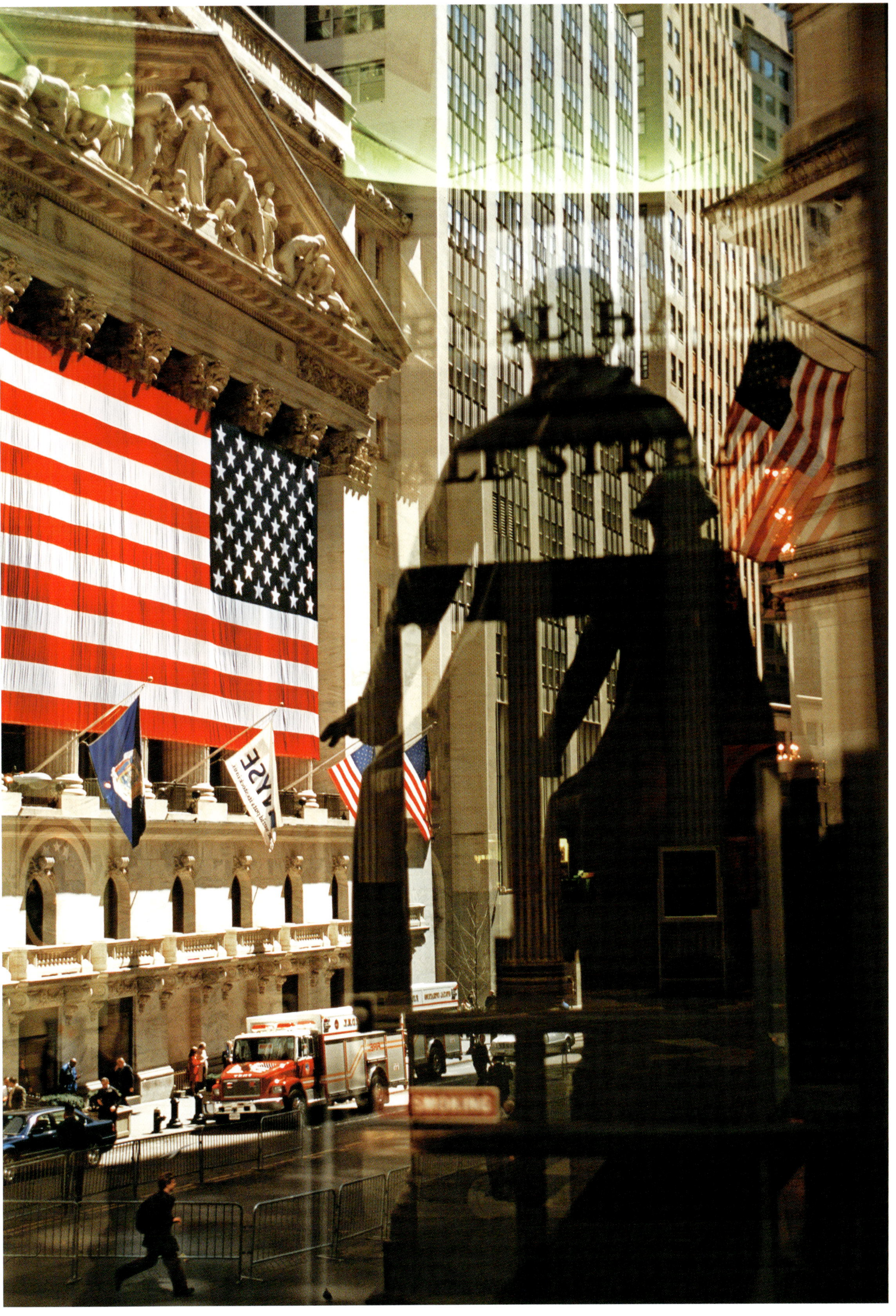

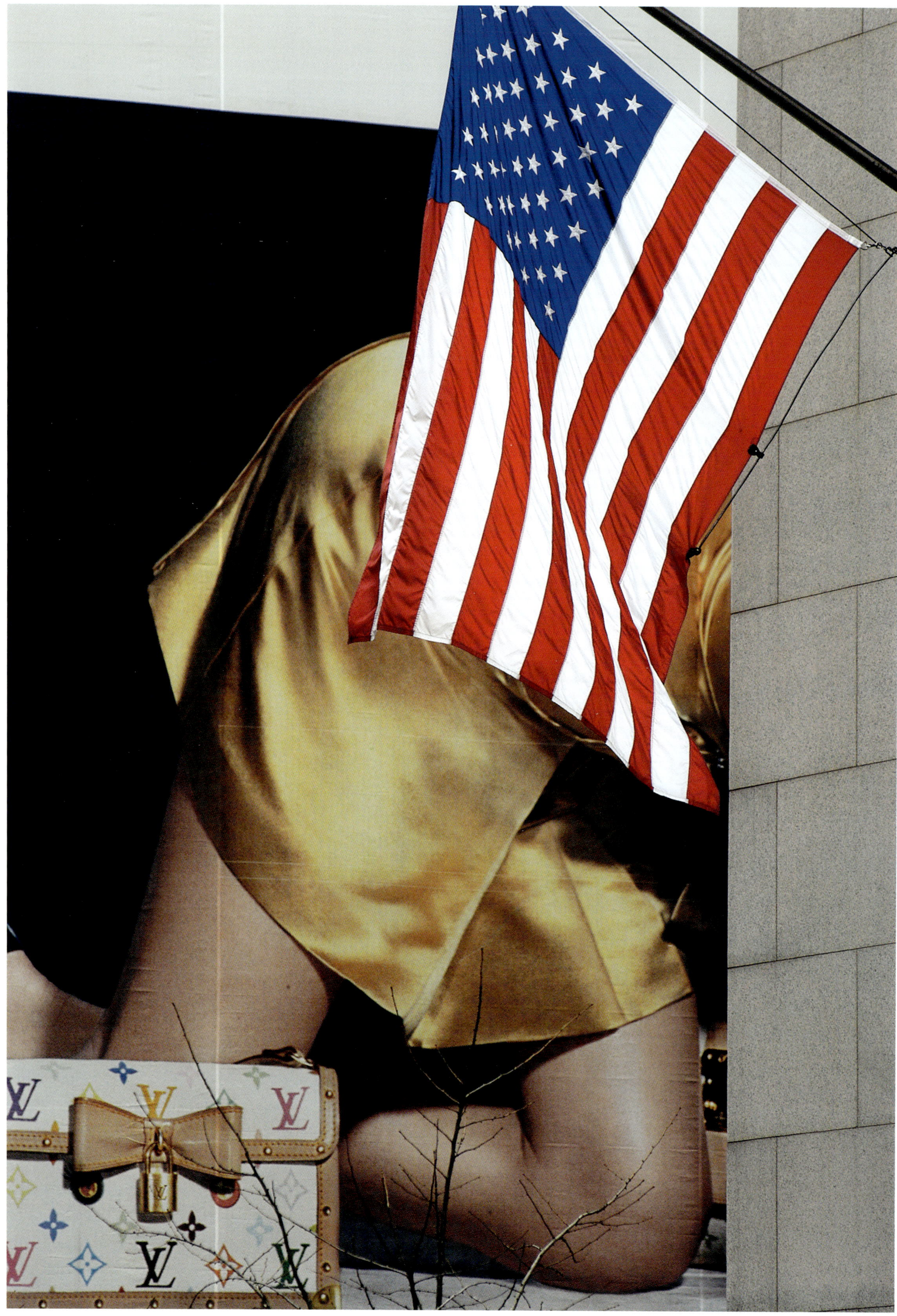

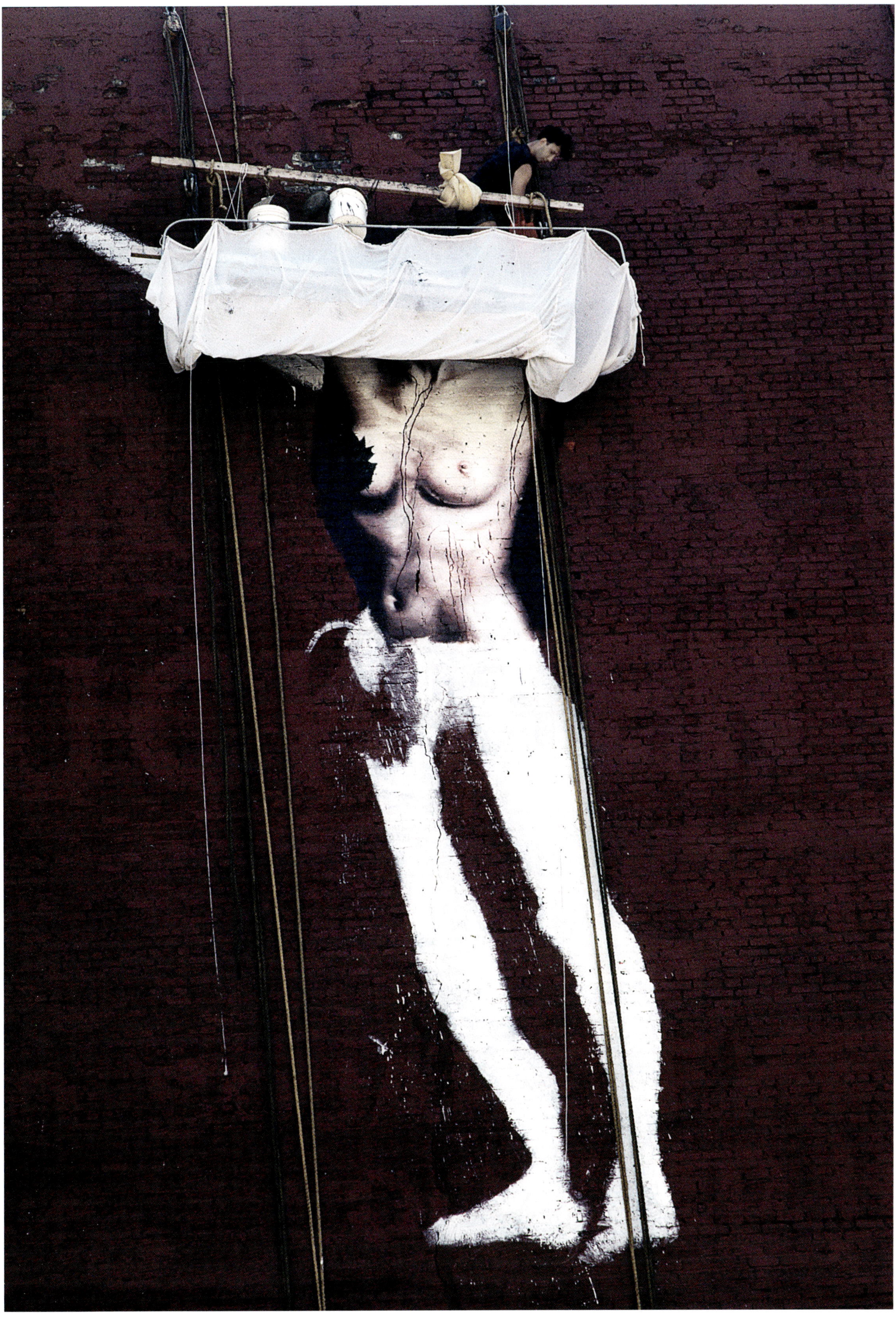

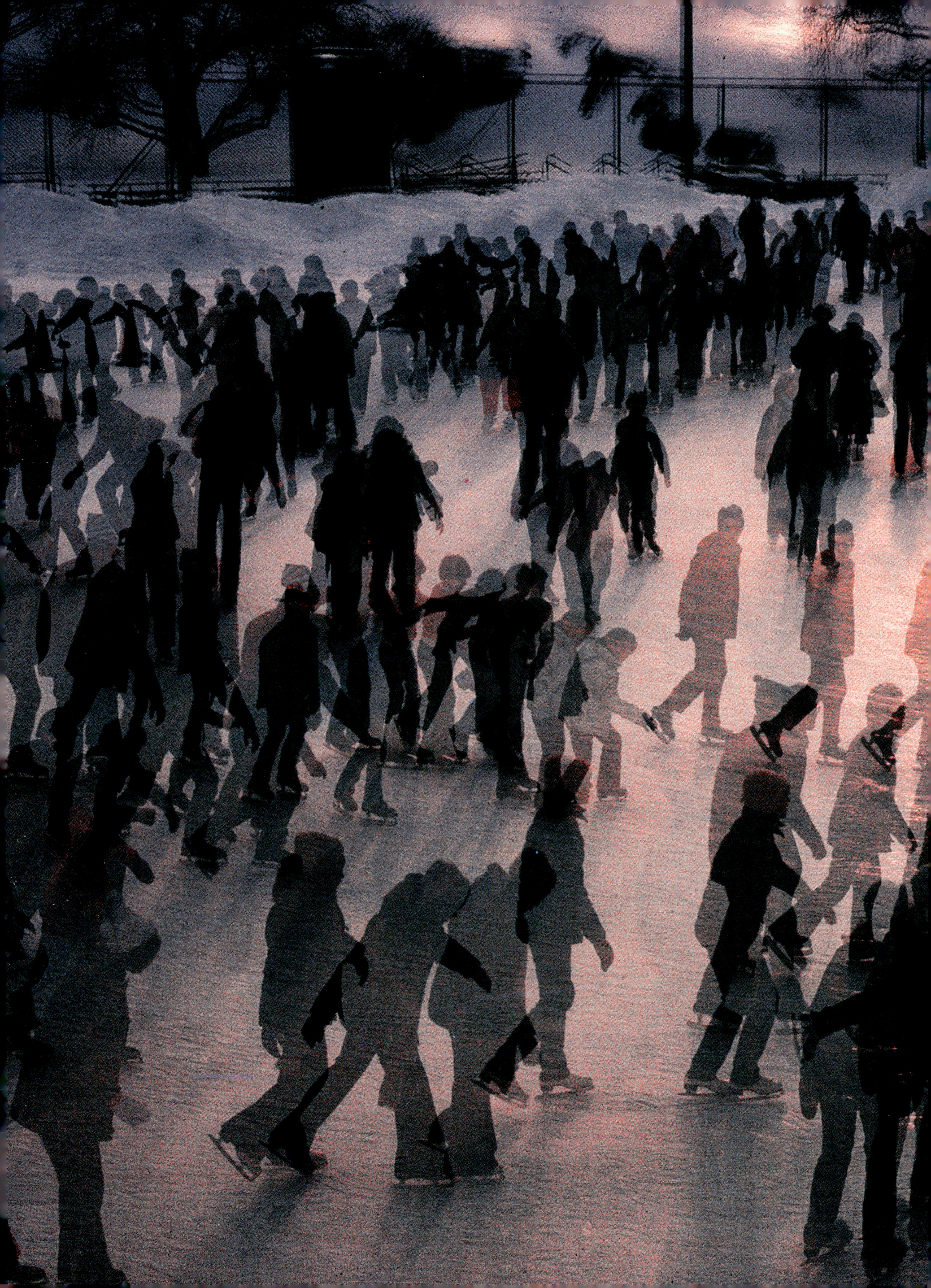

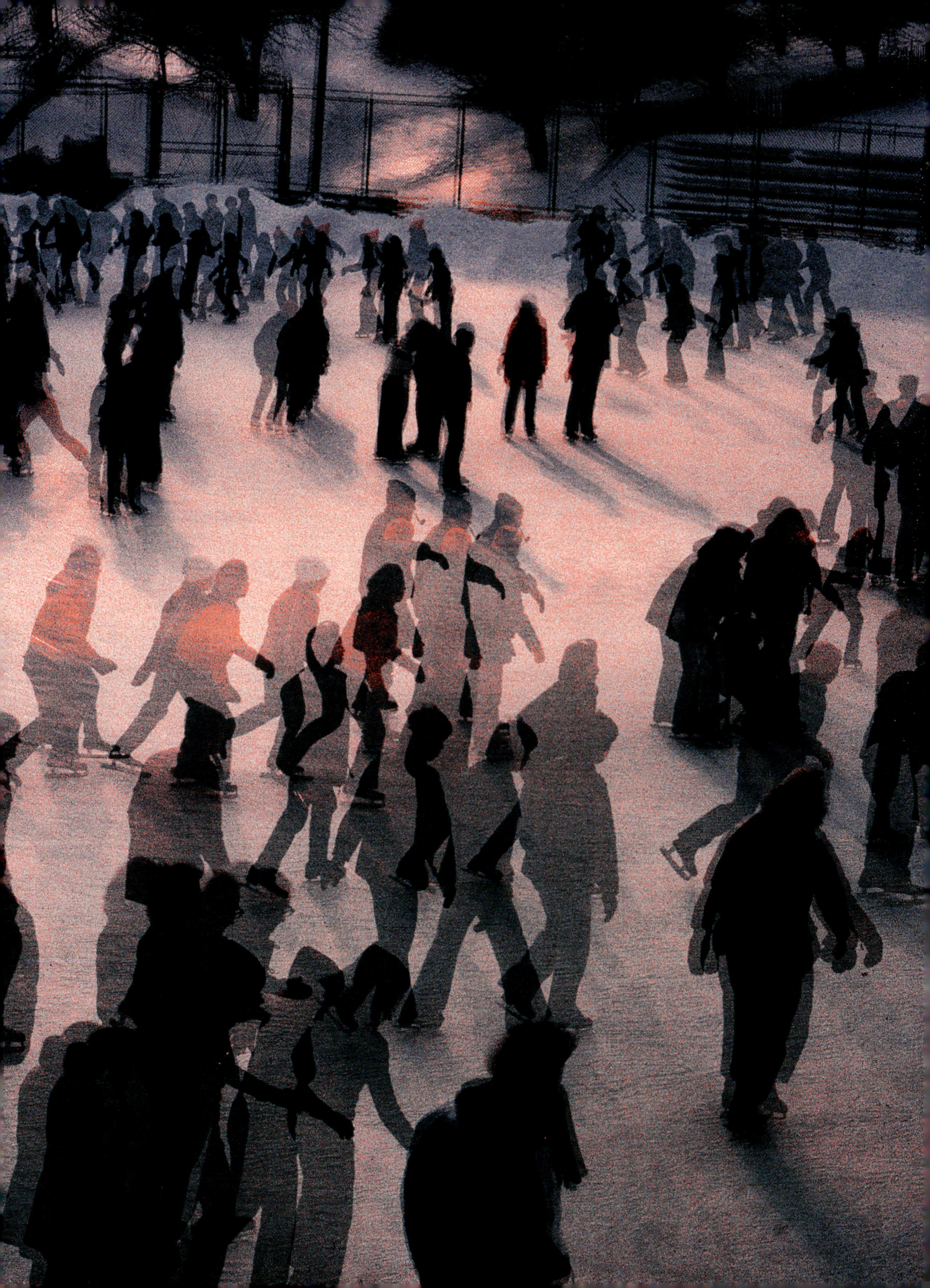

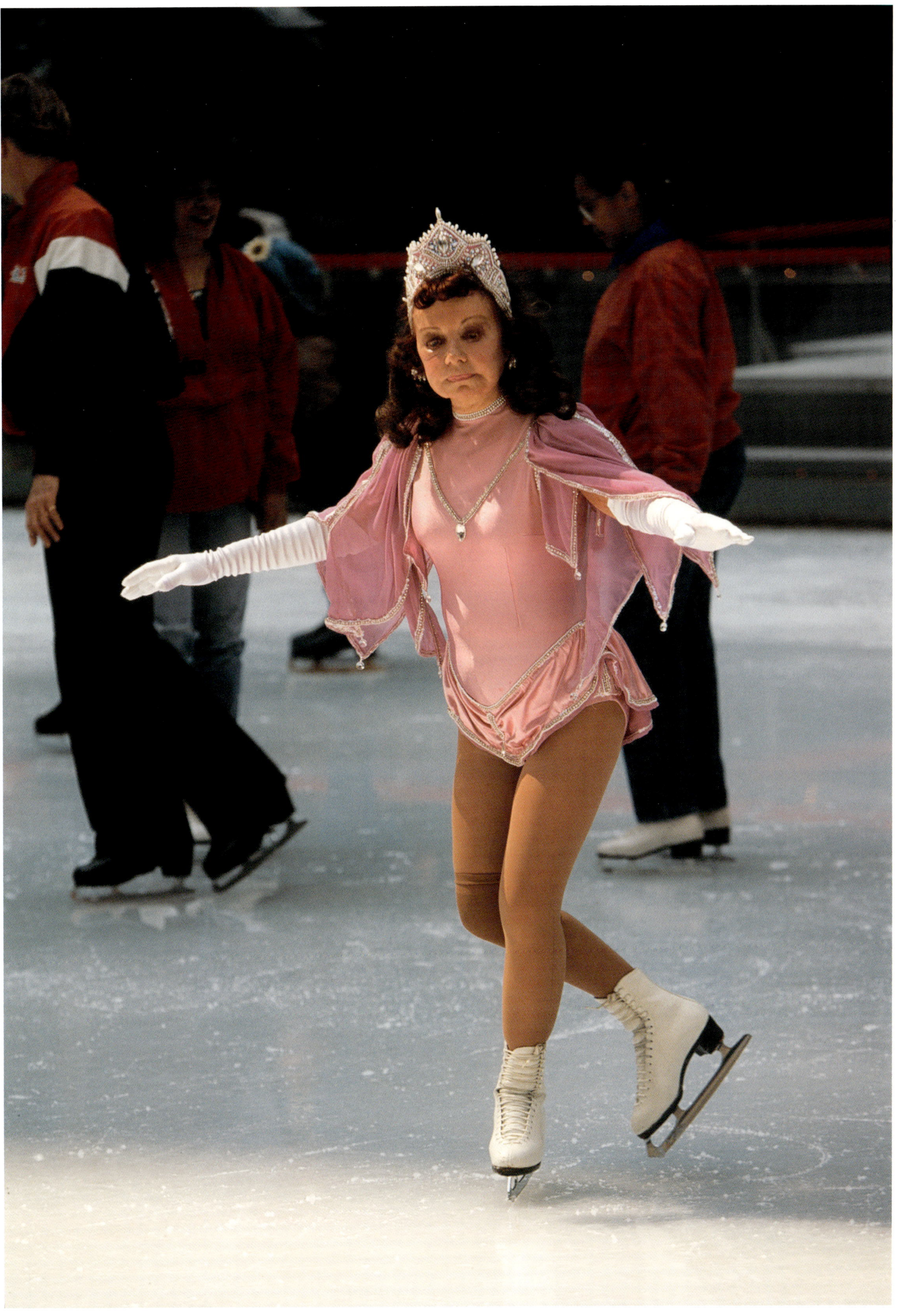

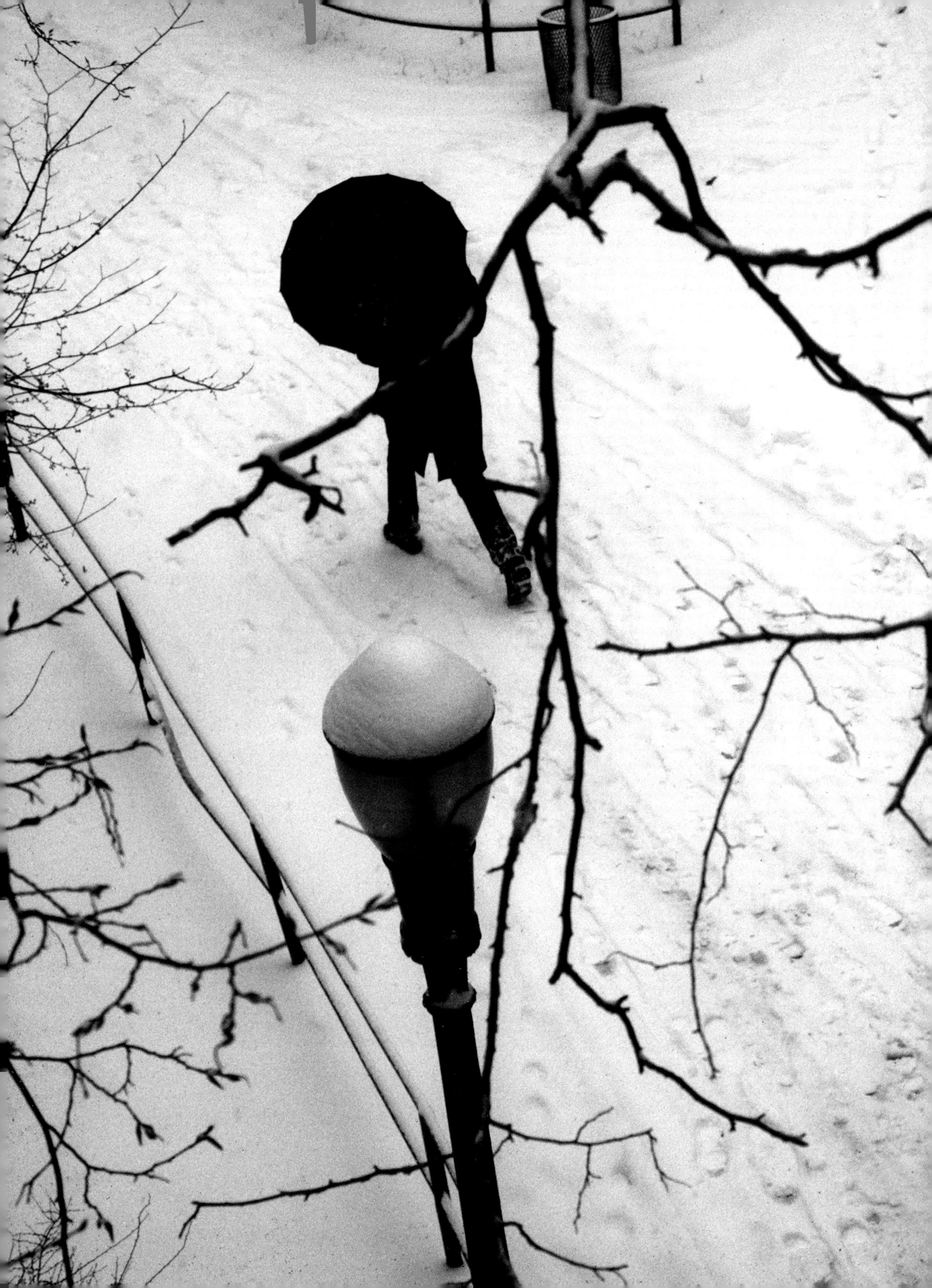

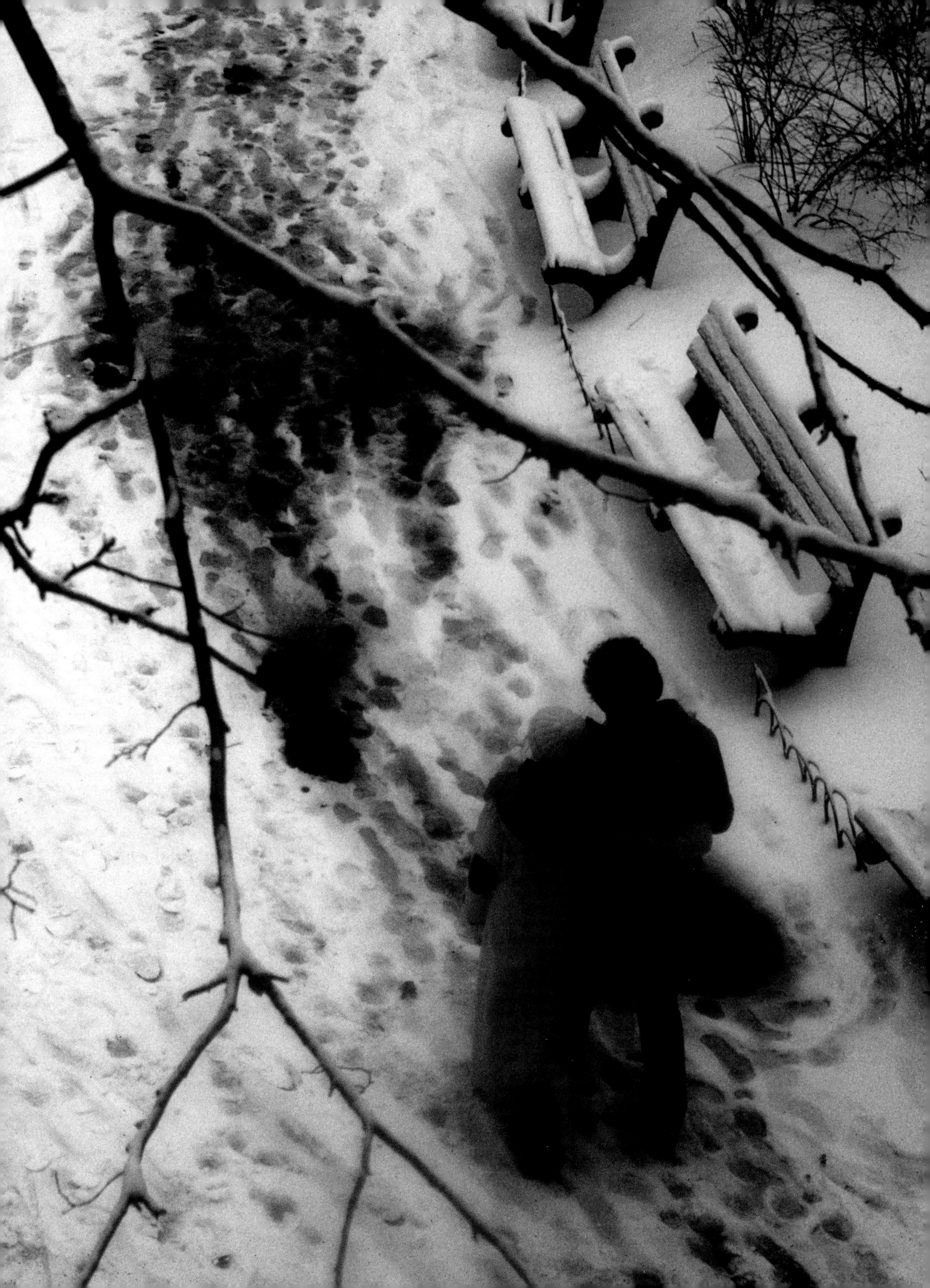

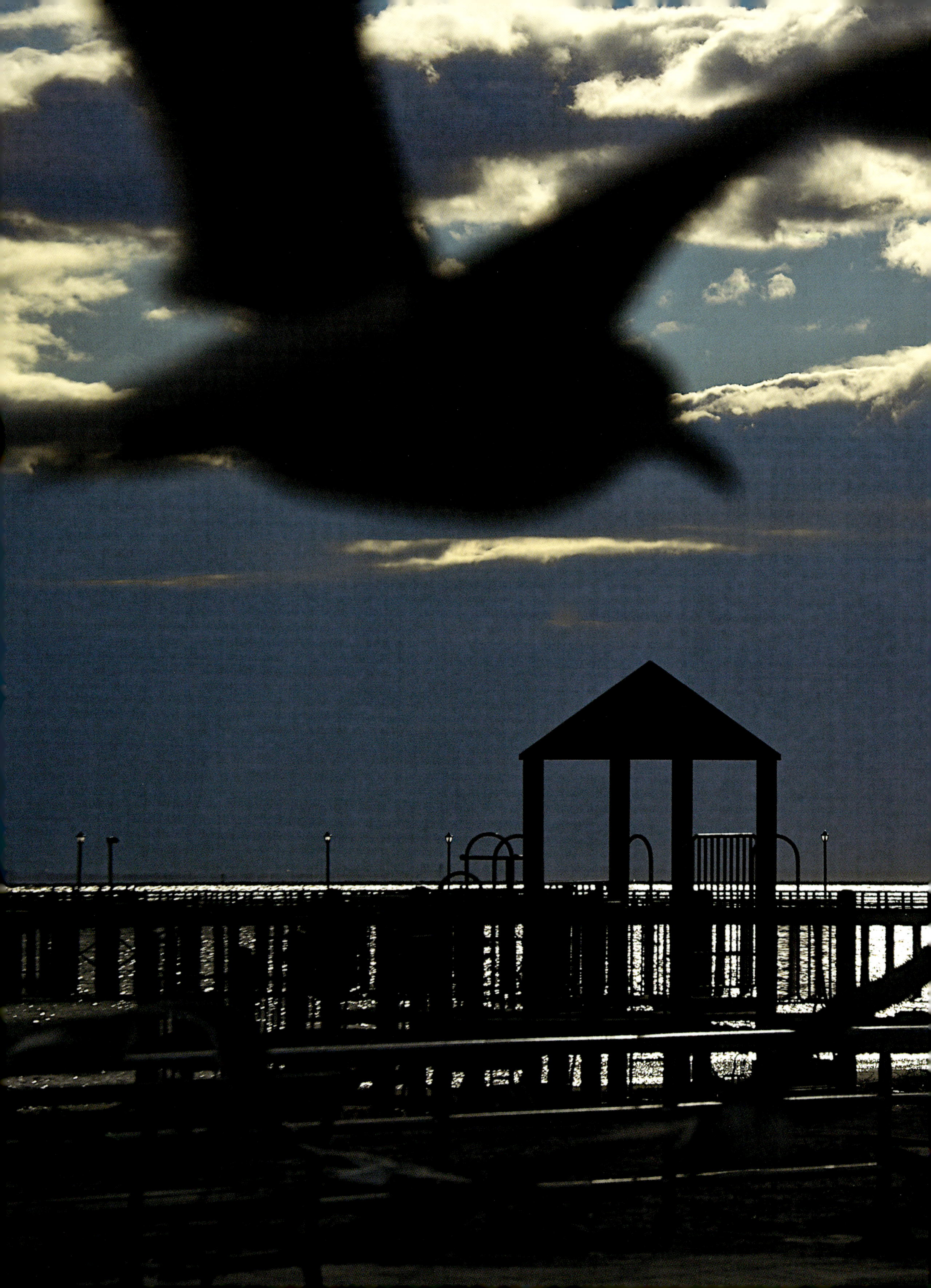

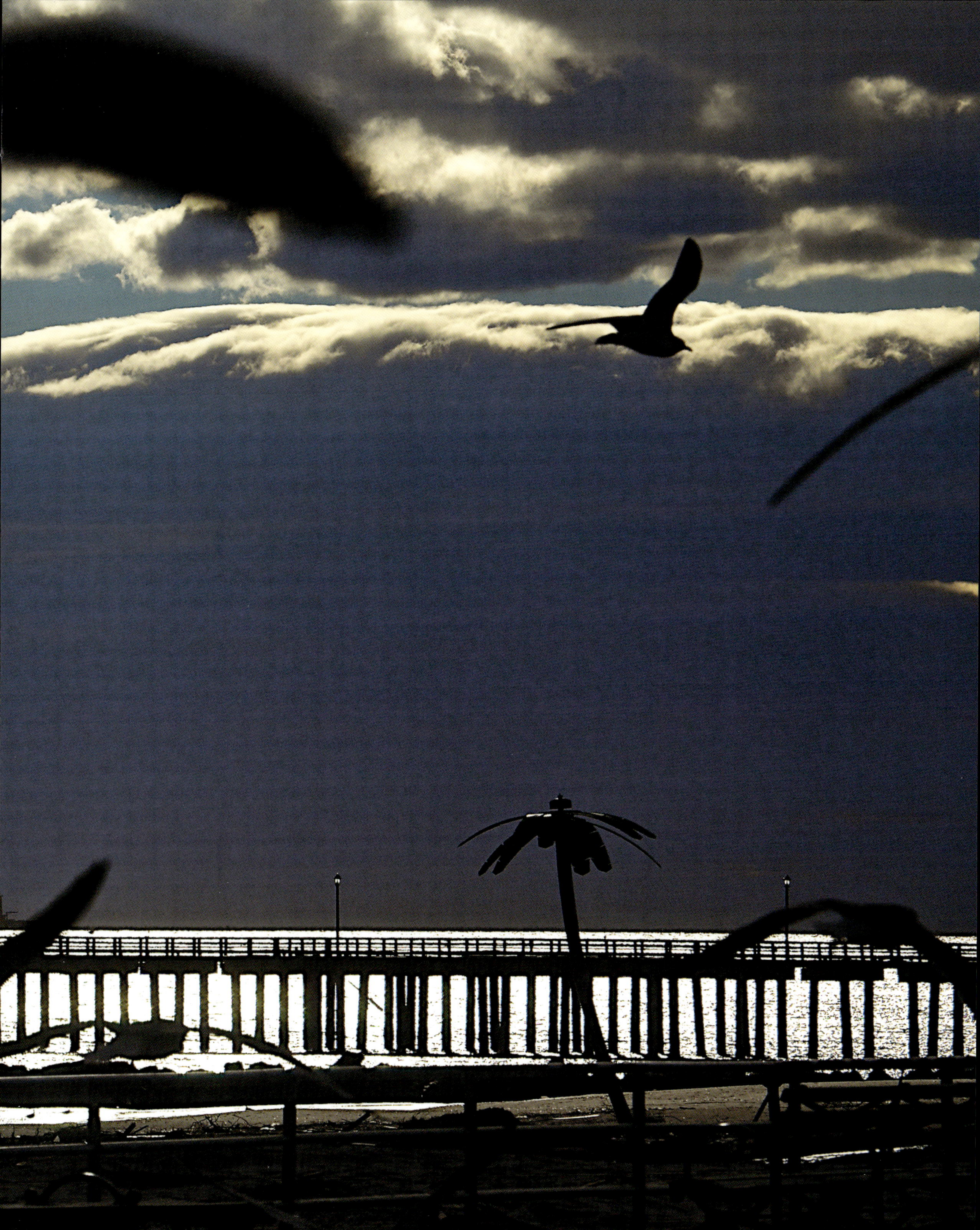

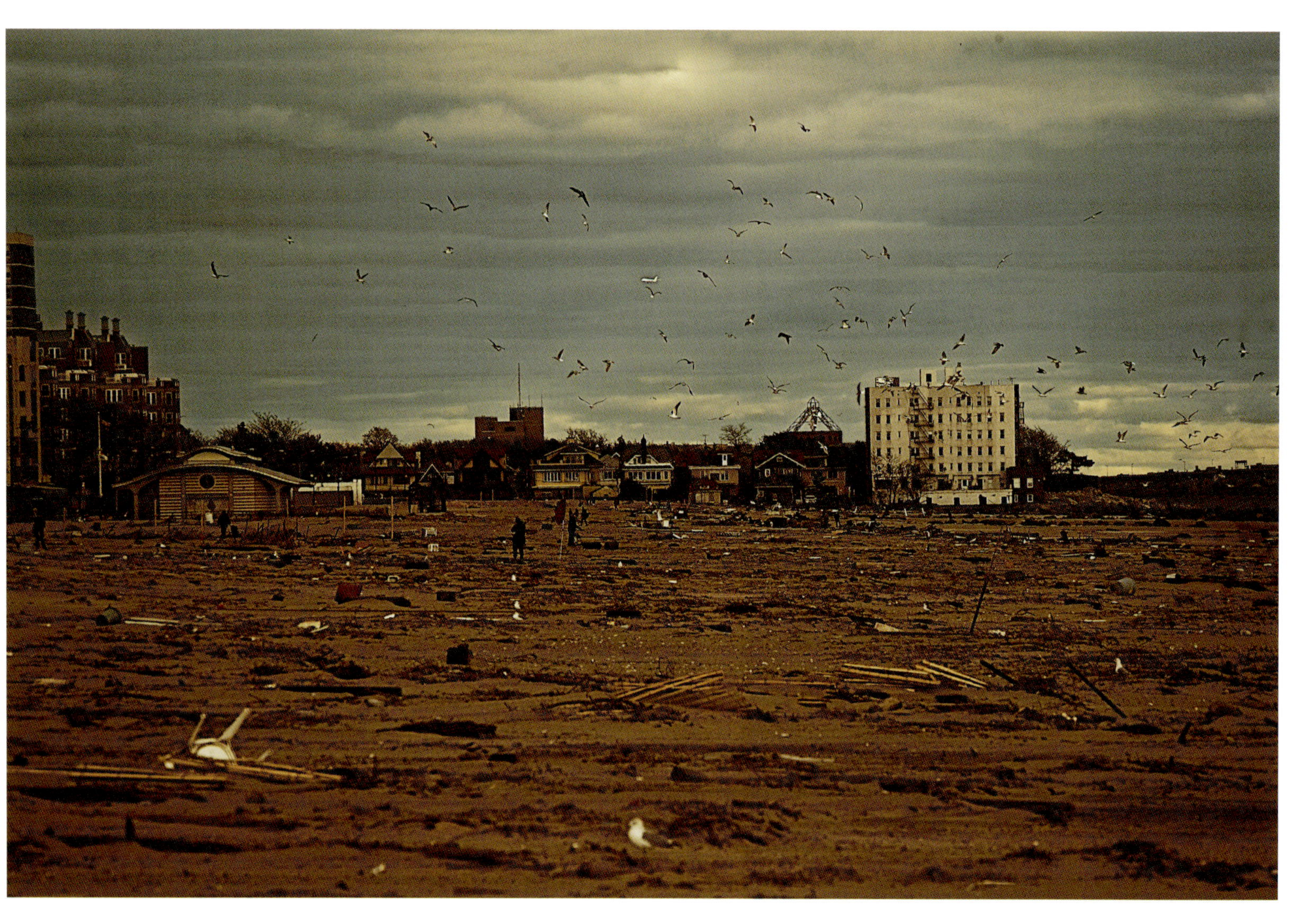

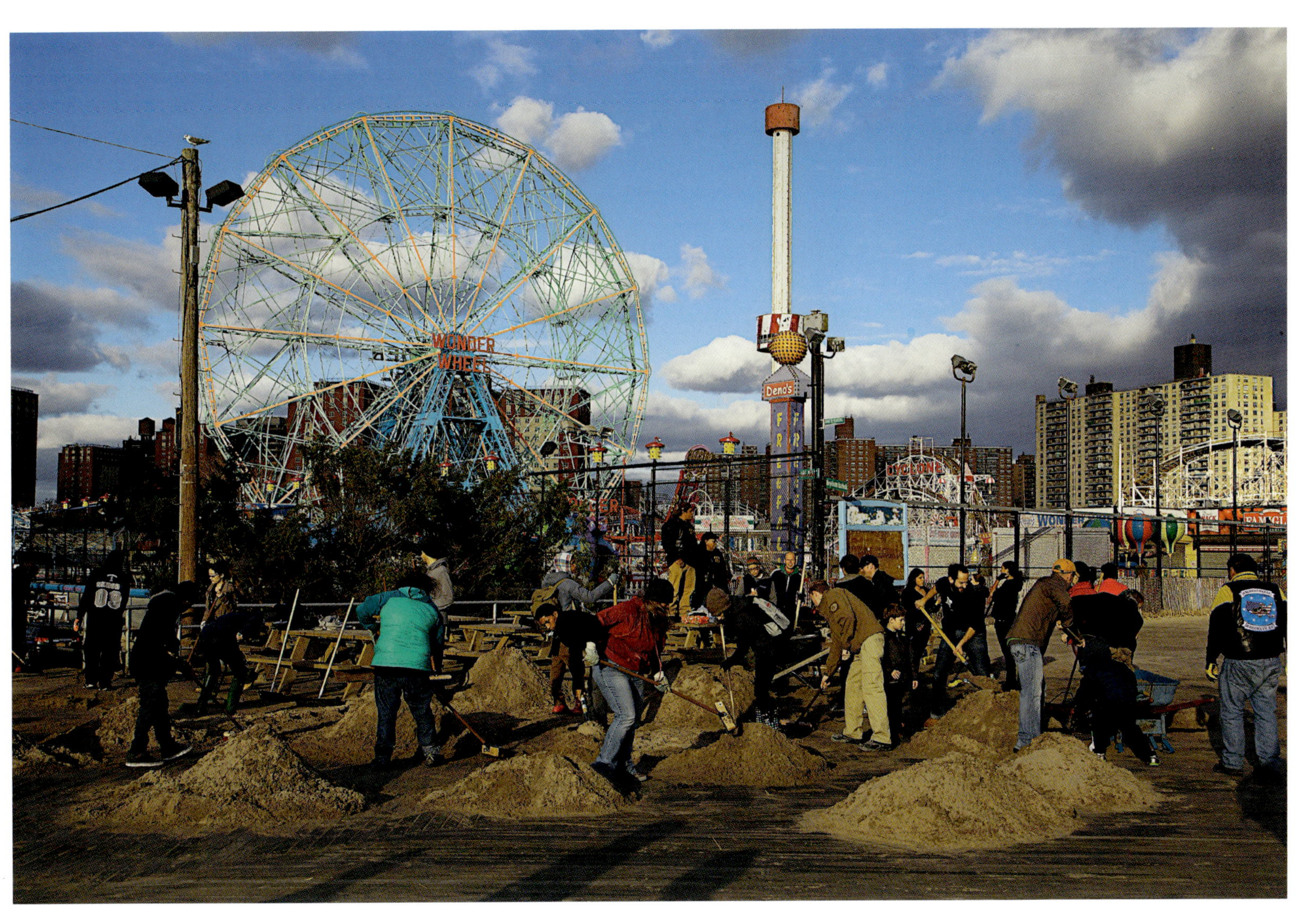
WONDER WHEEL
Deno's
CYCLONE
WON

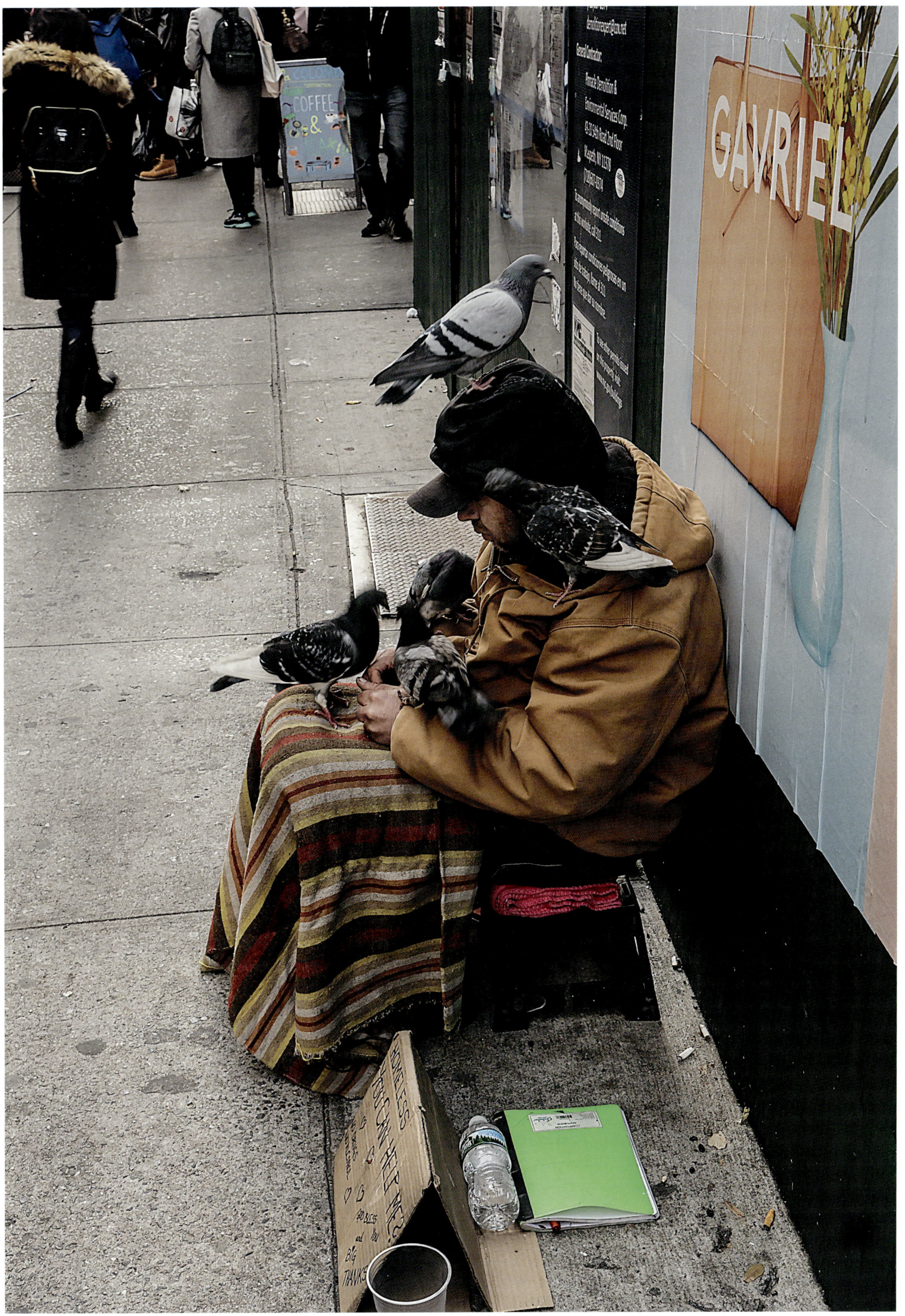
COFFEE
GAVRIEL
HOMELESS
YOU CAN HELP ME
GOD BLESS
and YOU
BIG
THANKS

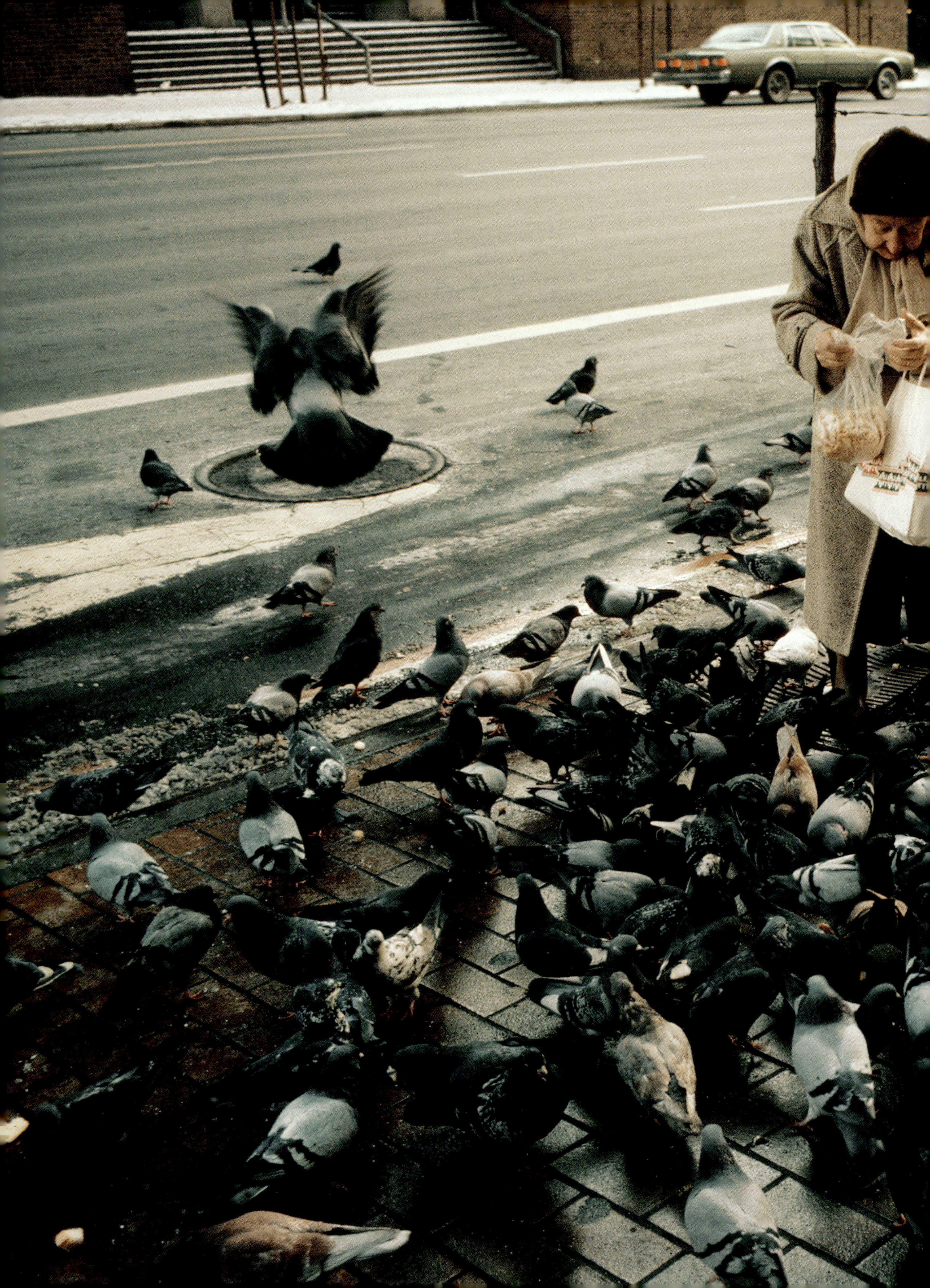

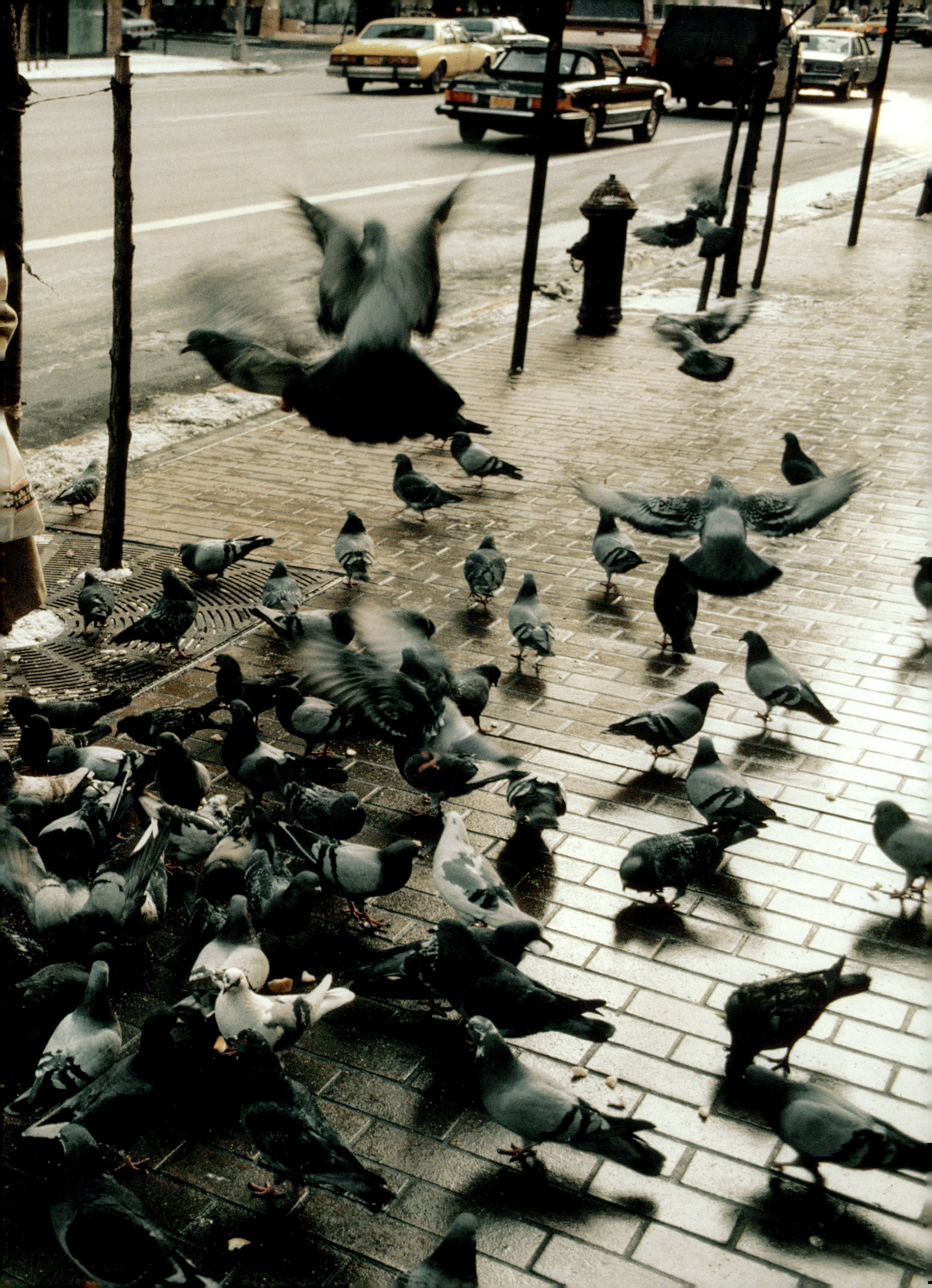

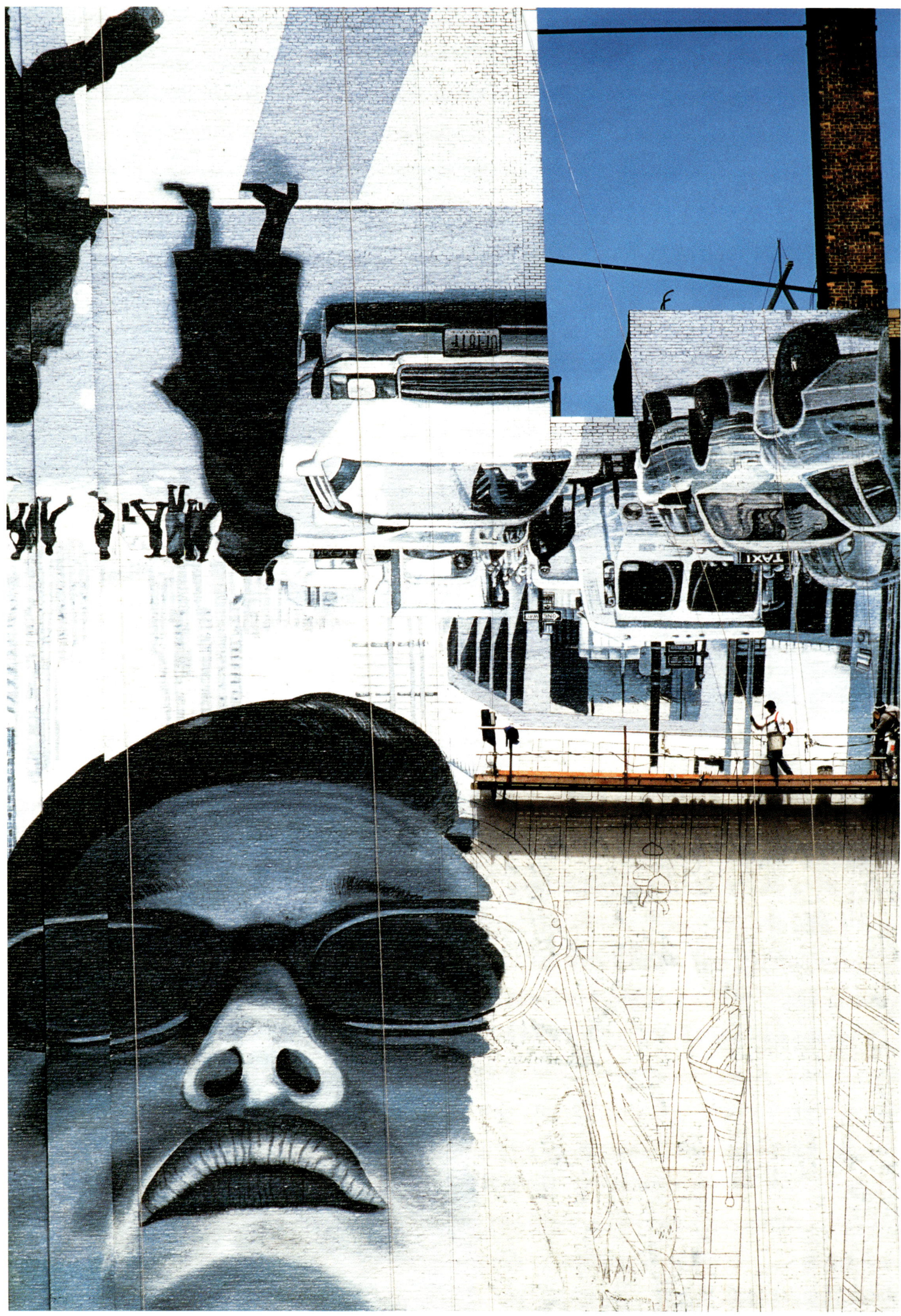

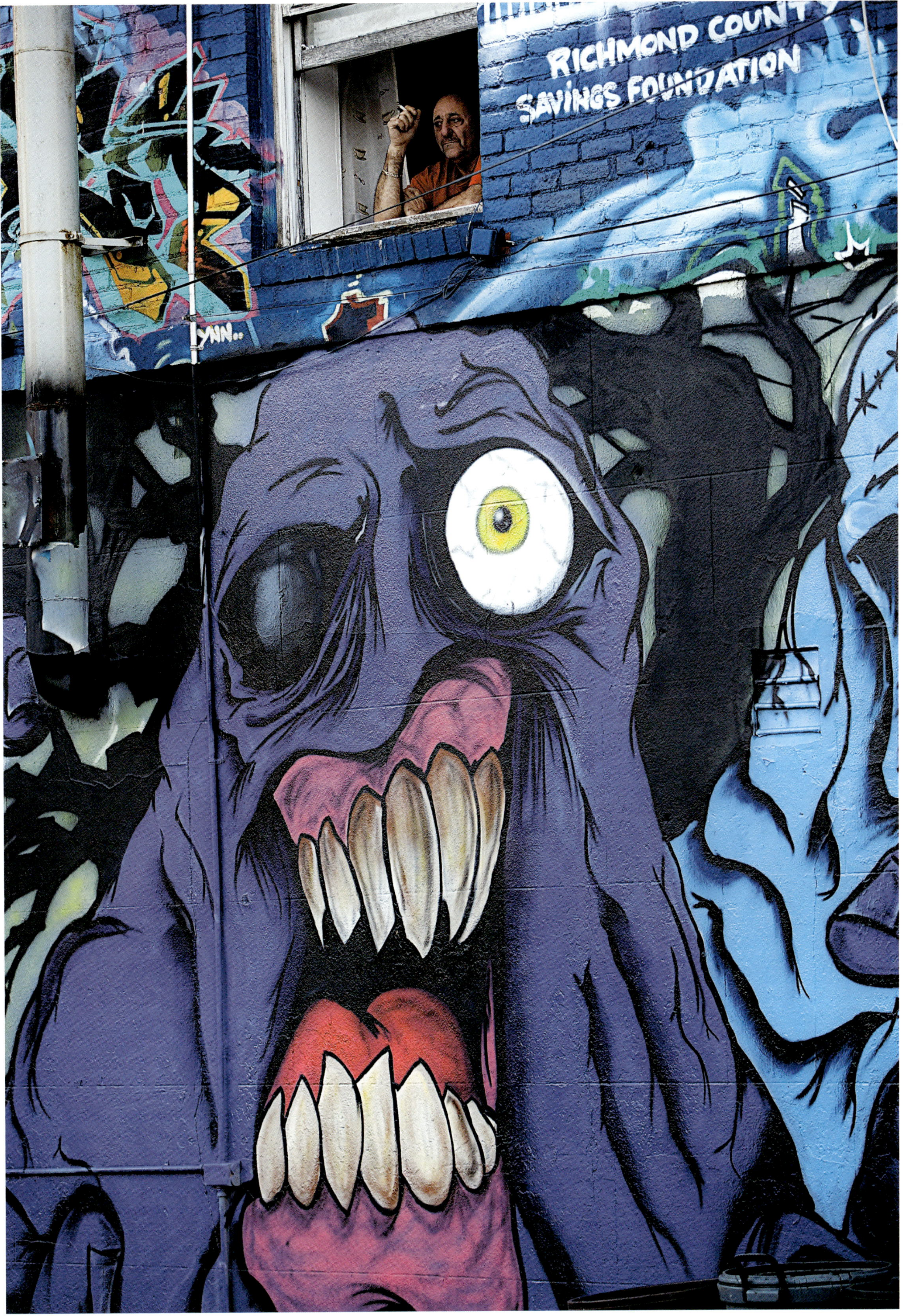
RICHMOND COUNTY
SAVINGS FOUNDATION
lynn..

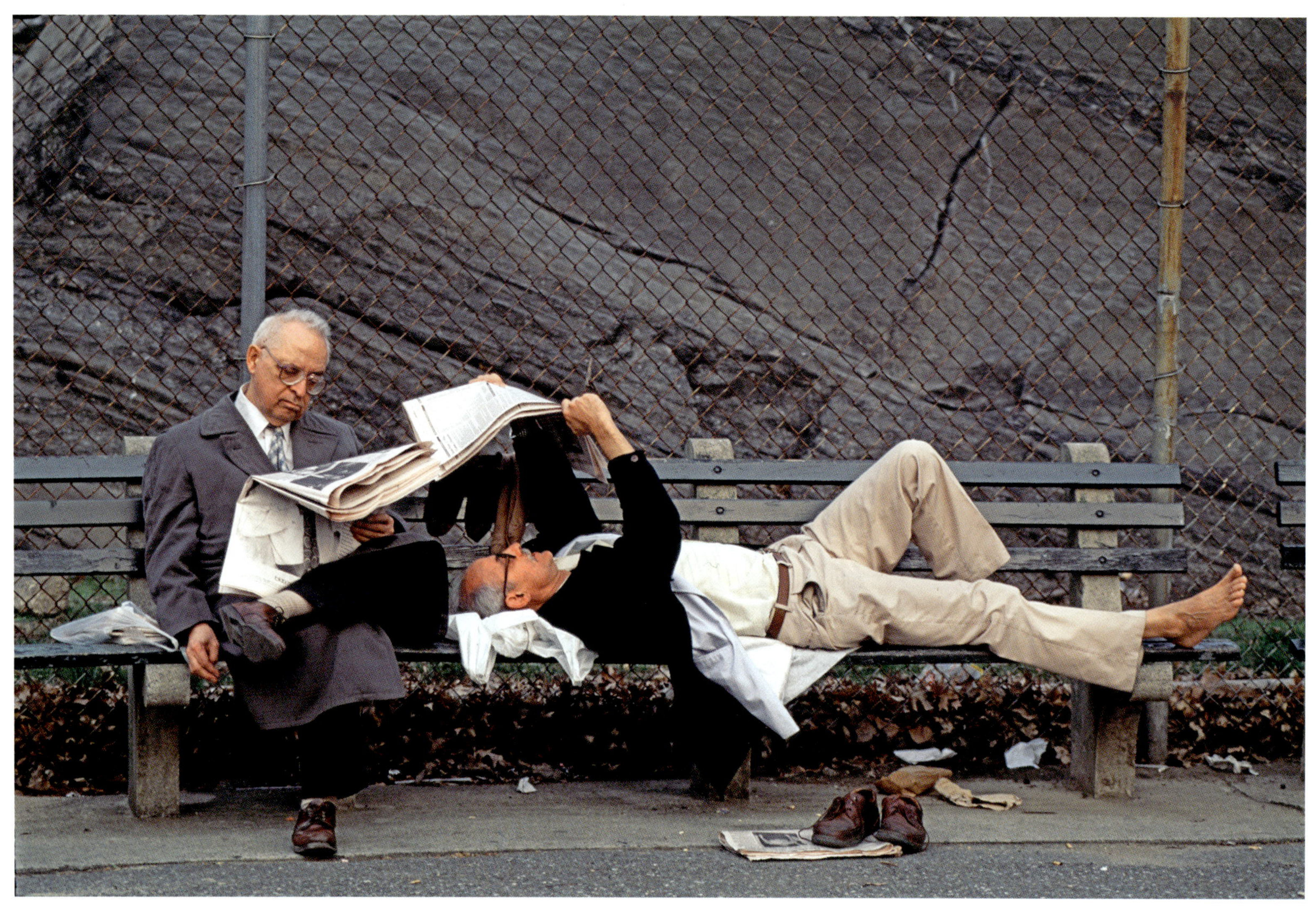

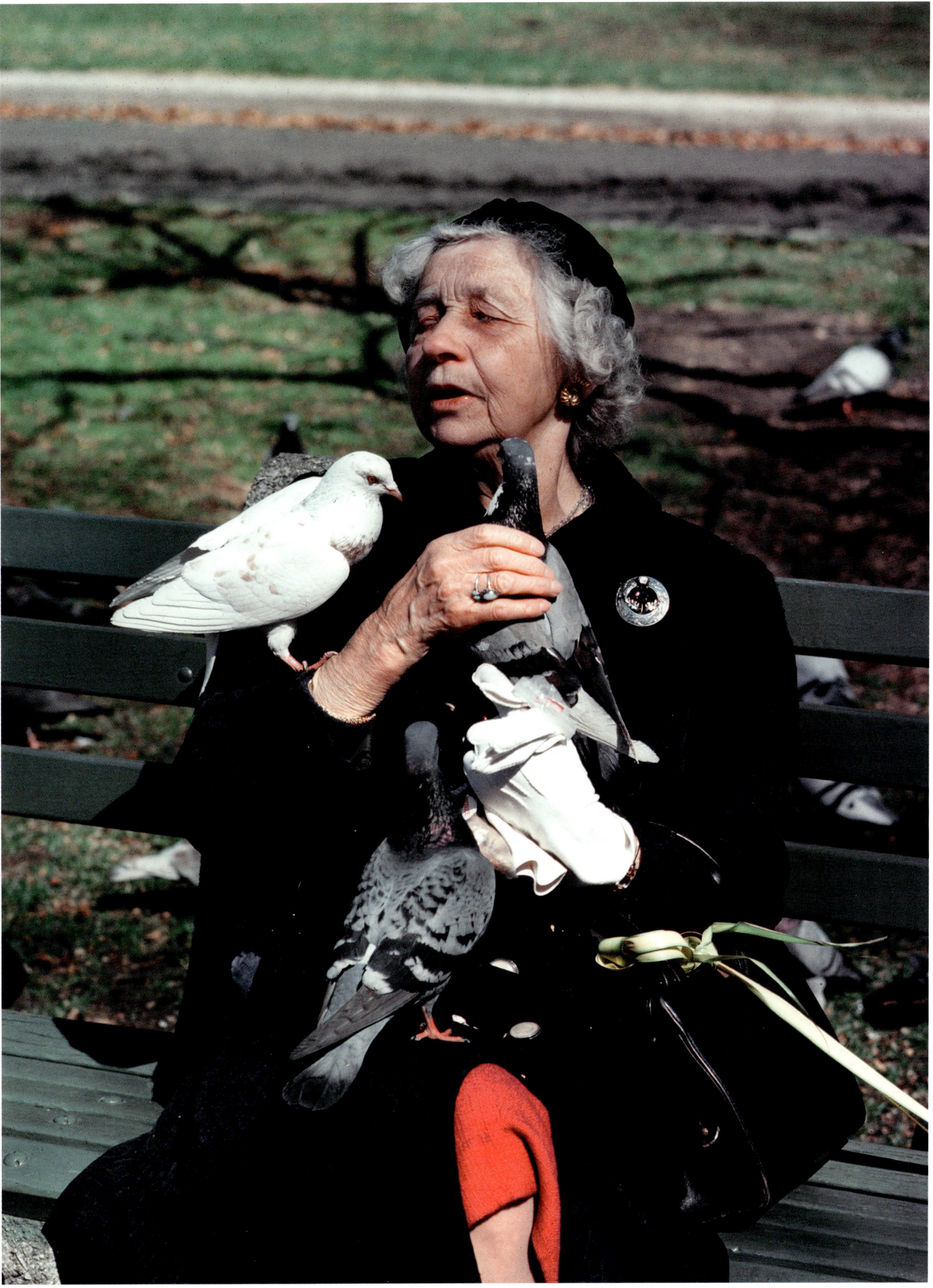

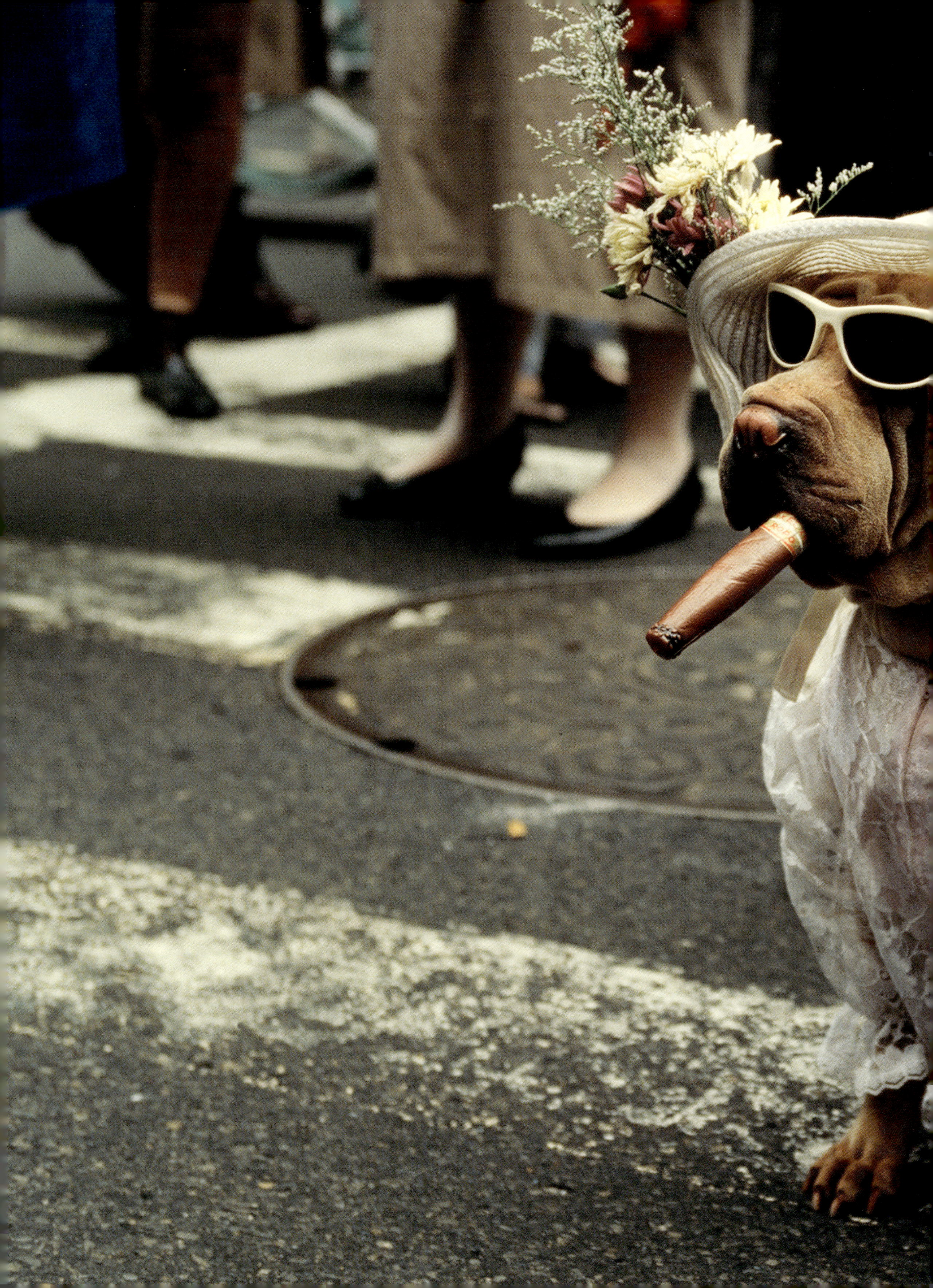

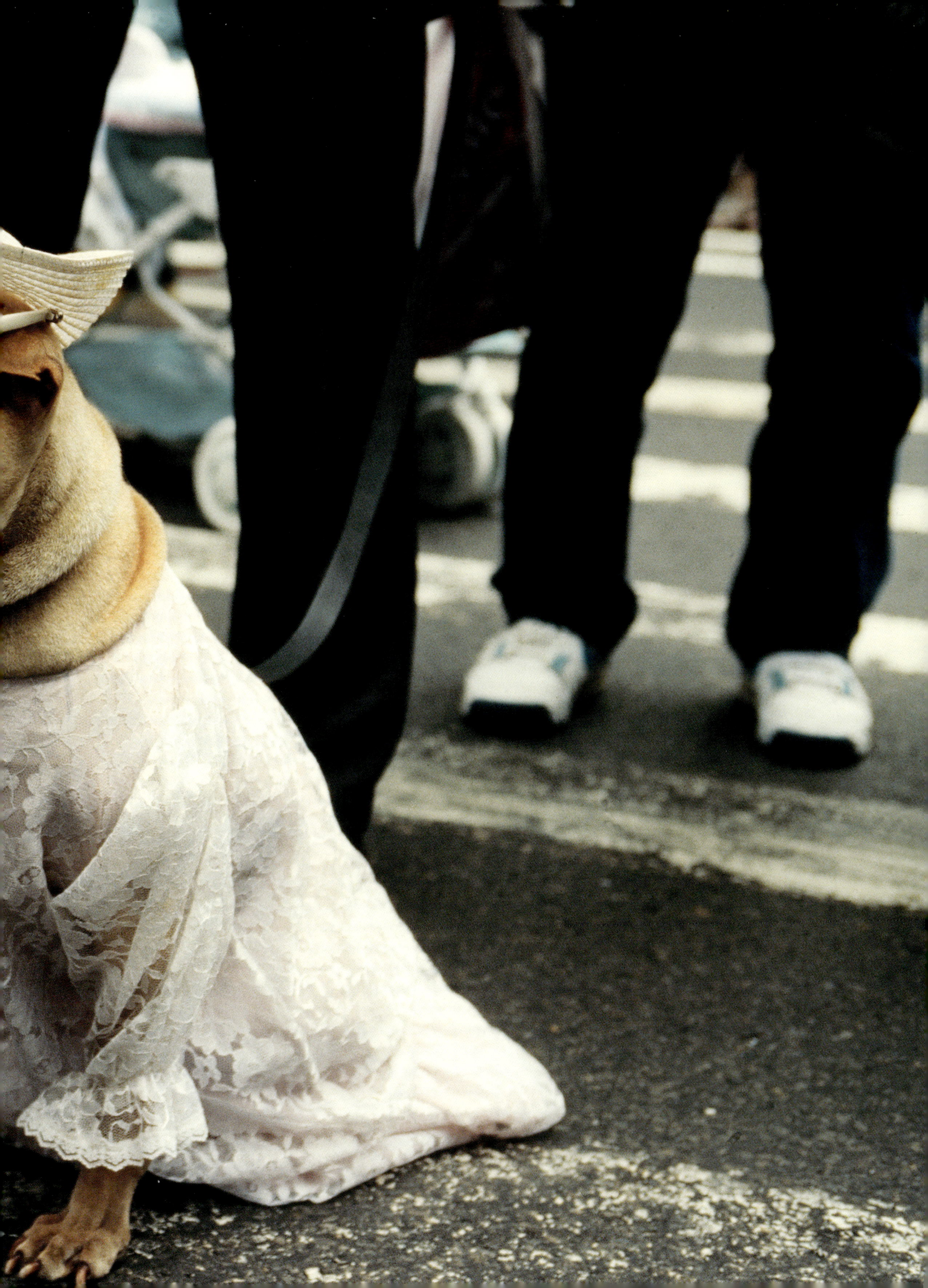

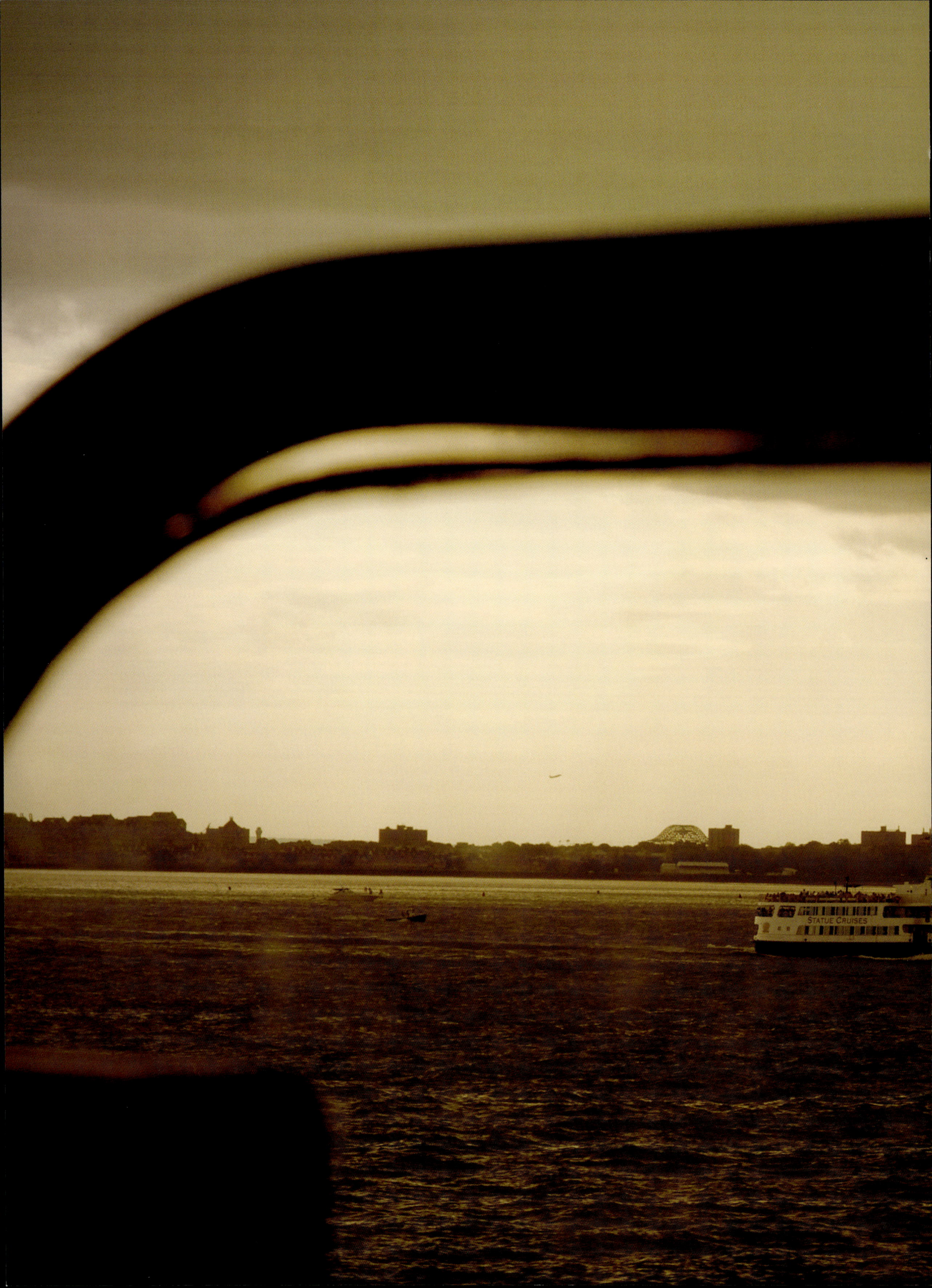
STATUE CRUISES

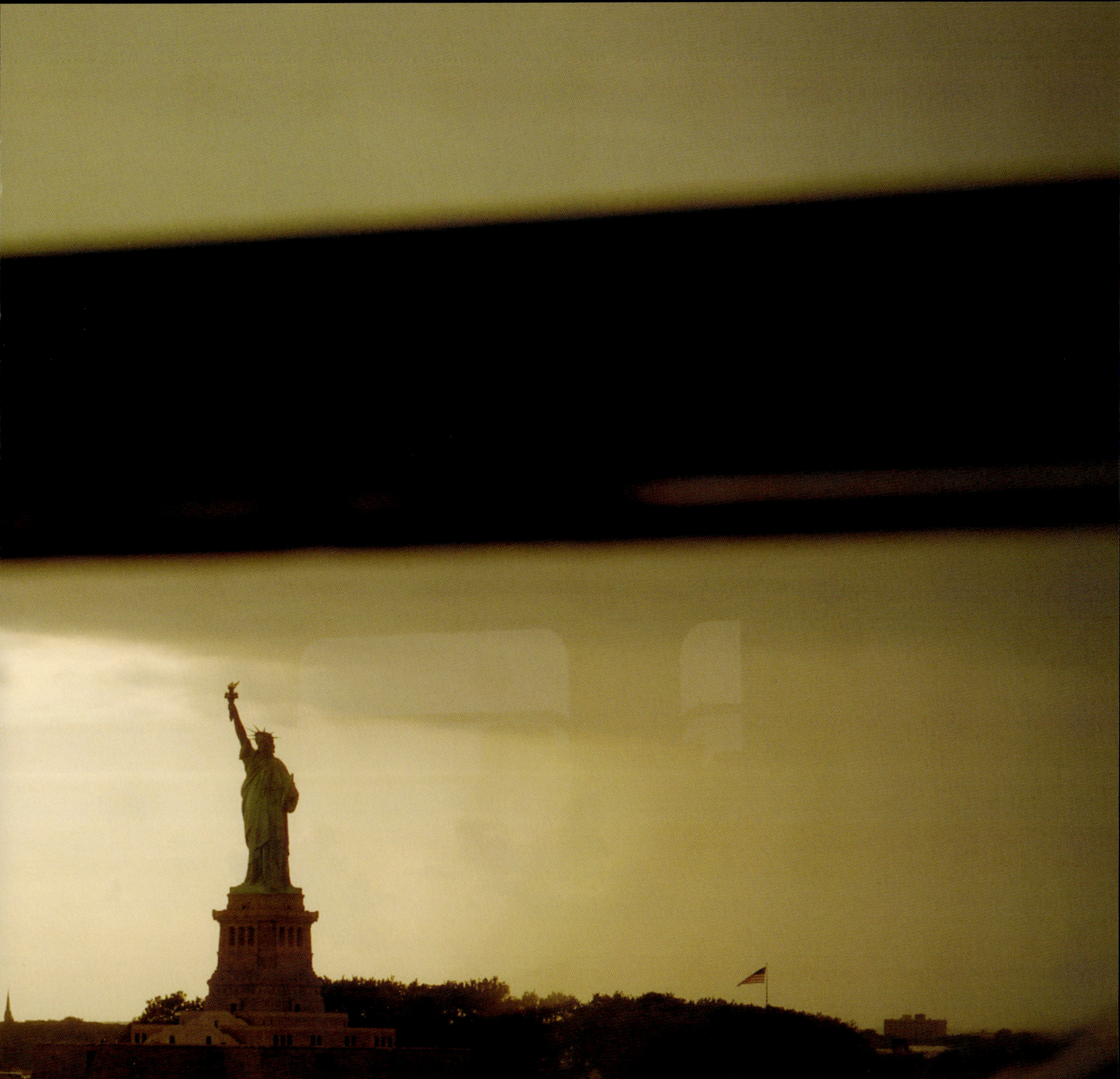

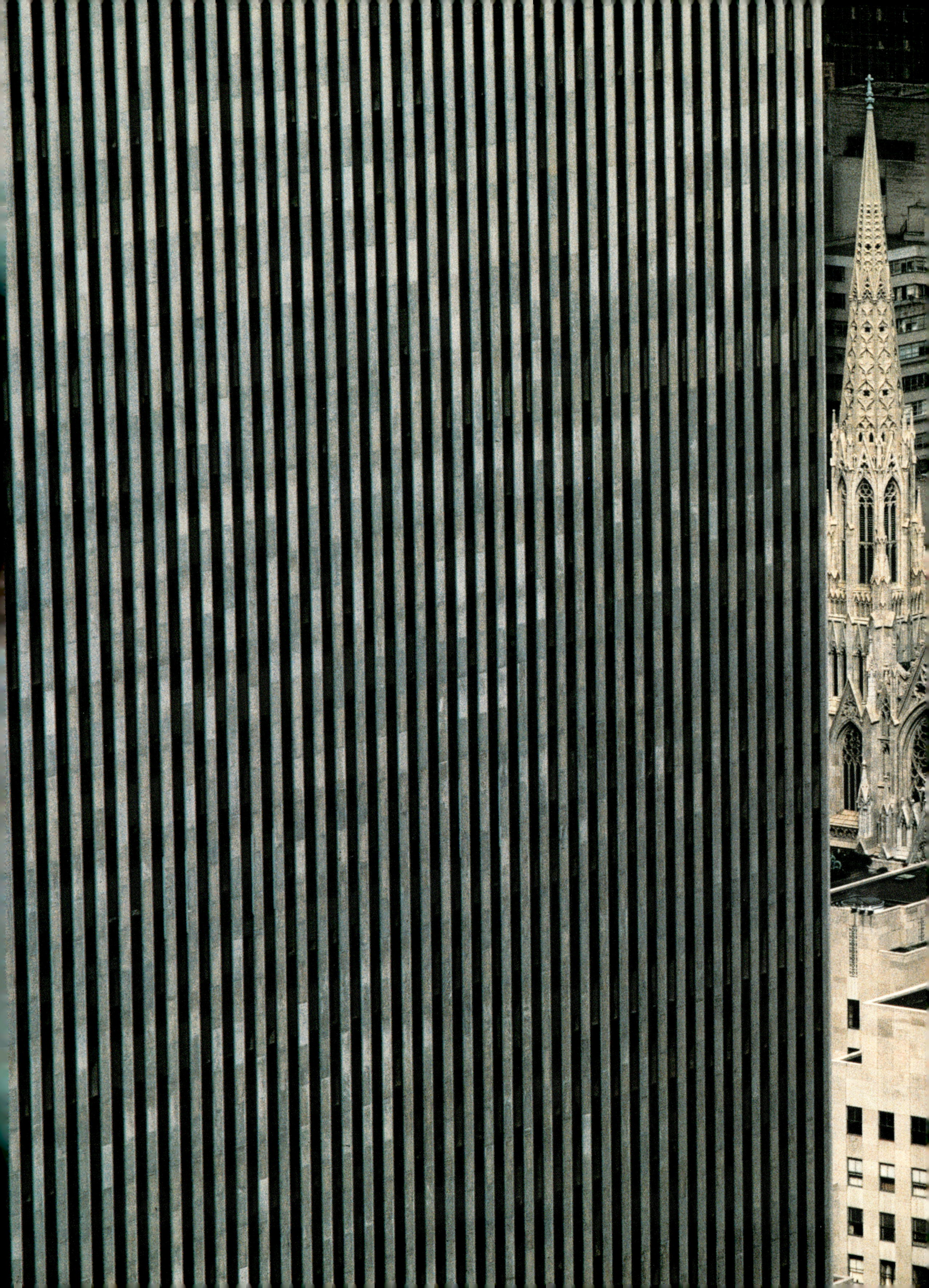

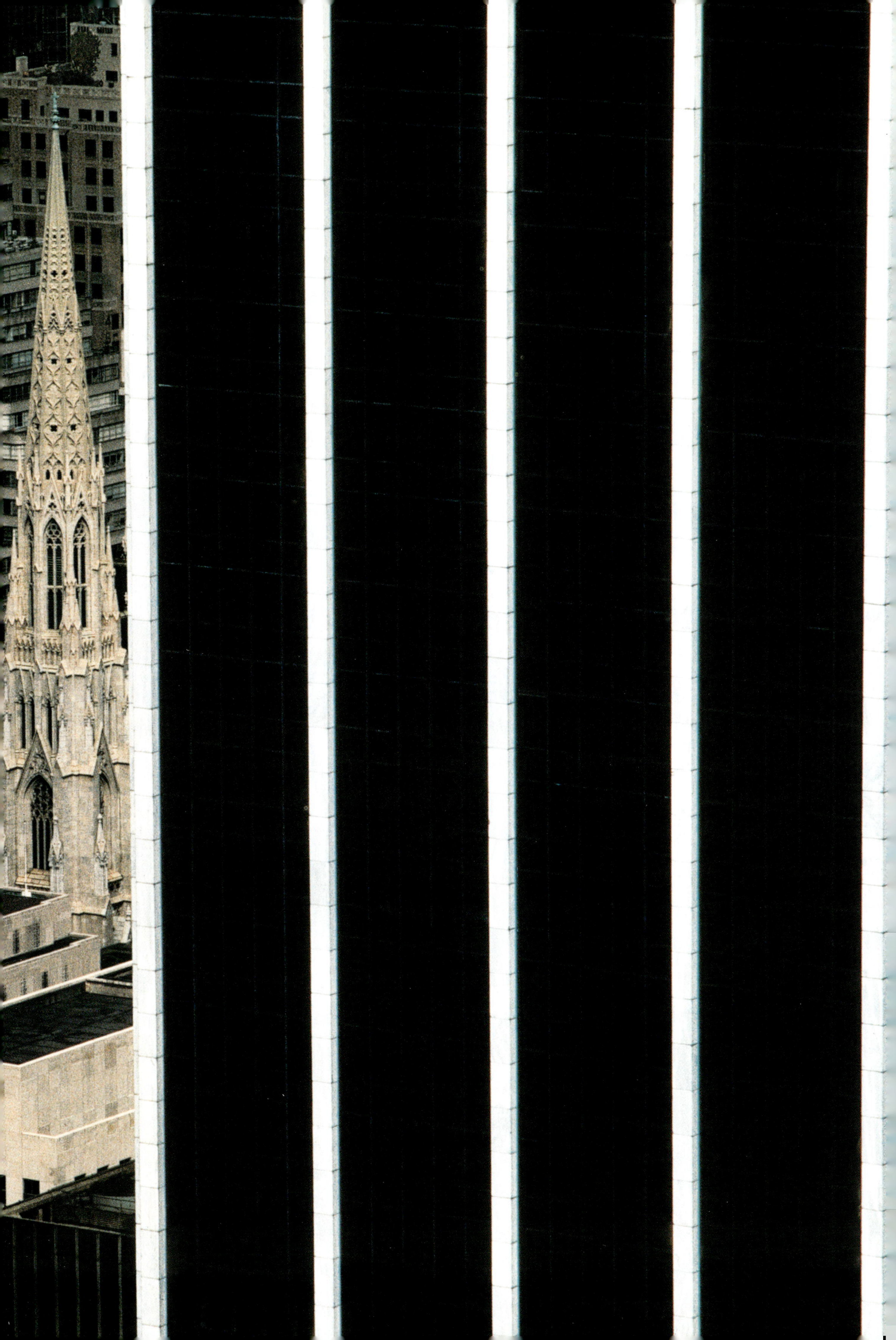

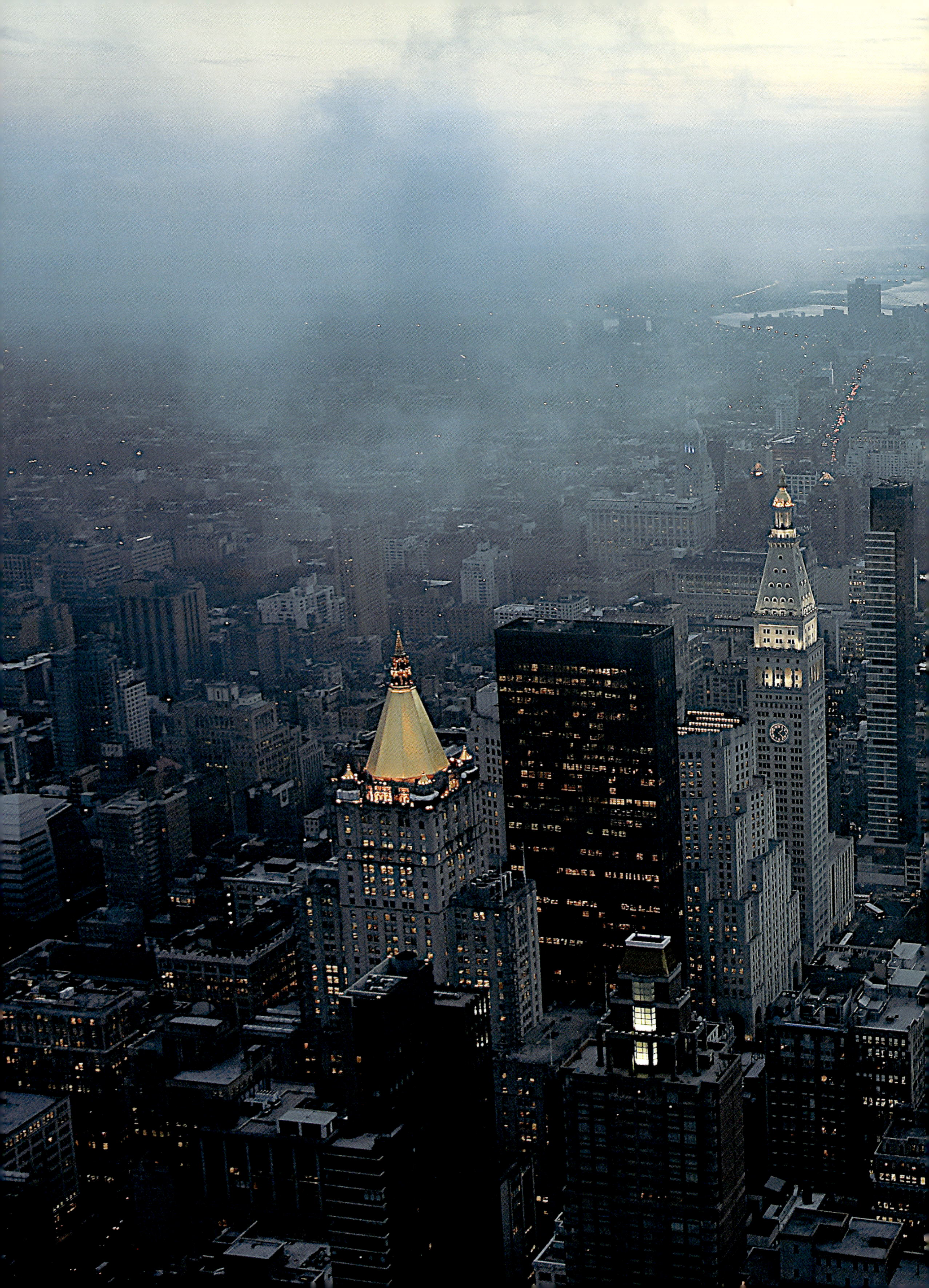

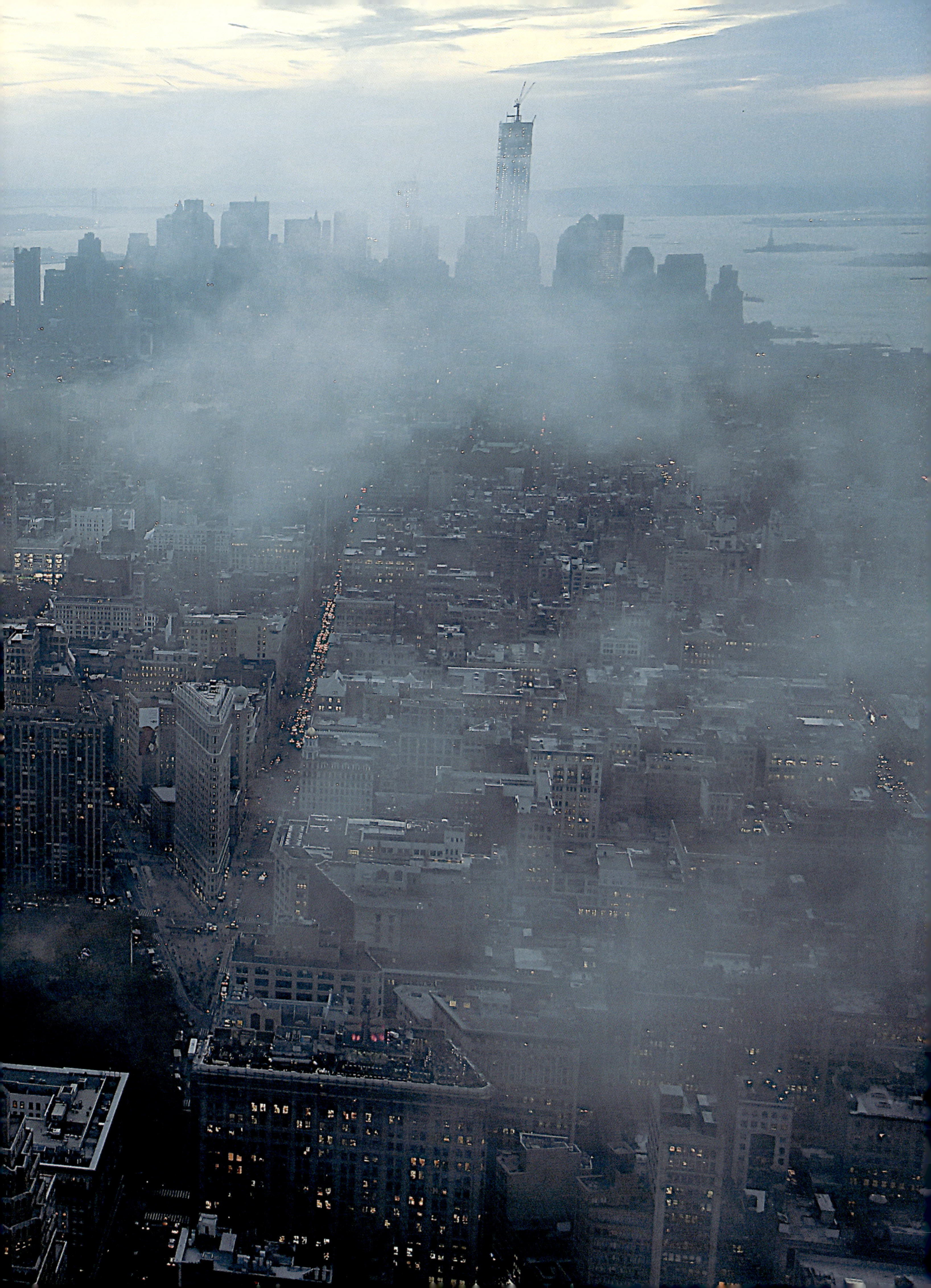

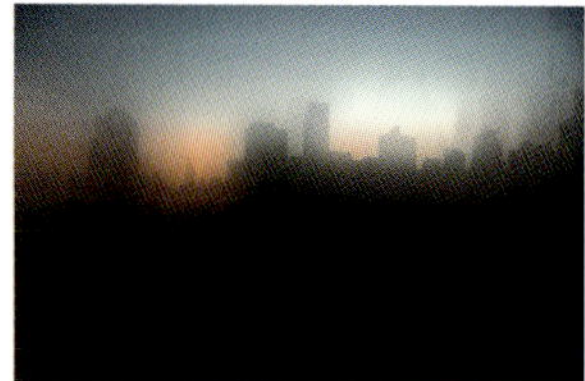

2–3  View from East 63rd Street downtown with Citicorp Building in the center, 1983

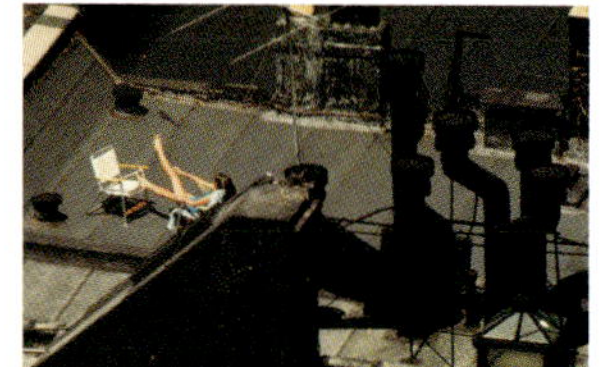

4–5  Sunbathing on a roof at 2nd Avenue and 63rd Street, 1983

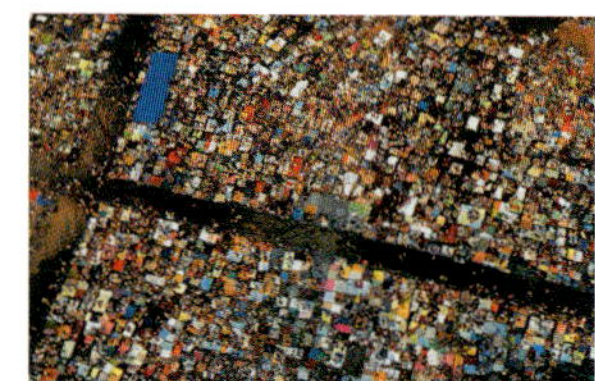

6–7  Helicopter view down on the Great Lawn in Central Park before a concert, 1983

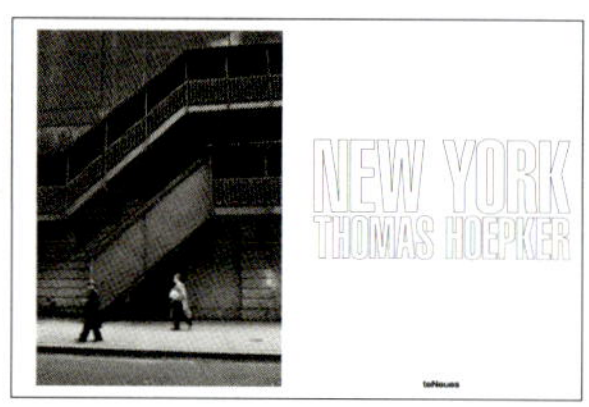

8  Manhattan, Financial District, 1960

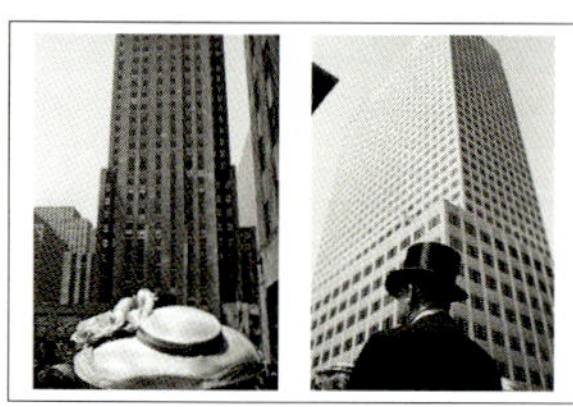

10–11  Festive hats at Easter Parade on Fifth Avenue, Rockefeller Center, 1960

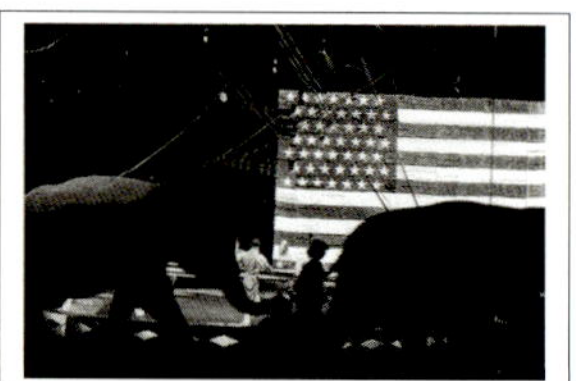

12–13  Ringling Bros. and Barnum & Bailey Circus setting up their big tent in lower Manhattan, 1960

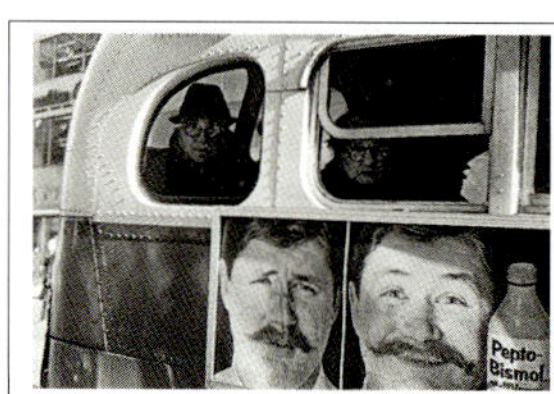

14–15  Advertising on a city bus, 1963

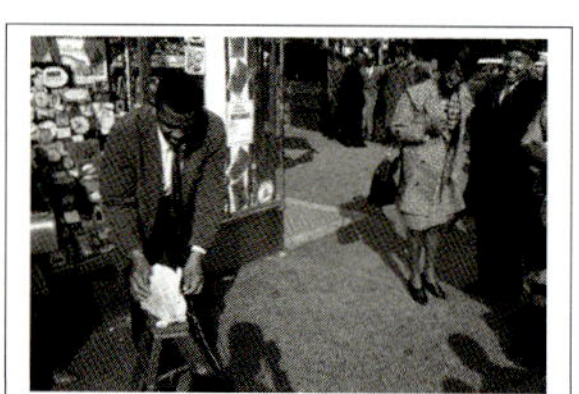

16–17  A street photographer sets up a white bunny as a prop on 125th Street in Harlem, 1960

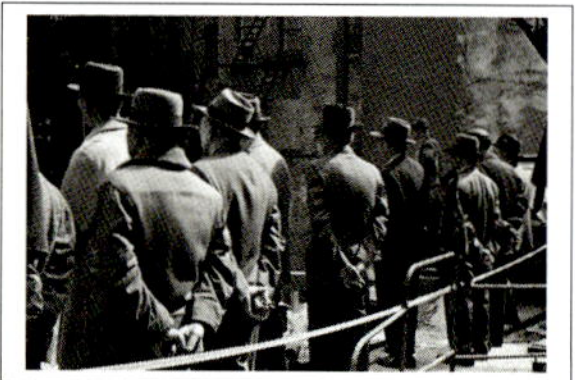

18–19  Men watching excavation workers in Chinatown, 1960

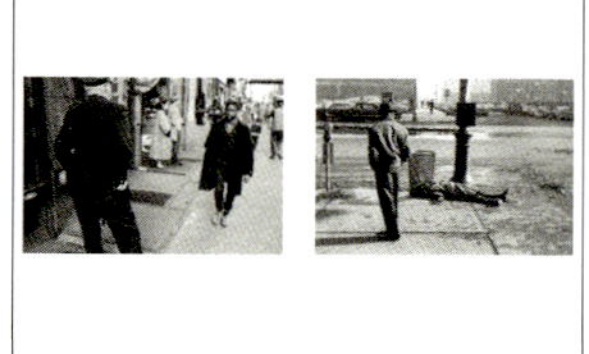

20  Policeman watches a black teenager in Harlem, 1960
21  A dead woman on a street in Harlem, 1963

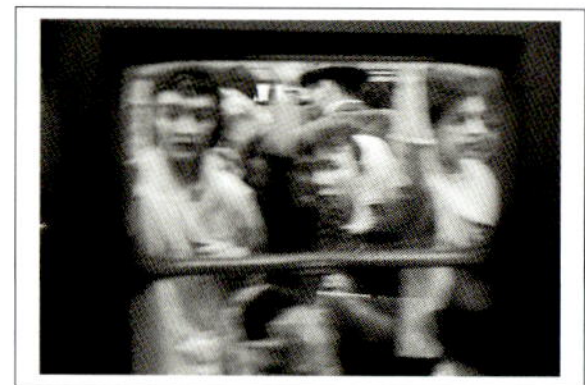

22–23  Subway riders at rush hour, 1960

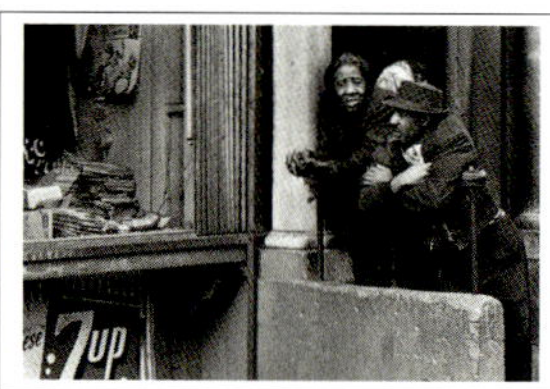

24–25  A black couple on a street in Harlem, 1960

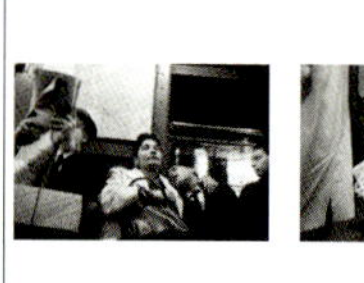

26–27  Subway riders in mid-Manhattan, 1960

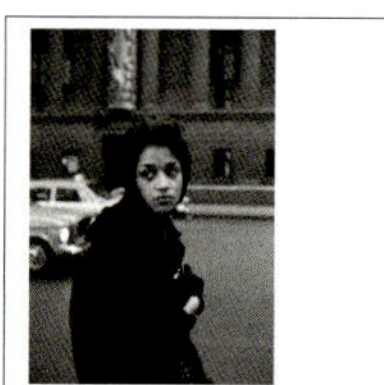

28  "Mona Lisa of Manhattan," Young woman in the streets of Manhattan, 1960

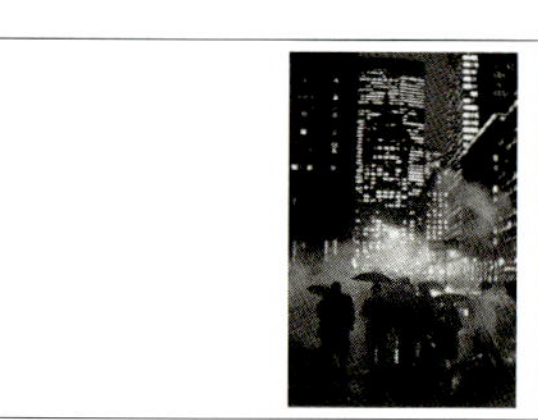

31  People walking on Park Avenue in the rain, 1960

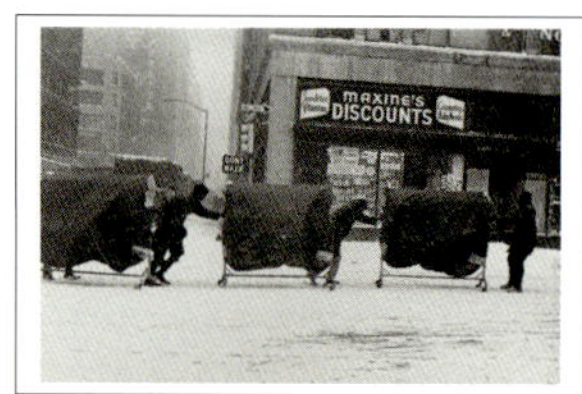

32–33  Blizzard in New York's Garment District, 1960

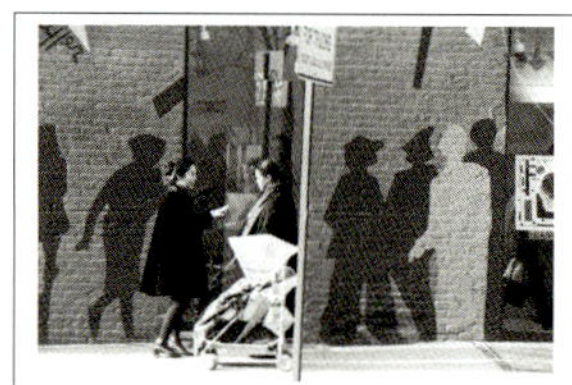

34–35  NY from story about Woody Allen's New York, 1990

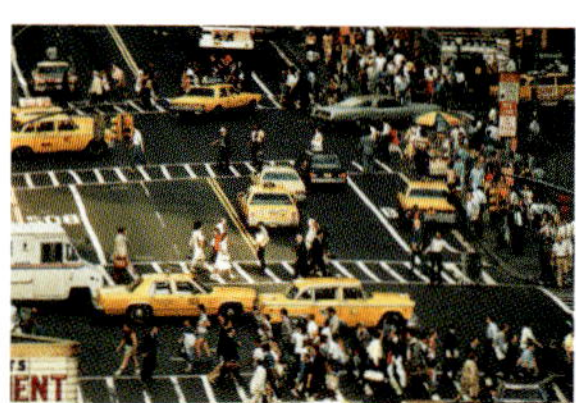

36–37  View of Times Square and Broadway at rush hour, 1983

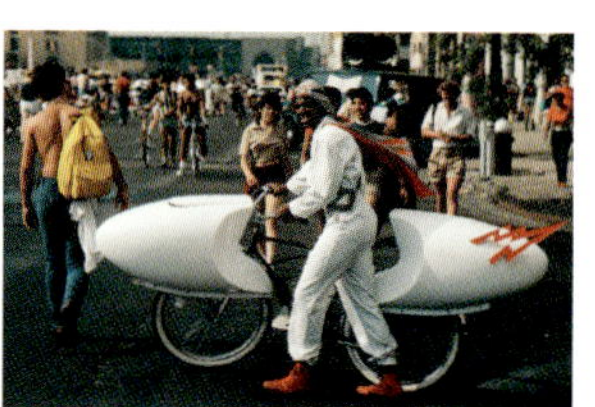

38–39  Man with home-built speed bike on Fifth Avenue, Manhattan, 1983

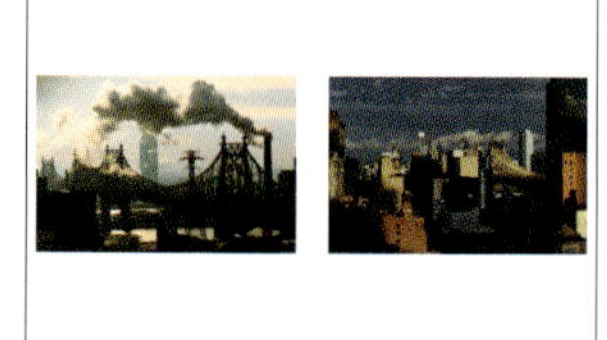

40  View of the Queensboro Bridge (now Ed Koch bridge) over the East River with CitiBank Building in Queens, 1994
41  View of the Queensboro bridge (now Ed Koch bridge) from Thomas Hoepkers Apartment, 2018

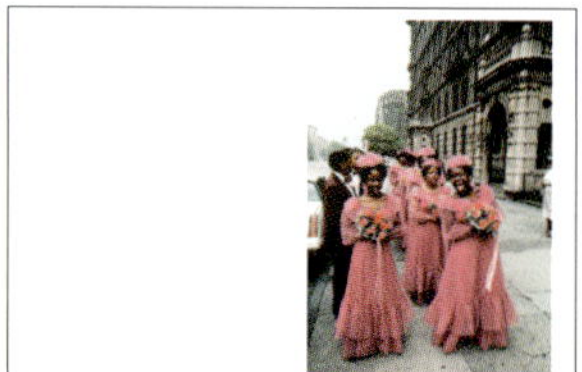

43  Bridesmaids in front of a church on Park Avenue, 1983

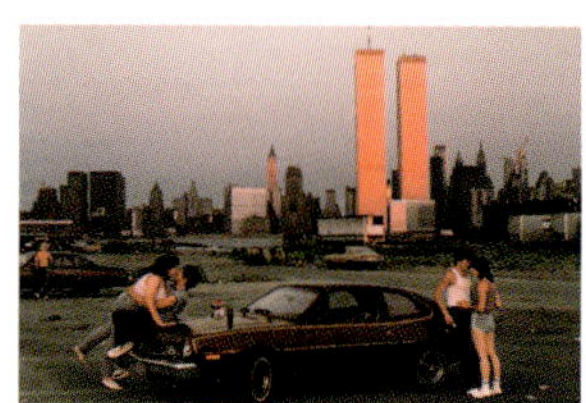

44–45  Lovers' Lane at the New Jersey docks with view of the World Trade Center at sunset, 1983

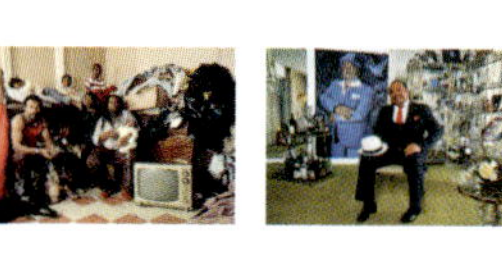

46  Earl and Joyce Griffin with their six children in their one-room apartment in Bedford-Stuyvesant, 1983
47  Curtis Sharp, janitor and fivefold Lotto millionaire in his new house, 1986

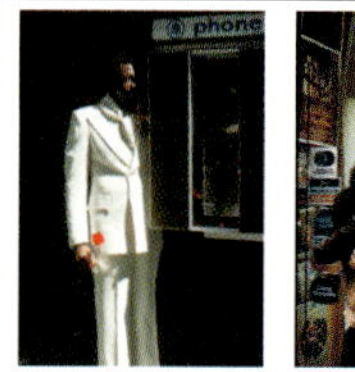

48  Man at a pay phone on lower Fifth Avenue, 1983
49  Lovers on St. Patricks Day in front of a store window on Fifth Avenue, 1983

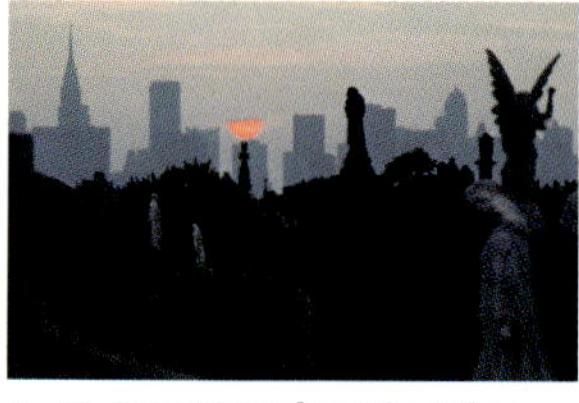

50–51  Sunset view from the Calvary Cemetery in Queens towards Manhattan skyline with Chrysler Building, 1983

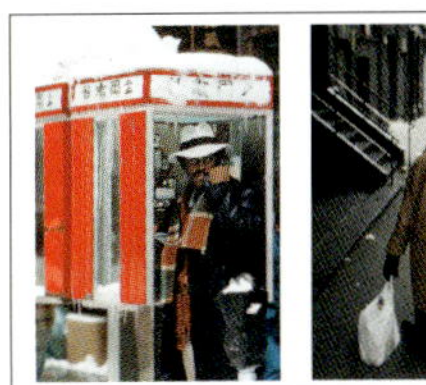

52  Man in phone booth in winter in Chinatown, 1983
53  Bag lady in Chelsea, 1983

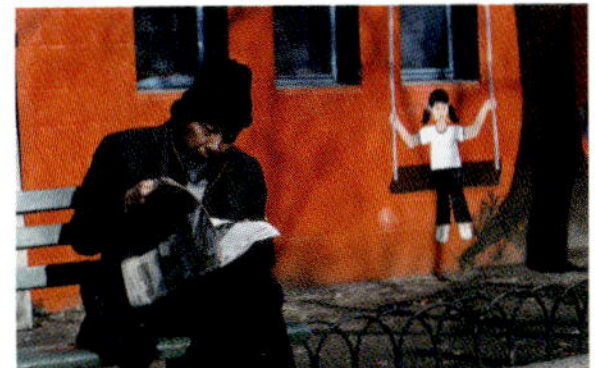

54–55  China Town, 1977

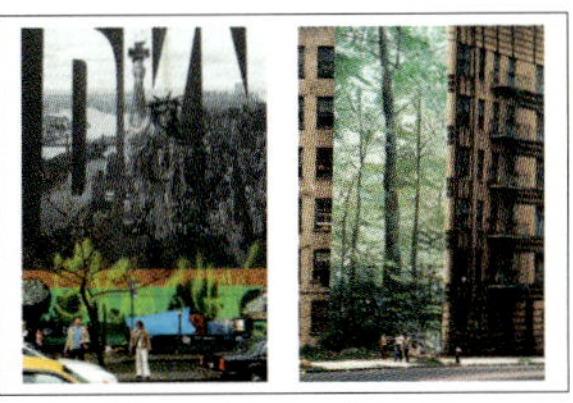

56  Billboard at Houston Street and Broadway, 2003
57  Mural with forest painting in the South Bronx, 1983

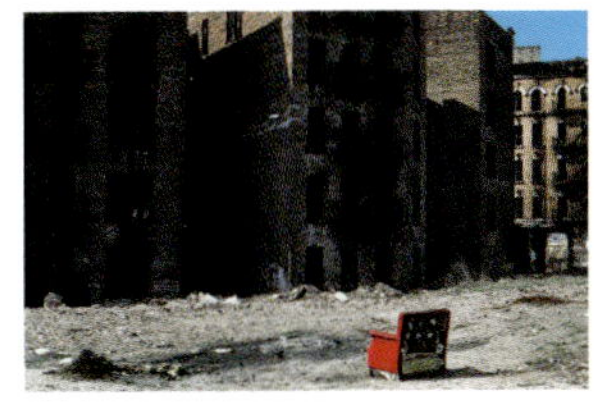

58–59  Burned out apartment buildings in the South Bronx, 1983

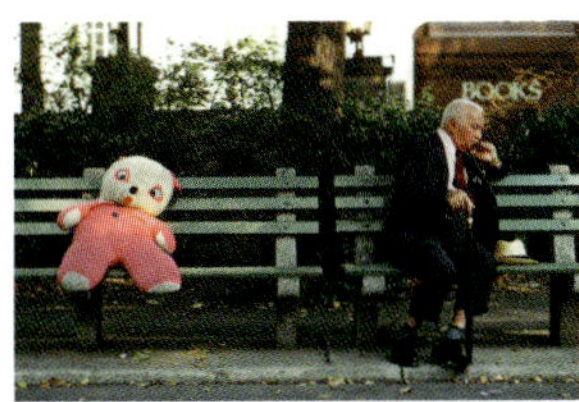

60–61  Old man sitting on a bench in Central Park. A stuffed animal gives him company, 1983

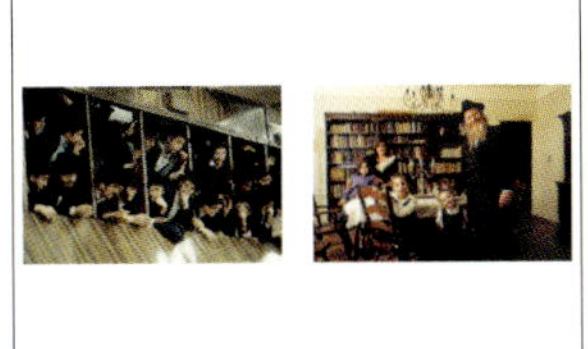

62  Orthodox Jews in Lubawitscher Synagogue in Brooklyn, 1983
63  Avroaum and Suri Crawford, librarian, and his Jewish-Orthodox family in Brooklyn, 1986

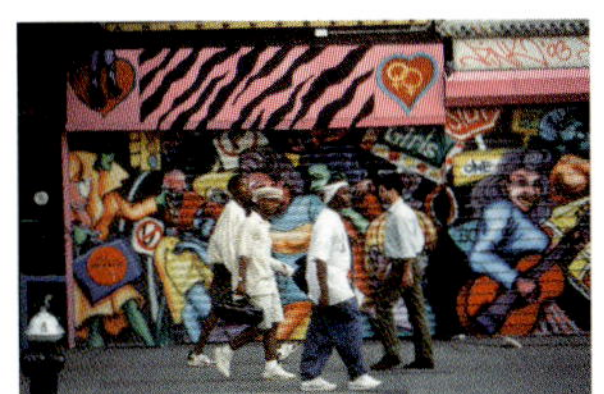

64–65  Latino paintings on store shutters in East Harlem, 1993

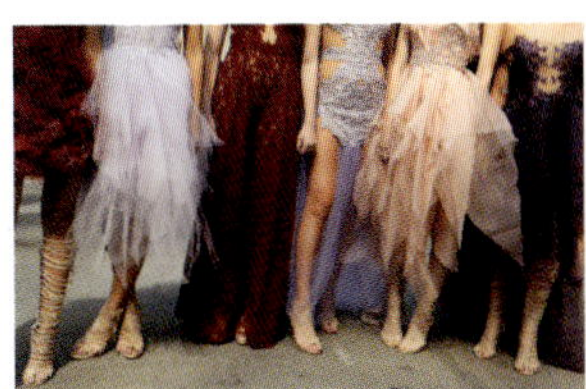

66–67  Fashion week in New York, 2016

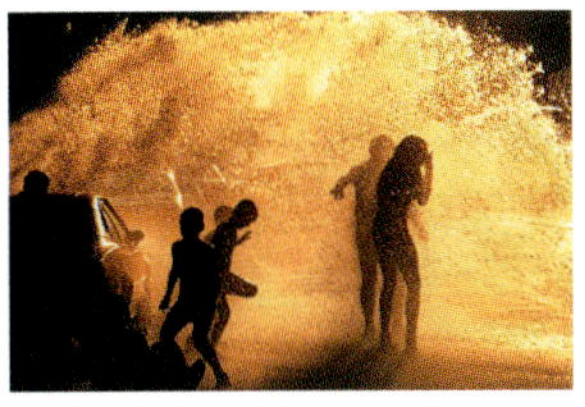

68–69  Harlem, children playing in the spray of a fire hydrant on a hot August day, 1983

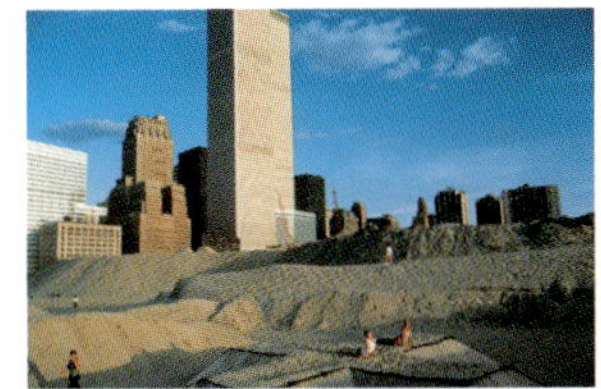

70–71  Construction site for the World Financial Center in downtown Manhattan. "Art on the beach" event with performances on the site, 1983

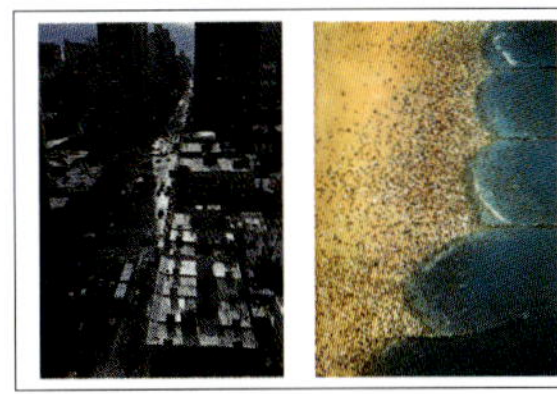

72  View of Second Avenue from 63rd Street to downtown, 2011
73  Beach at Coney Island on a July weekend seen from the air, 1983

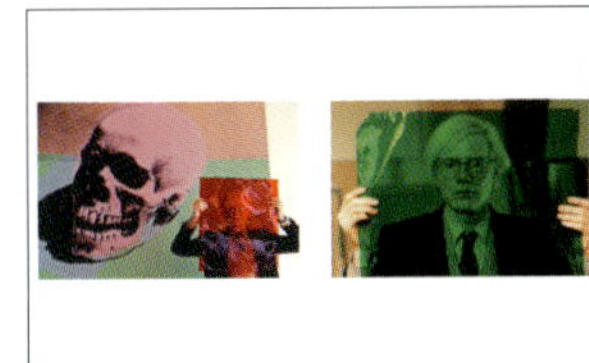

74–75  Andy Warhol in "The Factory" at Union Square, 1981

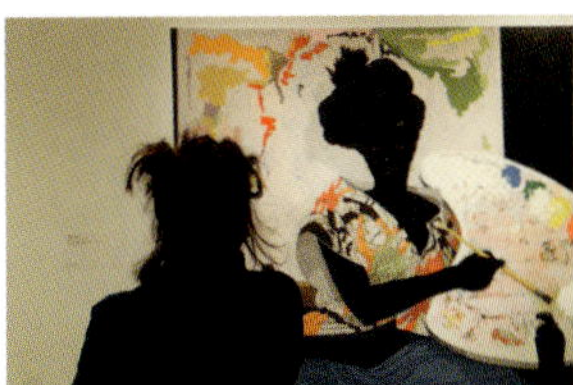

76–77  Woman watching Kerry Marshall painting at The Metropolitan Museum of Art, 2016

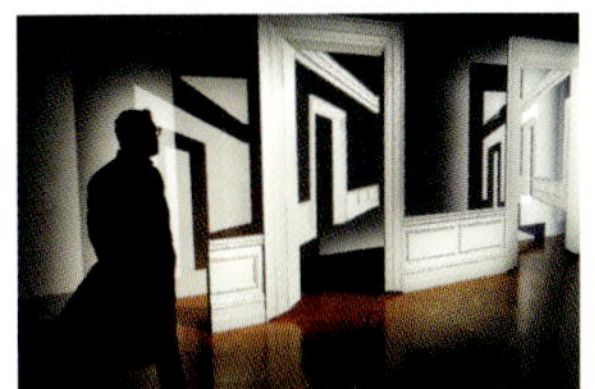

78–79  MoMA, 2015

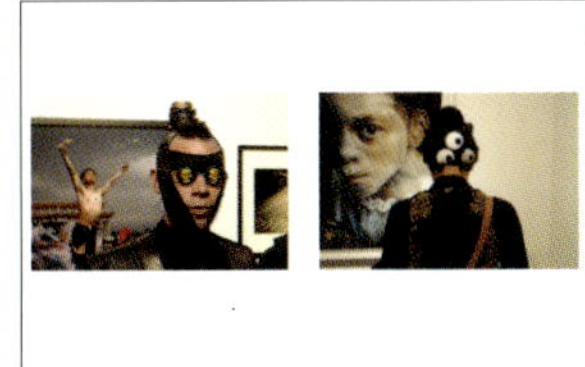

80  Staley-Wise Gallery, 2016
81  New York Art Fair, 2013

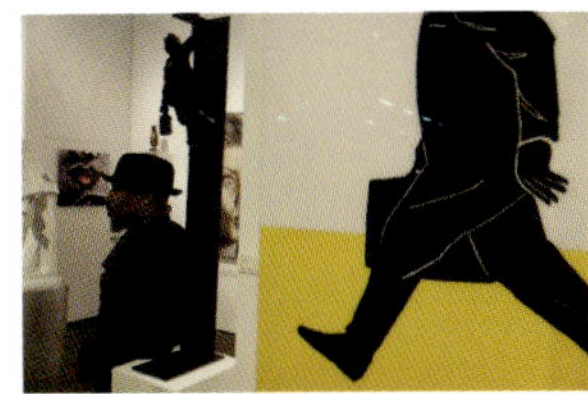

82–83  New York Art Fair, 2019

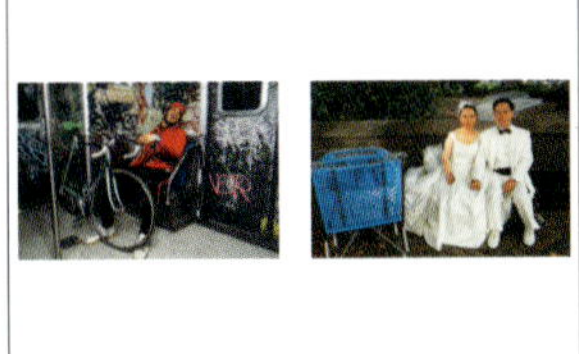

84  A bike messenger on a subway train, 1986
85  A Taiwanese couple after their wedding on a bench in Central Park, 2002

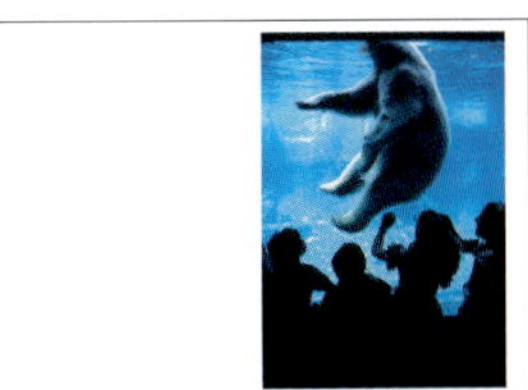

87  Polar bear in the Central Park Zoo, 1992

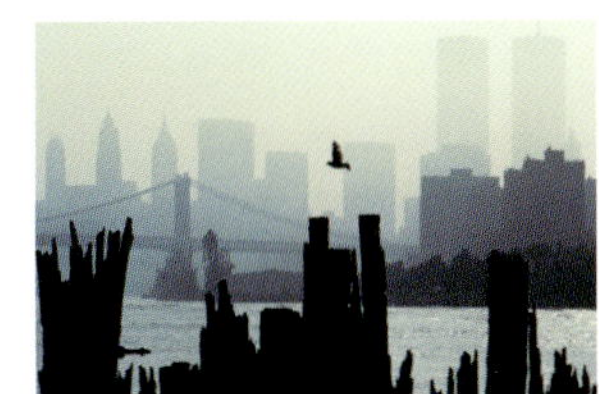

88–89  Manhattan skyline with Manhattan Bridge over the East River and World Trade Center towers, 1983

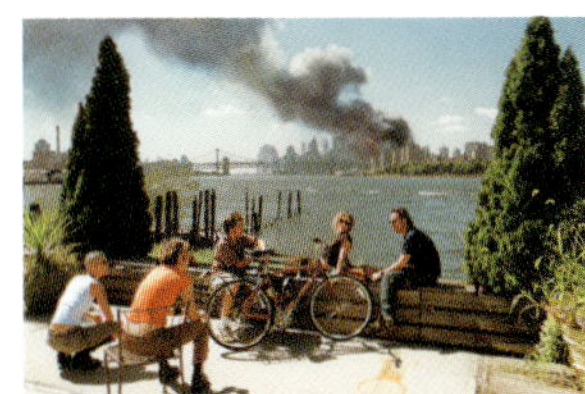

90–91  View from Williamsburg towards Brooklyn Bridge and downtown Manhattan in the aftermath of the World Trade Center bombing, September 11, 2001

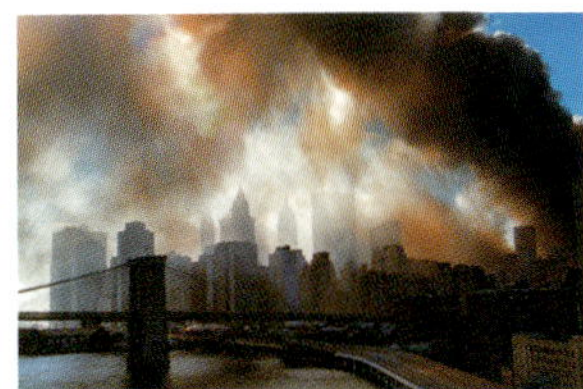

92–93  View from the Manhattan Bridge to the Brooklyn Bridge and downtown Manhattan during aftermath of World Trade Center bombing, September 11, 2001

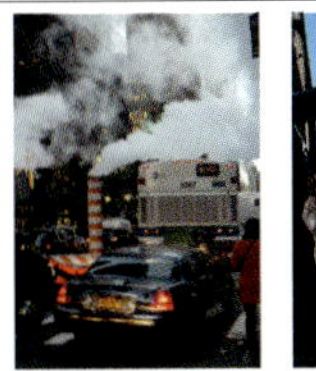

94  Walking through the streets in Midtown in October, 2018
95  Bagel truck, Manhattan, 2011

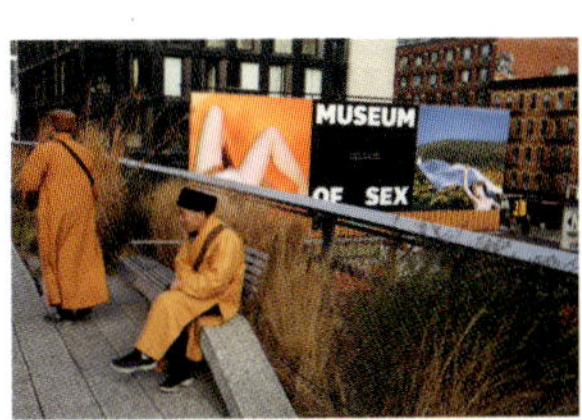

96–97  The High Line Park near Whitney Museum, 2016

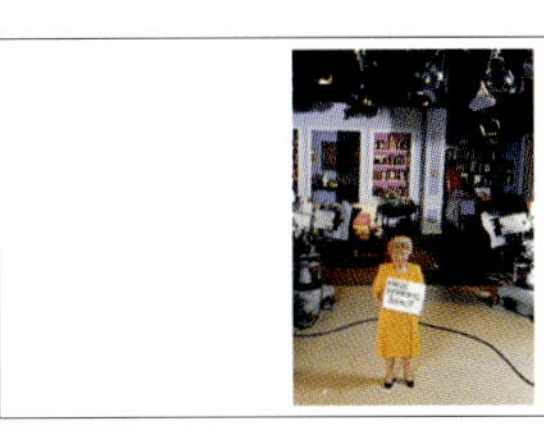

99  Dr. Ruth Westheimer, sexual therapist and TV personality, during a break in TV studio, 1986

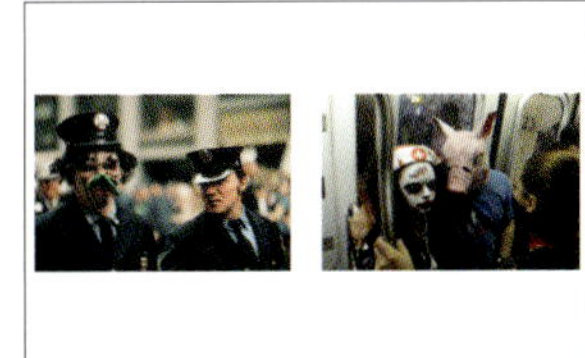

100  New York Police during St. Patrick's Day parade, Manhattan, 1983
101  Halloween, 2013

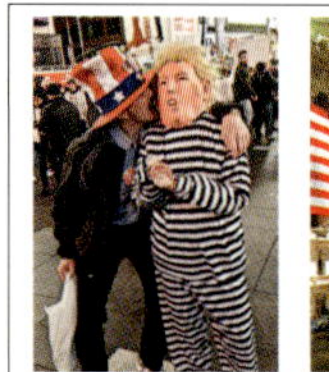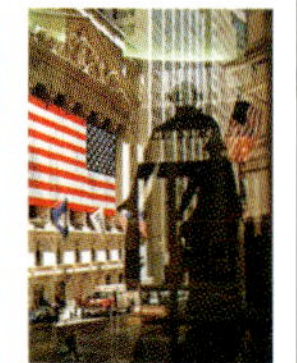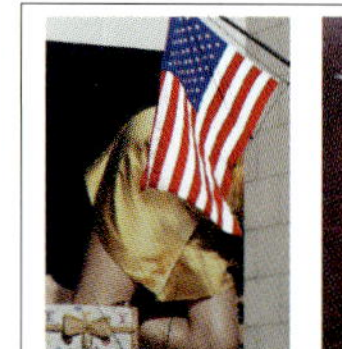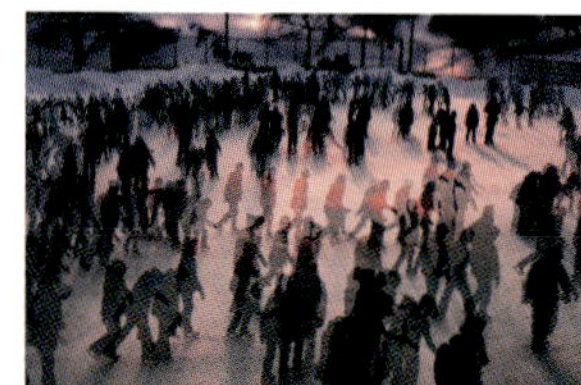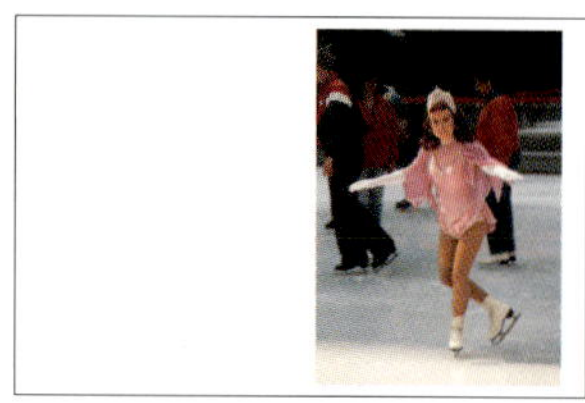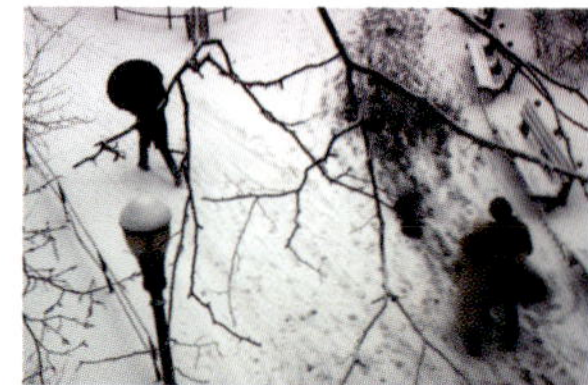

**102** Trump Protest, 2018
**103** Wall Street, New York Stock Exchange. The George Washington monument is reflected in glass doors, 2002

**104** Billboard on Fifth Avenue, 2003
**105** Painter working on billboard, 2012

**106–107** Skaters on the ice rink in Central Park, 1983

**109** The "Ice Princess" skating on ice rink in Rockefeller Center, Manhattan, 1994

**110–111** Central Park in winter, 1983

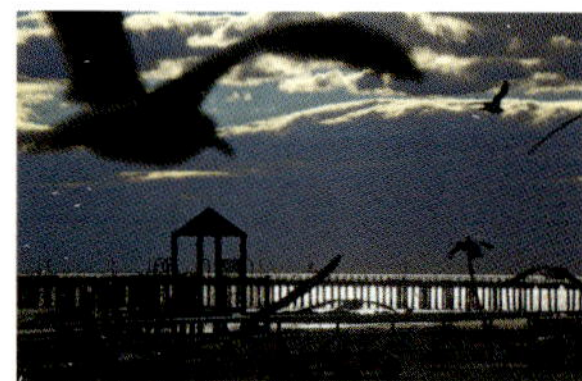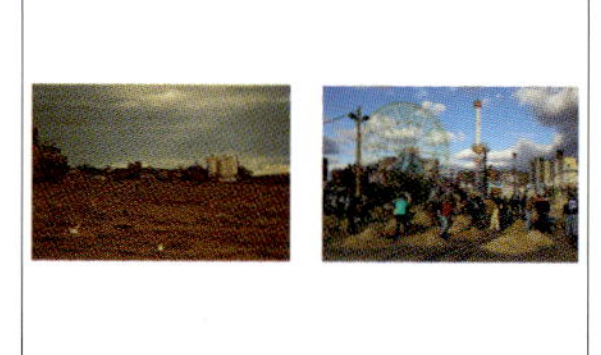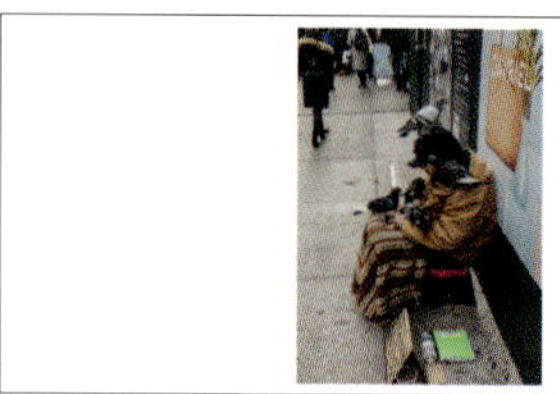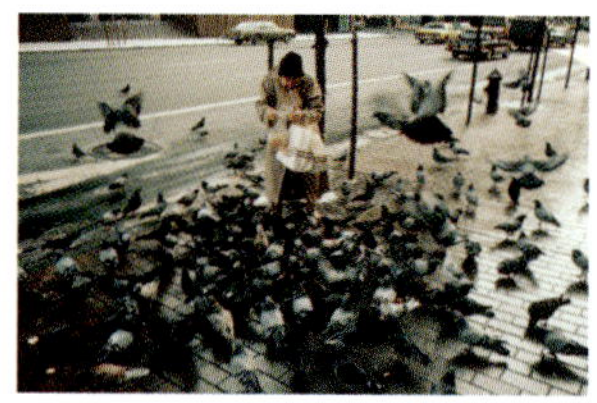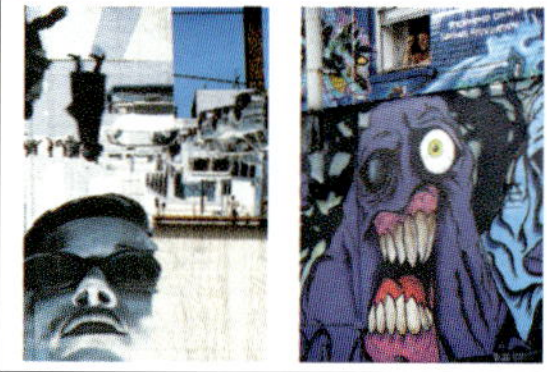

**112–113** The morning after Hurricane Sandy had hit the beach at Coney Island, 2012

**114–115** Hurricane Sandy hit the mid-Atlantic region of the USA on October 22, 2012. Images were taken at the beach at Coney Island

**117** Street views, Midtown, 2016

**118–119** Woman feeding pigeons on Second Ave, 1983

**120** A billboard painter works on a giant mural on 8th Avenue, 1999
**121** House with spooky mural in Red Hook, 2012

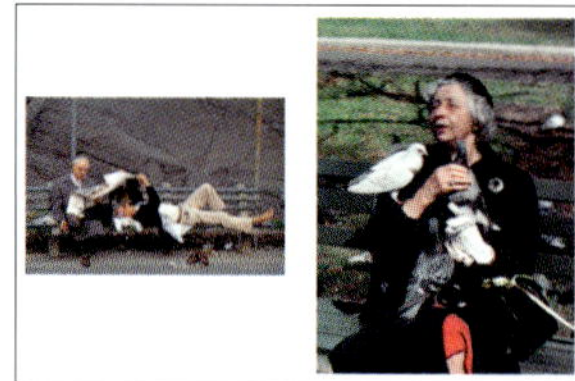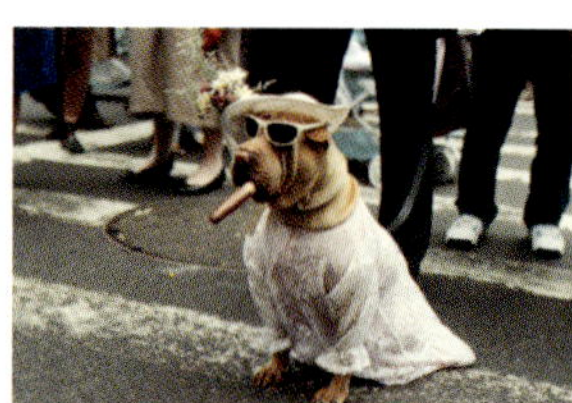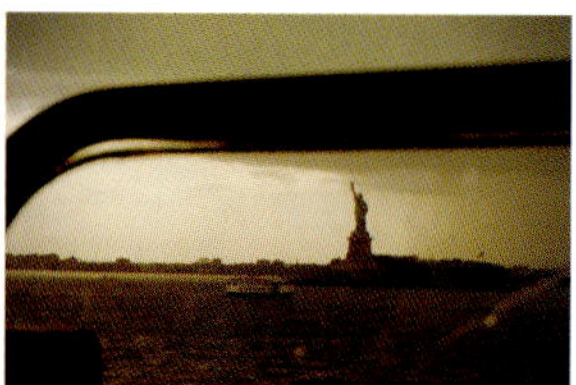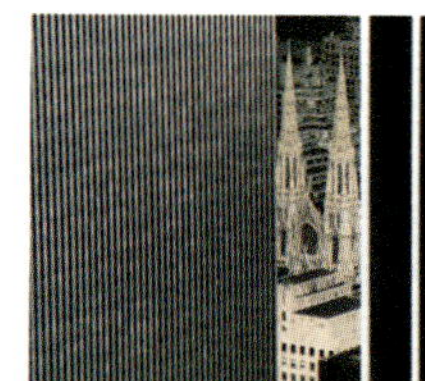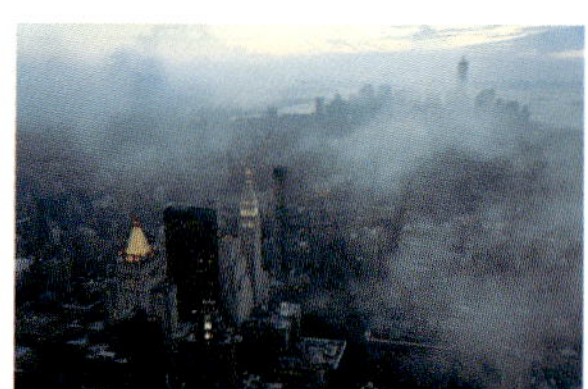

**122–123** Central Park, 1977

**124–125** Dog with cigar in Easter Parade, Fifth Avenue, 1983

**126–127** Statue of Liberty, 2019

**128–129** St. Patrick's church on Fifth Avenue, 1983

**130–131** View from the Empire State building towards lower Manhattan, during a storm, 2013

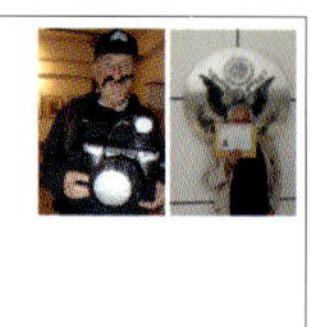

**135** left Getting ready for the Halloween Parade, 2013
**135** right Thomas Hoepker receiving his US citizenship, 2009

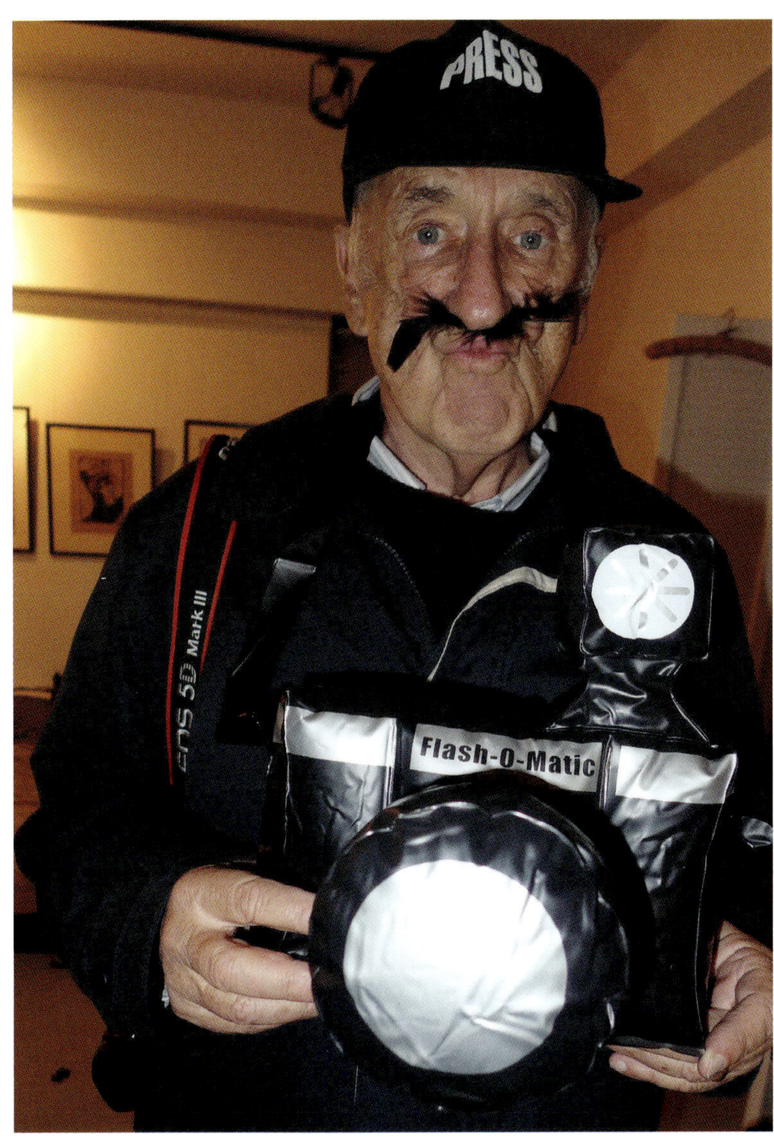 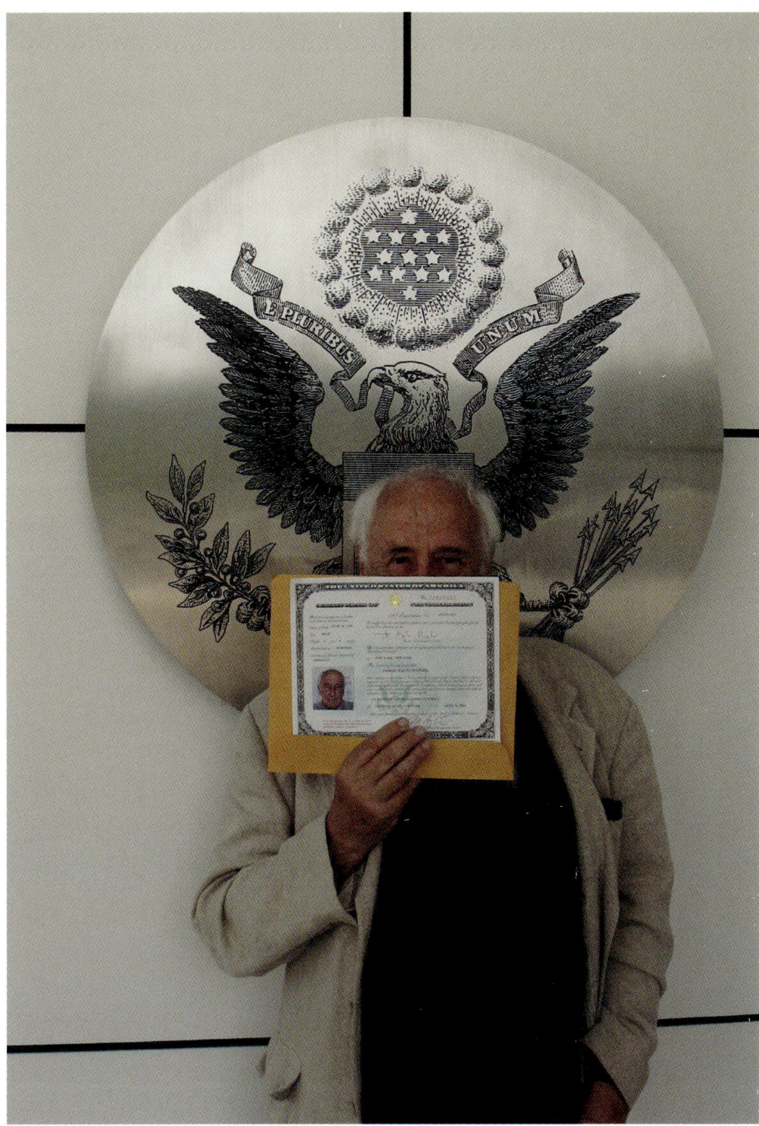

Thomas Hoepker, born in Munich in 1936, studied art history and archeology before working between 1960 and 1963 as a photographer for the *Münchener Illustrierte* and *Kristall*, reporting from the Middle East, Brazil, Peru, Ethiopia, and Iran, and traveling the U.S. from coast to coast. In 1964, he moved to *stern*, for which he described life in the GDR as a correspondent from East Berlin, among other things, and went to New York as a U.S. correspondent in 1976. From 1978 to 1981, Hoepker was Executive Editor for the American edition of *Geo*, and at the same time began working as a freelance photographer. From 1986 to 1989, Hoepker was Art Director for *stern* in Hamburg and became the first German photographer to become a full member of the renowned international photography cooperative Magnum. He specialized in reportage and stylish color photography and returned to New York in 1989. In addition to photography, Thomas Hoepker also devoted himself to documentary film and made films about Robinson Crusoe Island or Patagonia's glaciers, among others. In 1992 Hoepker became vice president of Magnum, and from 2003 to 2006 he was its president. His work has been presented in numerous exhibitions, including a retrospective exhibition of 250 images at the Fotomuseum in Munich, as well as published in several books. In 2013, teNeues Verlag published the first edition of *New York*, and in 2014 the book *Wanderlust*.

Thomas Hoepker, 1936 in München geboren, studierte Kunstgeschichte und Archäologie, bevor er zwischen 1960 und 1963 als Fotograf für die *Münchener Illustrierte* und *Kristall* aus dem Mittleren Osten, Brasilien, Peru, Äthiopien sowie dem Iran berichtete und die USA von Küste zu Küste bereiste. 1964 wechselte er zum *stern*, für den er u.a. als Korrespondent aus Ost-Berlin das Leben in der DDR schilderte und ging ab 1976 als USA-Korrespondent nach New York. Von 1978 bis 1981 war Hoepker Executive Editor für die amerikanische Ausgabe von *Geo* und startete parallel seine Arbeit als freier Fotograf. Von 1986 bis 1989 war Hoepker Art Director für den *stern* in Hamburg und wurde als erster deutscher Fotograf Vollmitglied der renommierten internationalen Fotografen-Kooperative Magnum. Er spezialisierte sich auf Reportagen und stilvolle Farbaufnahmen und kehrte 1989 nach New York zurück. Neben der Fotografie widmete sich Thomas Hoepker auch dem Dokumentarfilm und drehte Filme u.a. über die Robinson Crusoe Insel oder Patagoniens Gletscher. 1992 wurde Hoepker Vizepräsident von Magnum, von 2003 bis 2006 war er ihr Präsident. Seine Arbeiten wurden in zahlreichen Ausstellungen präsentiert, darunter eine Retrospektive Ausstellung mit 250 Bildern im Fotomuseum in München, sowie in mehreren Büchern veröffentlicht. 2013 erschien im teNeues Verlag die Erstausgabe von *New York*, 2014 das Buch *Wanderlust*.

NEW YORK by THOMAS HOEPKER
© 2023 teNeues Verlag GmbH
Photographs © 2023 Thomas Hoepker/Magnum Photos.
All rights reserved.

Foreword by Charles Simic
Design by SMITH, London, England
Alice Austin, Maria Juelisch, Justine Schuster
www.smith-design.com
Editorial coordination by Inga Wortmann-Grützmacher, teNeues Verlag
Production by Alwine Krebber, teNeues Verlag
Layout and color separation by Robert Kuhlendahl, teNeues Verlag

Translation by:
Dr. Kurt Rehkopf

ISBN 978-3-96171-558-9
Library of Congress Control Number: 2023951097

Printed in Bosnia and Herzegovina by GPS

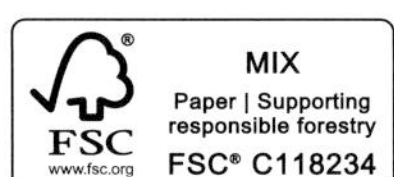




Bibliographic information published by the Deutsche Nationalbibliothek:
The Deutsche Nationalbibliothek lists this publication in the Deutsche
Nationalbibliografie; detailed bibliographic data are available on the
Internet at dnb.dnb.de.

Published by teNeues Publishing Group

teNeues Verlag GmbH
Ohmstraße 8a
86199 Augsburg, Germany

Düsseldorf Office
Waldenburger Straße 13
41564 Kaarst, Germany
e-mail: books@teneues.com

Augsburg/München Office
Ohmstraße 8a
86199 Augsburg, Germany
e-mail: books@teneues.com

Press Department
presse@teneues.com

teNeues Publishing Company
350 Seventh Avenue, Suite 1702
New York, NY 10001, USA
Phone: +1-212-627-9090
Fax: +1-212-627-9511

www.teneues.com

**teNeues Publishing Group**
Augsburg / München
Berlin
Düsseldorf
London
New York

**teNeues**